Adventure Guide

Bermuda

3rd Edition

Blair Howard

HUNTER

Hunter Publishing, Inc.
130 Campus Drive
Edison, NJ 08818-7816
☎ 732-225-1900 / 800-255-0343 / Fax 732-417-1744
Web site: www.hunterpublishing.com
E-mail: comments@hunterpublishing.com

IN CANADA
Ulysses Travel Publications
4176 Saint-Denis
Montreal, Québec H2W 2M5 Canada
☎ 514-843-9882, Ext. 2232 / Fax 514-843-9448

IN THE UK & EUROPE
Windsor Books International
The Boundary, Wheatley Road
Garsington, Oxford OX44 9EJ England
☎ 01865-361122 / Fax 01865-361133

ISBN 1-58843-392-7
© 2004 Blair Howard

All photos courtesy Bermuda Department of Tourism,
unless otherwise indicated.
Front cover: *Daniels Head* (see page 79;
Kerrick James Photography)

4 3 2

Contents

Maps

Introduction

I've now been writing about Bermuda for more than 10 years. What a joy. Over the years, things have changed slowly and mostly for the better. But, even if they hadn't changed, Bermuda is still the magical island I fell in love with all those years ago. It's still a real thrill to fly in from the west and gaze down at the great, fishhook-shaped atoll surrounded by the deep blue waters of the Atlantic Ocean. The pastel-colored buildings with their snowy-white roofs stand out like coral beads; the turquoise shallows and pale pink beaches never change; and Hamilton, the islands' tiny capital city on the shore of the Great Sound, is an oh-so-English anomaly unique in the Western Hemisphere.

To me, Bermuda is one of the most beautiful places on Earth, and I've been around. I don't know whether it's the combination of the English culture and its quasi-tropical setting, or something else I can't quite put my finger on. There's just something very special about this little group of islands in the middle of the Atlantic that, once experienced, is never forgotten. Perhaps it's because I'm English and feel very much at home among the little English-style shops, streets and churches. The cathedral, the bright red British pillar boxes, the food and especially the afternoon tea that's almost a religious experience all help to make Bermuda even more English than England itself. Add pink sandy beaches, with some of the most beautiful island terrain to be found anywhere, and you have something very special indeed.

There was a time when only the very rich could afford to vacation in Bermuda; not so today. Almost every budget can be accommodated here. From the small cottage colonies to the expensive luxury resort hotels, from the private yacht to the giant cruise ship, and from cook-for-yourself vacations to the all-inclusive package deals offered by any one of a growing number of operators, you'll find something to suit your taste and your wallet. You can do six nights, seven days on the islands for as little as $1,250 per person, or you can pay as much as that per night. Whatever your budget, you're sure of a grand time.

The Land

 Bermuda, a tiny collection of rocks in the Atlantic Ocean some 580 miles due east of Cape Hatteras, is isolated. Even so, this group of British islands is one of the most popular tourist resorts in the Western Hemisphere. On most maps, if it shows at all, it's no more than a tiny dot. Close up, Bermuda looks somewhat like a fishhook, with the curve at the southwest end and the stem extending to the northeast.

The flight in over the island is incredible. The view is never quite what you expect. The sparkling blue waters seen around any tropical island are mixed with eye-catching colors. Homes and shops painted pastel shades of pink, blue, green, yellow and other colors of the rainbow sit anchored under snowy white roofs. The effect is a patchwork quilt, thrown down on a field of green in the middle of the blue ocean.

Bermuda rests on the peaks of a volcanic mountain that rises steeply from the ocean floor to a point some 200 feet below the surface. Above this level, the islands consist mainly of limestone formed by seashells and corals. Along the shores rise huge rocks, sculpted by the action of the wind and water into improbable pinnacles, pillars and grottoes. The reefs surrounding the islands are made of coral, and the Bermudian archipelago is the northernmost point on the planet that supports its growth.

Coral stone, one of its great natural resources, provides Bermuda with an excellent source of road-building and construction material. The stone is so soft that it can be cut with handsaws, but it hardens with exposure to air. Bermuda's attractive white roads are nothing more than coral bedrock, which have been stripped of the surface soil, smoothed and then allowed to harden. Even the roofs of houses, which are unique to Bermuda, are built of coral stone. Some say they are designed to resemble upturned lifeboats, which were probably the first shelters of the early mariners shipwrecked here. Today, the roofs serve a second and extremely important purpose: they are used to catch rainwater and are the islands' chief source of drinking water. Because Bermuda has no rivers or fresh-water lakes, most of the island's fresh water falls from the skies and is stored in underground cisterns.

There are about 180 islands in the Bermudian archipelago, but they comprise a total land mass of less than 22 square miles. Only 20 of the islands are inhabited. Of those, the seven largest are joined by a series of bridges and scenic causeways. At its widest point, Bermuda measures just two miles. The sea is never far away and can be seen from almost anywhere. Great Bermuda, the Main Island, is larger than all the other islands combined. Its highest point, Town Hill, rises 260 feet above sea level.

The Bermudian community is divided into nine parishes, each managed by advisory councils. These include Sandy's, Southampton, Warwick, Paget, Devonshire, Pembroke, Smiths, Hamilton, and St. George's.

The delightful climate and great natural beauty of Bermuda attract thousands of visitors each year. The average temperature is 70°F. The winter seldom sees temperatures below 55°; in summer it rarely climbs above 87°.

Rainfall on the islands is often heavy, with almost 60 inches falling annually. That, accompanied by eight hours of brilliant sunshine 315 days on average each year, ensures an abundance of lush vegetation. Palms, casuarinas and swamp mangroves are among the common trees. Hibiscus, oleander, poinsettia, and many other flowering plants and trees bloom profusely. Easter lilies are cultivated for export and are also used to make perfumes. Two hundred species of birds have been catalogued here (although most of them are migratory birds blown off course). The waters off Bermuda literally teem with fish, many of which are remarkable for their striking colors and markings. Clear waters offer good visibility up to 200 feet and beyond.

Most of the island is residential, a fact that becomes readily apparent as you travel through town after town of neat, pastel-colored homes with white roofs and beautifully maintained English gardens full of hibiscus, oleander and Bermudiana. Beyond these areas, tiny farms create a magic quilt of tomatoes, sweet potatoes, onions and other vegetables. Bananas hang heavily from trees in great green and yellow bunches. Magnificent pink beaches, green golf courses and the eye-popping turquoise ocean combine to create a tropical utopia. And with 12 nature reserves on the Main Island alone, Bermuda is also a haven for naturalists.

The Attractions

 Tiny though it is, Bermuda has much to offer. For the modern adventurer there are diversions aplenty: diving, snorkeling, sportfishing, hiking, exploring, sailing, windsurfing, golfing, shopping, tennis, island hopping and parasailing. For the sightseer there's even more: great military forts, fine old churches, magnificent lighthouses, historic buildings, botanical gardens, a national aquarium, museums and the great **Naval Dockyard** at the West End of the island group.

The capital and chief port of Bermuda is **Hamilton**, located in Pembroke Parish on the Main Island. With a population of only 2,000 and a total area of less than 200 acres, Hamilton is one of the world's smallest cities. Bermuda's second city of **St. George** is a picturesque little port and is one of Bermuda's oldest settlements. It lies at the East End of the group on St. George's Island.

The People

 In total, Bermuda is home to about 60,000 people, 60% of them black. There is also a large Portuguese population.

Despite its isolation, lack of manufacturing industry and a cost of living that ranks among the highest in the world, Bermuda has almost no poverty or unemployment. No income tax is levied, nor does the government receive any foreign aid. More than 95% of the population is literate, with education free and compulsory between the ages of five and 16.

In an average year, about 600,000 tourists – largely from the US and Canada – visit the islands. The money they spend accounts for about 40% of the colony's total income. As international insurance and investment companies contribute ever more significantly to the economy through their foreign exchange earnings, tourism is becoming less important. Vegetables are still a key winter export, even though housing and industrial construction has significantly reduced farm acreage. Pharmaceuticals and extracted essences for perfumes are Bermuda's major exports. What little industry the island has is dedicated to boat building, ship repairing and furniture making. Meat and most other foods are imported; there are few commercial fisheries.

Early in World War II, Bermuda became important as an outpost commanding Atlantic sea lanes. In 1940, US President Franklin D. Roosevelt gave Great Britain 50 destroyers in exchange for advanced bases. In 1941, the US took over, on a 99-year lease, 526 acres for a base on Great Sound at the western end of the islands.

Prior to World War II, one of Bermuda's special charms was the absence of motor traffic. Motorized transport – both private and public – was banned and everyone traveled by bicycle, horse-drawn carriage, boat or railway. In 1946, however, the ban on private cars, buses, taxicabs and motorcycles was lifted and things began to move more quickly. Today, private cars are restricted to one per family and rental cars are still not available.

Life on the islands reflects Bermuda's very British traditions. Islanders adhere to a fairly strict code of social conduct and recreation. British pubs are truly British, fish and chips are the same in Hamilton as they are in London, cricket is the national sport, and tea is served every afternoon at four o'clock. The Queen's English is often spoken, especially by whites, with a clipped, upper-class accent more reminiscent of the quadrangles of Oxford and Cambridge than the sub-tropical island that is Bermuda.

Bermuda has always been an island of adventure. From the dawn of its history more than 380 years ago, explorers, castaways, rovers and opportunists have made for the islands. Today's adventurers – the outdoor enthusiast, skin diver, angler, sailor, hiker, bird watcher or shopper – are looking for something different.

Today, the adventurer is you.

Horseshoe Bay

About Bermuda

History & Government

On a balmy day in 1503, a Spanish explorer by the name of **Juan de Bermudez** became the first European to visit Bermuda, though not by choice, so

the story goes. Today, having undergone a number of name changes, including "Isle of Devils" and the "Somers Isles," the islands are named for the man who discovered them.

Bermudez was shortly followed by several more Spanish explorers but, due to the perceived unfriendly nature of the uninhabited islands, no one bothered to claim the islands for Spain. In 1609 an English flagship, *Sea Venture*, ran aground off what is now St. Catherine's Point. The *Sea Venture*, commanded by **Sir George Somers**, right, was bound for Jamestown in the American colonies. The vessel was carrying 150 people, including John Rolfe, who later married the Indian Princess, Pocahontas; Sir Thomas Gates, the Deputy Governor of Jamestown; and Christopher Newport, the leader of the first expedition to Jamestown. Fortunately, everyone made it safely ashore. Two ships were quickly built from the wreckage of the *Sea Venture* and they set sail once more for Jamestown. Sir George claimed the islands for England, and a charter was granted to the Virginia Company.

An interesting sidelight on the wreck of the Sea Venture *is that Shakespeare drew heavily upon the reports of its survivors for his work,* The Tempest, *written in 1611.*

But the story didn't end there. When the ships arrived in Jamestown, Somers found that most of the colonists had died of starvation. The winter of 1609-1610 became known as the "Starving Time." Somers immediately returned to Bermuda in search of food for the starving colony. It was to be Sir George's last voyage; he died in Bermuda. His heart was buried in the garden established by the survivors of the wreck of the *Sea Venture* and his body was transported back to England. For quite a while after his death, the Bermudas were known as the Somers Isles and, even today, the name is not uncommon among islanders.

In 1612 the **Virginia Company**, impressed by Somers' reports about Bermuda, petitioned King James for an extension to their charter, which was granted. Six months later, the company transferred its rights to the **Bermuda Company**. The same year, the first group of permanent settlers on the islands established the city of St. George's near St. Catherine's Point. Three years later, in 1615, a new charter was granted under the name of "The Governor and Company of the City of London for the Plantation of the Somers Islands," and a second group of settlers arrived from England. In 1620, the **British Colonial Government** was founded, a Royal Governor appointed, and a legislature was established in St. George. In 1684, however, the Bermuda Company's charter was forfeited, and government transferred to the English Crown. A new parliament was established, and Bermuda has been a self-governing British colony ever since.

For more than 200 years, **St. George** was the capital of Bermuda. Then, in 1815, the capital was moved to **Hamilton** in nearby Pembroke Parish, where it has remained.

From 1684 until 1775, Bermuda's main source of income was from timber production, mainly cedar, used extensively in shipbuilding. During that same period, Bermudians colonized the Turk Islands and established the salt industry there. When wooden ships gave way to steel in the 1800s, the island turned to tourism.

Movements for **independence** have surfaced repeatedly over the years, but in 1968 Bermudians ratified a new constitution, under which the British monarch, represented by a Governor, is the head of state. The Governor controls defense, internal security, external affairs, and the police. The 12-member cabinet, headed by the Premier, and including at least six other members of the majority party in the legislature, advises the Governor on other matters. The 11 members of the Senate are appointed. The 40 members of the House of Assembly are elected, two from each of the islands' constituencies. Bermuda's oldest political party, the Progressive Labor Party, was founded in 1963; the United Bermuda Party was formed a year later. Racial and political tensions increased in 1973 when Bermuda's Governor, Richard Sharples, was assassinated. Rioting in the late 1970s led to the Human Rights Act of 1981, which prohibits racial discrimination.

 *On Sept. 25, 1987, Bermuda was hit by the 'worst hurricane in many years. **Hurricane Emily** caused an estimated $35 million in damage.*

Independence continues to be a topic of debate. Members of the opposition recently proposed to take the decision to the people through a national referendum. Judging from the loyalist atmosphere on the island, however, Bermuda's long history of adherence to tradition, and even stronger ties to the homeland, it seems doubtful that independence will ever become a reality.

Economy

 Bermudians enjoy the highest standard of living in the world. Per capita income is extraordinarily high – made even more remarkable by the fact that Bermudians are not required to pay income tax. Unfortunately, the cost of living is high as well. Many Bermudians hold two or more jobs. Almost everything – food, electronics, household goods, clothing – is imported. Property, too, is extremely expensive; a modest two-bedroom home can easily cost a quarter-million dollars or more.

However, it seems that most young Bermudians with a will can and do own their own homes. For instance, during a conversation with one of my taxi drivers – great sources of local information – he explained how it is usually done. His son and daughter-in-law both spent the first several years of their marriage living in a rented apartment and working two jobs each, saving every penny they could spare. Three years later, and with some $60,000 in savings, they were able to purchase a small lot outright. This gave them collateral for a starter loan/mortgage and, still continuing to work two jobs each, they began to build. As the structure began to grow, so did the collateral and they were able to borrow a little more every several months along the way. The structure, a three-bedroom home with a two bedroom apartment attached, was completed in about two years. Still working two jobs each, they were able to move into the house and rent out the apartment. The rental money pays most of the mortgage, which will be paid off in 10 years, and they are now the proud owners of a property worth more than $600,000. Not bad for a couple still in their '30s. And that's the way most Bermudians grow into home ownership. Perhaps there are some lessons to be learned here.

As with most offshore vacation destinations, Bermuda has suffered from the effects of 9/11. At the time of writing this, tourism was off some 30%, and that has affected the attitudes of those most concerned with the industry. No longer complacent, the service industry has taken the downtrend to heart. The once cavalier attitudes of hotel staff, waiters, bus drivers and other members of the service industries toward their guests are no more. And, even though the attitudes of a few store clerks leave a lot to be desired, you can expect to meet friendly, helpful staff wherever you go.

With the new prosperity brought to the islands by the giants of international banking and insurance – more than 6,000 off-shore companies are now based here – and with the aftermath of 9/11 the hotel industry has had to learn to compete, and I'm happy to tell you that it has. Many of the major hotels on the islands have undergone extensive renovations and upgrades; restaurants, once more than a little complacent, are now up-to-date with the industry and, for the most part, compete on a level playing field with any of their international rivals. The cost of a hotel room has not been reduced, but value for money in those rooms has, in my opinion, more than doubled. Yes, you'll still find hotels that are sub-par at best, mostly the older, smaller properties, and conditions have a nasty habit of deteriorating over even a short period of time. So, if you're not satisfied with the service, the food that's put before you, or the condition of your hotel room, be sure to make your feelings known, not only to the people directly concerned, but to those who can do something about it at the Bermuda Ministry of Tourism (see page 13).

People

Although Bermuda's roots are buried deep within its British heritage, the people have also been heavily influenced over the past three hundred years by its location. While the average Bermudian is very British, one finds the Caribbean influence and its African roots here, especially among the black population. The colorful clothing and many of the important festivals reflect beginnings born in slavery. Caribbean music, reggae and calypso, wafts gently across the islands, bringing with it a feeling of well-being and a happy attitude.

Daily life on Bermuda is much the same as in England. Darts are played in pubs; fish and chips, sausage rolls, and meat pies are on most menus; and afternoon tea is a tradition that's inviolable. Everything stops for tea.

On an island nation this small, no place is exclusive to locals; where they go, you go. And, as most people use the public transportation system, you'll find yourself in close contact with the residents. Today's Bermudian is, for the most part, an extremely friendly soul, easy to like and easy to get to know. Locals have no qualms about striking up a conversation with visitors on buses, the ferry, in pubs or on the beach. If you need help of any sort, you have only to ask. Bermudians are well educated and extremely articulate; you'll have no trouble understanding them. Treat them with courtesy and respect.

Holidays

Bermudians enjoy their holidays. Given an excuse, gombay dancers in colorful garb will turn out to dance through the city streets, especially on Boxing Day (December 26th), New Year's Day, Good Friday, Easter Monday, and during May (Heritage Month). **Gombay** (the

African word for drum or rhythm) was born of slavery and is celebrated throughout the Caribbean and the West Indies in various forms. During the celebrations you will see gaily-colored feathered headdresses, elaborate costumes, fantastically carved masks, acrobatic leaping and dancing, all set to throbbing, hypnotic island music. If you are lucky enough to experience gombay, you'll be hooked. Locals and visitors alike find themselves joining in, dancing to the beat, and following along as the parade meanders slowly through the city streets.

Perhaps the strongest holiday tradition on the islands is the **Cup Match**, a cricket match between St. George's and Somerset. This two-day tradition was born at the turn of the century to celebrate Sir George Somers and the abolition of slavery. It's difficult to believe a cricket match could stir up so much emotion. Rivalry between the two teams, and the communities, borders on the obsessive. It takes place in either late July or early August and has developed into a carnival of the first magnitude. While the cricket match is the center of the celebration, socializing has become just as important. The event brings intense competition on the field, along with wild island music, dancing, food, and much more. If you can make it to Bermuda for the Cup Match, you're in for a treat.

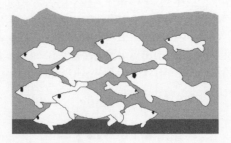

Travel Information

Bermuda Department Of Tourism

In the **United States**, for brochures and automated information, ☎ 800-237-6832 or visit www.bermudatourism.com. You can call or write the Bermuda Department of Tourism office at 205 E. 42nd Street, New York, NY 10017; ☎ 212-818-9800.

In **Canada**, contact the Bermuda Department of Tourism at 1200 Bay Street, Suite 1004, Toronto, ON, Canada M5R 2A5; ☎ 416-923-9600.

In the **United Kingdom**, contact the Bermuda Department of Tourism at 1 Battersea Church Road, London, SW11 3lY; ☎ 020-8410-8188.

When To Go

Peak Season

 There's no doubt that the high season – April through September – is the best time to head to Bermuda. That's when the weather, events, activities and attractions are all at their peak. The beaches are open (though often crowded), and there are lots of organized tours, barbecues, cricket matches and evening entertainment options.

In summer the days are balmy, the evenings warm and romantic, and the nights cool. The temperatures during the day rise into the mid-80s to low 90s, and fall in the evenings to the high 60s or low 70s.

HURRICANE CATEGORIES

Atlantic hurricanes are ranked by the Saffir-Simpson hurricane intensity scale to give an estimate of the potential flooding and damage. Category three and above is considered intense.

Category	Min. Sustained Winds	Damage
One	74-95	*Minimal:* Damage primarily to shrubbery, trees and foliage.
Two	96-110	*Moderate:* Considerable damage to shrubbery and foliage; some trees blown down. Some damage to roofing materials.
Three	111-130	*Extensive:* Foliage torn from trees; large trees blown down. Some structural damage to small buildings. Mobile homes destroyed. Flooding along the coastline.
Four	131-155	*Extreme:* Shrubs and trees blown down. Complete failure of roofs on small residences. Major beach erosion. Massive evacuation of all homes within 500 yards of shore possibly required. Hurricane Andrew, which smashed into South Florida in 1992, is an example of a category four.
Five	155+	*Catastrophic:* Some complete building failures. Small buildings overturned or blown away. Low-lying escape routes inland cut by rising water three to five hours before the hurricane's center arrives. Hurricane Camille, a category five, struck Mississippi and Louisiana in 1969.

When it rains (sometimes quite heavily), it does so mostly in the evenings. Rain, of course, is extremely important to the islands. Having no other natural source of water, the occasional downpour is always welcomed for it fills up the storage tanks.

Hurricane season runs from June through November, but Bermuda has been lucky for many years. Big winds do blow, but most hurricanes seem to skirt the island. Tropical storms with winds of up to 75 miles an hour can make for an exciting day or two. The architecture on the islands, though, is built to withstand all but the most intense category five hurricanes. Interestingly, the islanders always seem to know instinctively, well in advance, when there's a "big blow" coming. Apparently it has something to do with the activities of insects and spiders, birds, the atmosphere, and even the action of the sea on the South Shore.

Off-Season

Bermuda's slow season, from November through February, has advantages all its own. Although the climate is always inviting, it is cooler and more comfortable in the off-season. The beaches, shops and hotels are less crowded, and there are package deals that, along with special offers at many restaurants, can save you money. The swimming, diving, hiking and fishing are just as good – perhaps even more enjoyable with the lack of tourists.

Be aware, though, that many popular attractions, restaurants, museums and hotels close, or at least operate on reduced hours during this slow period. On the plus side, a number of golf tournaments, special events and walking tours are organized especially with winter visitors in mind.

Book your vacation during the winter months and you're likely to get a good deal. Hotels – those that remain open – usually reduce rates as much as 40% to fill some of the empty space. Package rates on the public transport system are also lower. The cooler weather makes golf and tennis that much more enjoyable.

If you like solitude, windswept beaches, cool sea breezes, quiet streets and shops, then the slow season may be just right for you. I've made several visits in the off-season and I always have a good time. Daytime temperatures are in the high 60s to low 70s most of the time, and there's more than enough to see and do to keep you busy.

If you do decide to visit in the low season, you'll need to take a warm jacket for the evenings and a light sweater in case it gets chilly during the day.

Getting There

There are a number of ways to reach Bermuda. Almost all major US and Canadian airlines offer service from most of the larger cities. The United Kingdom is also well-served, both by British and American airlines, although using an American carrier usually means being routed through one of the hubs on the American mainland.

Another option is to arrive by sea, and Bermuda is on the itinerary of most cruise lines. Increasingly popular is the package vacation offered by a growing number of companies in the US, Canada and Europe. Package tour operators may be the airlines themselves or independent companies, each offering a variety of products designed to suit every budget.

Vacation Planning Online

There are bargains to be found online; it's just a matter of knowing where to look. I do have one major reservation, though. When going it alone, not only do you often get precisely what you pay for; you might just find you get a lot less. For instance, whom do you appeal to when things go wrong? And they may. A good travel agent will often have first-hand knowledge of many of the popular resorts and will be able to recommend good hotels and restaurants. Better yet, the same travel agent may be able to steer you away from the traps. He/she will be able to provide trip insurance, day trips and itineraries. In short, a good travel agent will ensure you get value for money and real back-up when you need it.

But, if you're determined to go it alone, I recommend you use only well-established companies, such as **Expedia.com, Orbitz.com** and **Travelocity.com**. These sites cater to the true "independent" traveler. Here you can book airline tickets hotels and rental cars – often at a discount. If you've not used a direct booking service before, make sure you understand exactly what you're buying. First, are there restrictions on your airline tickets? Can you cancel or are they non-refundable? What penalties would apply if you needed to cancel close to the departure date? You should understand that a cheap airline ticket almost always means there are restrictions. Second, be sure to shop around; there's always a better deal no more than a couple of clicks away. Third, don't forget such websites as **hotels.com**, **hotelclub.com** and **hoteldiscounts.com.** Combine an inexpensive airline ticket with a discounted hotel stay and you should have a total cost you can live with.

In addition, most of the **major airlines**, and some of the larger **package operators**, have websites. Many, if not all, of the advantages of using an online booking agent are available at these sites. Delta Airlines, American Airlines, USAir, and many more, all offer extensive package options that include airfare, car rental, hotel rooms, trip insurance, and airport/hotels transfers, often at big discounts (depending upon when you want to go). These companies are very good at what they do. They have inspectors visiting resorts on a regular basis to make sure that things are just as they should be. They own the airline, which means if a flight is cancelled you are their first priority for the next available flight. True, you might run into a small hitch here and there but, on the whole, you can rest assured that what you pay for is exactly what you get. And it's true one-stop-shopping. A few clicks and you're done. If you want to book online yourself, I think this is the way to go.

ADDITIONAL TRAVEL WEBSITES

American Airlines Vacations. . www.aavacations.com

Delta Vacations . . . . www.deltavacations.com

Insight Vacations . . . . . www.insightvacations.com

Travel Information

US Airways Vacations   www.usairwaysvacations.com

British Airways Vacations . www.britishairways.com

Classic Custom Vacations . www.classicvacations.com

Apple Vacations . . . . www.applevacations.com

Vacation Express. . . . . . www.vacationexpress.com

Travel Impressions . . . www.traveimpressions.com

Horizon Tours . . . . www.horizontours.com

Hotel Information . . . . www.wheretostay.com

Most independent package tour operators, such as Vacation Express and Travel Impressions, prefer that you book your vacation through a travel agent. The theory is that they have less trouble dealing with an agent, with whom they will already have built a long-term relationship, than they do when dealing directly with the general public. Even so, many will deal with you directly, but only online. For that reason, most operators, including the airline vacation companies, prefer not to publish phone numbers.

By Air

Commercial Airlines

Bermuda is served by **Air Canada** (☎ 800-776-3000), **American Airlines** (☎ 800-433-7300), **British Airways** (☎ 800-247-9297), **Continental** (☎ 800-525-0280), **Delta** (☎ 800-221-1212) and **US Airways** (☎ 800-428-4322), many with direct flights from Atlanta, Baltimore, Boston, London, Miami, New York, Newark, Raleigh/Durham and Toronto. Of these, Delta offers the most comprehensive service and the most convenient schedule of flights (with direct, non-stop flights from both Atlanta and Boston). American Airlines offers a complete non-stop flight schedule departing from New York and Boston, often at the best rates.

Private Aircraft

Bermuda International Airport accepts privately owned and corporate aircraft. However, the government requires that all private and commercial air traffic make arrangements for ground handling with an approved agency on the islands. **Bermuda Aviation Service Ltd.** can be reached at ☎ 441-293-2500, by radio on VHF 131.6 MHz, or by mail at PO Box HM 718, Hamilton, Bermuda HM CX. Or try **Mid-Atlantic Aviation Ltd.**, ☎ 441-293-4622, VHF 131.65 MHz, or PO Box 11, Bermuda, GE CX. These two agencies will act as representatives for you, your crew and passengers, handling all customs and immigration procedures, documentation, hanger facilities, aircraft services and ground transportation.

By Sea

Cruise Ships

Cruise ships dock either at the Royal Naval Dockyard or at St. George's. Either way, getting around is easy. The ferries run convenient services between the RND and Hamilton, and also serve Paget, Warwick and Somerset counties. Best of all, service is frequent, fun and inexpensive. You'll find ferry schedules at the end of this guide, page 199.

If you are on a cruise ship, you leave all the major decisions to your travel agent and the cruise line. All your wants and needs while on vacation can be found on-board ship, and most of what you'll consume (meals, snacks, soft drinks at the table) is included in the package price. The only extras are souvenirs, day trips at ports of call, and your flight (if necessary) to get you to your port of departure. Most often the best airfares can be found through the cruise lines themselves. They book block space on aircraft departing from all major airline hubs such as New York, Chicago, Atlanta, Miami, and Charlotte. Connector flights however – those providing transport between your hometown and the airline's hub – will run the airfare up appreciably.

Accommodations on-board range from cramped, windowless cubicles deep in the bowels of the ship, to large, luxury suites on an upper deck, complete with balcony, lots of space to spread out, and all modern conveniences – even butler service.

 *My advice is to book a mid-priced outside stateroom. You'll have a little more room than in cheaper staterooms, a view of the ocean and port of call as you arrive and leave, and the rate is not that much more.*

Ship pursers can arrange a variety of day trips and fun things to do – activities such as scuba diving, snorkeling and windsurfing, to name a few. You can also rent motor scooters to explore the island. My advice is to book through your travel agent whatever you think you'll need or want to do in advance, before you leave. If you wait until you're on board, it's first-come, first-served, and you may not get what you want. If you do decide to leave it that late, book as soon as you can. It's possible to book some of these activities independently, outside of the cruise line, at one of the Tourist Information Centres in Hamilton or at the Royal Naval Dockyard. Since the cruise lines make a profit on offered extras, you'll pay less if you book your activities and rentals direct. Your travel agent may be able to help. If not, use the phone numbers listed in this book.

Cruising to Bermuda is not an inexpensive vacation. Most cruises last for six or seven nights, with at least three nights spent on Bermuda. Sometimes a cruise special can be found for as little as $850 per person, not including airfare to the port of departure. Without a special, and at peak travel times, you may well find yourself paying at least double that.

Of all the cruise lines serving Bermuda, **Celebrity** – now a part of the Royal Caribbean Cruise Line – usually offers the least expensive options. At the high end, upward of $4,000 per person, cruising is still regarded as a very special experience. Luxury and formality are the main features of such lines as **Cunard** and **Crystal**. Whatever the price range or cruise line you choose, however, you can expect to be well looked after – all food and snacks are provided, along with soft drinks at the table. Most cruise lines now charge for soft drinks at the pool and for ice cream. Beer, wine and liquor are an additional cost (that will often bring on sticker-shock).

But cruising is a great way to visit any exotic location. Long, lazy days on deck, lounging poolside, being waited on hand-and-foot every waking moment, makes cruising an unforgettable experience. Feel like really pampering yourself? The spa and salon are only a deck away. Tropical sea breezes, watching the moon rise over the ocean, with the trackless sea stretching to the horizon in every direction – these are moments you can experience no other way.

The Food on Board

 The food on any cruise, no matter the line, is always a little out of the ordinary. Most ships have a master chef on-board to oversee the menu, cuisine and overall standard of excellence. The dining rooms are large, airy and offer grand views of the ocean. But it's the food that's special. Lobster is the highlight of Celebrity's main menu (at least it was at the time of writing). Afternoon tea is an experience not to be missed – homemade, freshly-baked scones with strawberry jam and clotted cream. Then there are the midnight buffets, extravaganzas of goodies where all-you-can-eat is the watchword. Want to dine in your room? No problem. Order room service from the menu or have gourmet pizza delivered to your door.

Paying for Extras on Board

You'll be expected to provide a credit card number or to pre-pay for a ship-board charge card. This means you'll hand over several hundred dollars (or British pounds), and they'll give you a credit account for charging all your extras. (Don't worry, they let you know as soon as your credit is up and you need to give them some more money.) It's easy to run up your bill. Several rounds of drinks will hit you hard, and you may lose track when you're having a good time.

Casinos on Board

Again, the watchword here is caution. I've heard horror stories of couples on honeymoon losing all they had on the outward-bound leg of the cruise. A vacation with little or no spending money can be a harrowing experience.

A Typical Cruise Schedule

The following gives you an idea of a Bermuda cruise schedule.

Celebrity's *Zenith* cruises to Bermuda from New York 28 times each year, from early May through the end of October. The itinerary is as follows:

- Saturday: Depart New York 4:30 pm
- Sunday: At sea
- Monday: Arrive Hamilton, Bermuda at 8 am
- Tuesday: Hamilton
- Wednesday: Depart Hamilton at 6 am
- Wednesday: Arrive St. George at 9 am
- Thursday: Depart St. George at 3 pm
- Friday: At sea
- Saturday: Arrive New York at 8 am

Cruise Lines

Bermuda is served by:

- **Carnival Cruise Lines,** ☎ 800-327-9501 or www.carnival.com
- **Celebrity Cruises,** ☎ 800-327-6700 or www.celebrity-cruises.com
- **Norwegian Cruise Line,** ☎ 800-327-7030 or www.ncl.com
- **Royal Caribbean Cruises, Ltd.,** ☎ 800-327-6700 or www.rccl.com

Private Yacht

 If you're one of those true nautical types – an adventurer of the old school – you may want to visit Bermuda under your own steam, or sail. And it's a great way to go if you have a vessel big enough and sturdy enough to make the journey. Small boats (under 30 feet) have made it without incident. The weather is obviously an important factor when making sail for Bermuda. The hurricane season – June through November – brings untold hazards, and December through April can be equally harrowing due to sudden storms and high winds that strike with little or no warning.

Bermuda's port of entry for all visiting yachts and small vessels is **St. George's**. All crew members and passengers must clear Customs and Immigration. There's a 24-hour facility on Ordnance Island, St. George's, but if you arrive after dark, it might be best to wait until dawn before entering port. To approach port, you must contact **Bermuda Harbour Radio** and give your ETA. The facility listens 24 hours a day on 2182 Khz USB and on VHF 16 (distress channel). Use these channels only for contacting Bermuda Harbour Radio. All passengers and crew are required to have valid documentation, such as a passport or, for US and Canadian citizens, a certified copy of your birth certificate and a photo ID – your driver's license is ideal.

If you plan to stay more than a week and live on board your boat, all Bermudian health regulations must be complied with. Notify the Department of Marine and Ports of your plans. They will then supply you with a copy of the regulations. Contact them after clearing Customs and Immigration. ☎ 441-295-6575.

Navigable Bridge

The swing bridge between Ferry Reach and Castle Harbour is opened upon request from 7:30 am to 7 pm, daily, April through September, and 7:30 am to 5 pm, October through March. If you intend to make sail from St. George's to Hamilton, this route can cut as much as 30 minutes from the normal two-hour sail, and make it more interesting. Contact the Department of Marine & Ports, ☎ 441-295-6575.

Marinas

St. George's

Captain Smokes Marina, McCallan's Wharf 13, Wellington St., Town of St. George. ☎ 441-297-1940. Fresh water, 110- and 220-volt electrical hookups, fuel.

Sandy's Parish

This comprises four small islands at the western end of the archipelago. Among other attractions, you'll find the Royal Naval Dockyard and Maritime Museum housed in what was once the largest fortress on the island. Together, the fortress and the Dockyard comprised one of the most important strongholds of the British Navy during the 18th and 19th centuries. Today, the West End is a tourist attraction; it's also home to the Dockyard Marina.

Dockyard Marina, 9 Dockyard Terrace, Royal Naval Dockyard, Ireland Island, Bermuda. ☎ 441-234-0300. The marina is housed within the confines of the Dockyard breakwater. Facilities include fresh water, fuel and a clubhouse. Daily, weekly and monthly rates are available.

Hamilton

Royal Bermuda Yacht Club, Albouy's Port, Hamilton, Bermuda. ☎ 441-295-2214. As its name implies, the Royal Bermuda Yacht Club holds a royal warrant granted by Queen Elizabeth II and has held such warrants continuously since the reign of Queen Victoria. What does this mean to you, the erstwhile mariner from across the ocean? Not much, I'm afraid. It does mean that it's a very exclusive club, with memberships received more on inheritance than application. Still, you can take advantage of the club's berths and services simply by tying up and registering. An account will be opened, allowing you and your crew full advantage of most of what's available. The club is situated on Albouy's Point in the city – all the sights and sounds of Hamilton are close at hand. Vessel size is limited to 80 feet maximum. The rate without electricity is $1.50/foot per night; with electricity it's $1.75.

If you are indeed going to sail to Bermuda, consider buying a copy of *The Bermuda Yachting Guide*. This extremely informative book, published by the Bermuda Maritime Museum Association, provides most of the information you'll need during your stay in the islands, including anchorages. In the US, purchase it from Bluewater Books and Charts, 1481 SE 17th Street Causeway, Ft. Lauderdale, FL 33316, www.bluewaterweb.com. Or order it direct from the publisher, Bermuda Maritime Museum Association, PO Box MA 273, Mangrove Bay, MA BX, Bermuda. ☎ 441-234-1333.

Package Vacations

While the information included in this section was correct at the time of writing, rates and content change without notice. Be sure to check by calling the appropriate phone numbers or visiting the websites.

The package vacation is perhaps the ideal way to visit Bermuda, or any other destination for that matter. The only decisions you'll need to make are when to go and how much you can afford to pay.

So what exactly is a package vacation? Well, they come in various shapes and sizes, tailored to offer something for almost everyone. Most include, as a minimum, airfare to and from the islands, airport/hotel transfers, and accommodations. The accommodations can be luxurious or barebones: you get what you pay for. Some packages may include activities such as golf. Some may include the use of a motorscooter or bicycle. Some may include food, alcoholic drinks, soft drinks and afternoon tea; these are the so-called "all-inclusive" packages, a term that's often a little misleading. Always find out exactly what your package includes before you pay for it, so you won't get any nasty surprises when you reach the islands.

No matter what type of package vacation you choose, you will need to take some cash, credit cards and perhaps travelers checks, along with you. There's no packaged holiday yet invented that covers all you'll need or want to do when you get there. How much should you take? That, of course, depends on your budget, but do remember that Bermuda has to import almost everything and, with the exception of duty-free goods, most items will cost a little more than they do at home, no matter where you hail from.

The following packages are just a few culled from the inventories of some of the major operators, and the prices were accurate at the time of writing. Bear in mind, however, that, depending on the season, and the individual needs of the particular operator, there are deals to be made beyond what's quoted here that can save you a significant amount of money.

Package Operators

There are a number of package operators I am very familiar with and can recommend. They have been in the business for a number of years and have ironed out the wrinkles and inconsistencies. They all make regular on-site visits to check on the overall condition and ambiance of the hotels they use, hotel restaurants, amenities and the quality of the service. Two of the operators are airlines, and so can offer somewhat better schedules, though not necessarily better rates. Two are independent companies that use a variety of airlines; often they can provide a similar package to those of the major airlines but at better rates.

All packages should include the following minimum services:

- Airfare from a major hub – Atlanta, New York, Chicago, Boston, etc. (airfare from your hometown can be provided with any package at extra cost).
- Hotel accommodations.
- Roundtrip airport/hotel transfers.
- Hotel tax.
- A local island representative.

Some operators may include chambermaid gratuities (Travel Impressions does). All offer some sort of travel protection **insurance**. This protects your investment if you have to cancel your vacation. You don't have to take insurance, but you should. I wouldn't consider investing two or three thousand dollars without this protection. Who knows what might happen? You could fall sick, meet with an accident, or even have a relative die.

Some operators offer "**all-inclusive**" vacations. These include all of the above, plus breakfast, lunch and dinner daily; unlimited bar drinks, themed night buffets, afternoon tea, a weekly cocktail party, all taxes and gratuities, non-motorized water sports (sailing, snorkeling, kayak, windsurfing, etc.), an unlimited Bermuda public transport pass (which includes buses and ferries), tennis, nightly entertainment, and daily activities. Are these all-inclusive packages worth the extra cost? Yes, especially if you enjoy a drink. Time was when only one hotel on the islands offered the all-inclusive option. Today, the idea is catching on, and more and more hotels are getting involved.

Some operators offer a range of **specialty packages** – golf, spa, or honeymoon. You'll find some of them listed below.

So as not to be repetitive, if I've listed package options under one package operator, but they are also offered by other operators, I've detailed only the essential differences, then referred you to the listings for the previous operator.

For more information on the individual hotels, check the *Accommodations* section of the book.

Most package tour operators prefer to deal through travel agents. Your agent can book you on any of these packages. Delta and American Airlines will, however, deal direct with consumers. See their contact information below.

Delta Vacations

Delta offers a number of packages to Bermuda, including hotels rated from standard to deluxe. They'll fly you non-stop to Bermuda on Boeing 767 aircraft either from Boston or Atlanta. Their air schedule is comprehensive and, provided you book far enough in advance, they can certainly meet any timetable you might want.

Contact Delta at ☎ 800-221-1212 and ask for Delta Vacations. You can also book directly on their website at www.deltavacations.com.

Delta also offers what they call their "MoneyPlus Guarantee." This states that "if any tangible component of any Delta Vacations packages is not delivered as promised (except under circumstances beyond the reasonable control of the tour operator), we will refund the value of the undelivered component plus issue a travel credit of equal or greater value which may be used for future Delta Vacation packages."

Delta's travel protection plan costs only $49 per person and allows you to cancel your vacation for any reason, including poor weather conditions, illness, or a sudden change of plans, with a full refund of the package price.

Also included in Delta's Bermuda packages are several nice bonus features: a free tour of the Bermuda Triangle Brewery, 2-for-1 entrée at La Trattoria Restaurant, 10% discount on Oleander Cycle Rentals, as well as discounts on glass bottom boat, snorkeling, and dinner cruises from Bermuda Water Tours.

The following three- and five-night Delta Vacations (low-season rates, 11/16 through 4/30) include airfare from Boston. Rates from Atlanta range between $40 and $80 extra, depending upon the season.

SANDPIPER APARTMENTS
Three nights $419; five nights $489

Located on the South Shore only 200 yards from the beach. These are studio apartments with fully equipped kitchens. There's also a swimming pool and Jacuzzi. The South Shore is where you'll find all the best beaches. Everything is easily accessible using the public transport system; buses run every 20 or 30 minutes. Inexpensive and very nice, if you don't mind the walk to and from the beach. Delta rates it a "standard" property.

PALMETTO HOTEL & COTTAGES
Three nights $529; five nights $629

This is actually a small hotel with several cottages on the grounds. It is situated on the shore and has a small beach. There's a pool, a restaurant and they also have mopeds for rent. There's a nice pub (English-style bar) on the property. The rooms are comfortably furnished and have patios and balconies. Delta rates this one as a "standard" property, but I think it's a little better than that.

GROTTO BAY BEACH RESORT
Three nights $449; five nights $709

Grotto Bay is one of my own favorite spots on the islands. The full-service resort is priced for the average budget and is rated "preferred" by Delta. All rooms have private balconies or patios and ocean view, though the more expensive rooms are actually on the water's edge while the more moderately priced rooms are on the hill overlooking the water.

I've stayed at Grotto Bay several times. On my most recent visit in 2003 I was pleasantly surprised to find that the resort, always one of my favorites, had undergone major renovations and now can easily hold its own with any of its competitors. The pastel shades of the guest units (pale yellows, blues and greens) I found pleasing, not to say soothing. The rooms have all been refurnished, are comfortable and relaxing. The rates offered by Delta make it even more appealing.

MUNROE BEACH COTTAGES
Three nights $479; five nights $619

Situated on its own private beach on the South Shore, this cottage colony is one of the best-kept secrets on the islands. It sits on five acres of waterfront property and is surrounded by Port Royal Golf Course, which makes it ideal for a golfing vacation. Delta rates this as a "preferred" property. I agree. This is pretty much a self-catering situation, but don't let that put you off. All of the cottages have fully equipped kitchens and the local grocery store will deliver every day except Sundays and public holidays. The cottages themselves are a short walk from the beach – about 100 yards – but it's a very pleasant stroll, especially in the early morning. The

Travel Information

cottages are all well furnished and have full bathrooms with tubs and showers.

SURF SIDE BEACH CLUB

Three nights $489; five nights $639

Again, a self-catering property on the South Shore, but with a small poolside restaurant and bar. The elegant one- and two-bedroom studio cottages and apartments feature fully equipped kitchenettes and each has a balcony overlooking the ocean and private beach. The furnishings border on the luxurious; the beach is secluded and inviting. This is a delightful property. Delta rates it "preferred." You won't be disappointed. I spent several days here in 2003 and I can highly recommend it.

THE FAIRMONT HAMILTON PRINCESS & THE FAIRMONT SOUTHAMPTON PRINCESS

Three nights $589; five nights $809

These two resorts could well be considered Bermuda's flagship properties. I've grouped them together for this section, but you'll find in-depth information about the individual properties in the *Accommodations* section of this book. Suffice it to say that they both offer the ultimate in resort amenities, with luxury accommodations, high-class restaurants, and service second-to-none. The Hamilton Princess overlooks the harbour and doesn't have a beach. The Southampton Princess does have a beach, but to reach it you have to walk across the golf course. Guests staying at one hotel can enjoy the amenities of both. Both have world-class restaurants, luxurious rooms, and everything else you could want for an exciting vacation. Golfers, too, are well cared for. The course at the Southampton Princess is a championship-rated facility, picturesque and challenging. Delta rates the Hamilton Princess "preferred" and the Southampton Princess "ultimate."

HARMONY CLUB

Three nights $809; five nights $1,189

This is Bermuda's only true "all-inclusive" resort. This means that not only the basics – flight, transfers, etc. – but all meals and alcoholic drinks, scooter, even public transport, as well as free golf at the Belmont Hotel and Golf Club are included in the cost. Newly redecorated and furnished, the hotel offers a comfortable, yet inexpensive hideaway. The sprawling complex's only drawback is its lack of beach. The closest one to the hotel is Elbow Beach, some 15 minutes away on foot, but only a couple of minutes by bus and, as they say, there's one passing every 15 minutes or so. Still, the rooms are comfortable, the gardens pleasant, the booze plentiful, and afternoon tea is served every day. Not really for the younger set. All of this makes the rates quoted above quite attractive, especially if you enjoy a drink now and again. Delta rates the resort "preferred." I would go one better. *Couples only –* any gender.

SONESTA BEACH RESORT
Three nights $529; five nights $709

Rated "ultimate" by Delta, this is an exceptionally well-appointed resort: 400 luxury rooms, three pools, three restaurants, three lounges, three beaches, all with pink sand on the South Shore, six tennis courts, golf, watersports, kids programs. It's difficult to elaborate on all that Sonesta has to offer without rambling. Suffice it to say that one never really needs to leave the property. If you like to enjoy an afternoon relaxing at the spa, you can do it here. Like to take long walks along the cliffs or beach? That, too, you can do, and without leaving the property. Do you have a large family? Sonesta will welcome you all, including the kids. Add a multi-million-dollar renovation and you have a resort that compares favorably with the best on the island. You name it, Sonesta has it all. It's not inexpensive, but if you're looking for something special, this is it.

Travel Impressions

During my time as a travel agent I became very familiar with Travel Impressions and I booked hundreds of vacation packages through them. I found them to be helpful in every way possible. They could be relied upon to deliver a good package at a reasonable price. Sometimes they are the cheapest, sometimes not, but you are sure to receive value for money, as well as peace of mind. Travel Impressions' Passenger Protection Program (insurance) costs $49 per person and includes the following:

Trip Cancellation/Interruption. Reimbursement for any non-refundable cancellation penalties incurred if you must cancel or curtail your trip due to covered medical reasons affecting you, your immediate family members or traveling companions.

$200 Trip Delay. Your luggage and personal belongings are insured for the duration of your trip against loss or damage up to $800.

$1,000 Medical Expense. Reimburses you for doctor or hospital charges should you become ill or injured during your trip.

Worldwide Emergency Assistance. 24-hour access to the services of American International Assistance Services, including legal and medical referrals, emergency cash transfers, lost documents, etc.

All Travel Impressions packages include:

- Advance seat assignment
- Airfare (not quoted in the rates below) from the city of your choice: rates vary from city to city.
- Hotel accommodations
- Hotel Tax
- Gratuities

Their website is www.travelimpressions.com.

FAIRMONT HAMILTON PRINCESS
Three nights from $330 per person (airfare extra)

Package includes transportation to and from Southampton Princess; also exchange facilities at the Southampton Princess.

FAIRMONT SOUTHAMPTON PRINCESS
Three nights from $334 per person (airfare extra)

Package includes transportation to and from Hamilton Princess; also exchange facilities at the Hamilton Princess.

SONESTA BEACH RESORT
Three nights from $266 per person (airfare extra)

Deluxe accommodations, indoor and outdoor pools, private beach, tennis courts, European beauty spa, casual and fine dining.

GROTTO BAY BEACH RESORT
Three nights from $204 per person (airfare extra)

First-class resort hotel in Hamilton Parish overlooking a secluded cove with two beaches, five grottos and a cavern. All rooms have panoramic ocean views. Two restaurants, tennis courts, watersports center.

POMPANO BEACH CLUB

Three nights from $260 per person (airfare extra)

Adjacent to Port Royal Golf Course. All 54 rooms feature ocean views. Breakfast and dinner is served daily. Heated pool, two Jacuzzis, restaurant, two bars, water sports, tennis courts, nightly entertainment. The on-site watersports center is a great convenience for those who like to spend time in, on and under the water. The dining and cuisine are highly rated, and the resort was recently voted one of the top 100 honeymoon resorts in the world.

ELBOW BEACH RESORT

Three nights from $321 per person (airfare extra)

A deluxe resort with an informal British atmosphere, set on 34 acres overlooking its own pink sand beach. The 300 guestrooms are all climate-controlled and have balconies. There are three restaurants, a beach café, exercise room, shopping arcade, satellite TV, free in-room movies, five all-weather tennis courts, and a heated freshwater pool.

ROSEDON HOTEL

Three nights from $351 per person (airfare extra)

Rosedon is a small private hotel, surrounded by lush botanical gardens, just a five-minute walk from Hamilton and the ferry. Even though this once was one of Bermuda's finest private residences, the atmosphere is relaxed and informal; the locale is convenient, and the setting exquisite. Breakfast and afternoon tea are served in your room, poolside, or on the hotel veranda. If you're looking for something intimate, even romantic, close to town and all the action, this is the place for you. As to the ocean and the beach, Rosedon has an arrangement with the Elbow Beach resort; for an extra $4 per day you can use the facilities there and enjoy free taxi service between Elbow Beach and Rosedon.

Travel Information

PALMETTO HOTEL & COTTAGES

Three nights from $287 (airfare not included)

A small, family-owned and -operated hotel and cottage complex overlooking the ocean and conveniently located in Flatts Village. All guestrooms and cottages are air-conditioned, have clock radios, telephones and either a balcony or patio. There's a nice saltwater pool, a small but inviting man-made beach, a great little restaurant, an English-style pub, and there's golf available nearby.

Insight All-Inclusive Packages

All-inclusive packages usually mean a well-budgeted vacation. Other than those little extras for gifts, ice creams, and the like, you know exactly what you're going to spend well before you leave the mainland. Insight offers two such packages. www.insightvacations.com.

HARMONY CLUB

Three nights from $546 (airfare is extra)

The Harmony Club is Bermuda's one and only true all-inclusive vacation spot. The Insight package includes breakfast, snacks and dinner daily, afternoon tea, unlimited wine, spirits and liquors, privileges at a private beach club, use of the putting green, use of all hotel sports and recreational facilities, including a two-seat motor scooter. The package also includes round-trip airport/hotel transfers, free bus and ferry passes (a great little extra), and all taxes and gratuities. This is a well-thought-out and comprehensive package, suitable for all types of vacationers, be they watersports or golf enthusiasts, honeymooners, or just about anyone else.

GROTTO BAY BEACH RESORT

Call Insight or your local travel agent for rates.

Although Grotto Bay is not a true all-inclusive resort, the package offered by arrangement with Insight is. It includes breakfast, snacks and dinner daily, unlimited wine, spirits and liquors, afternoon tea, nightly entertainment, daily activities and most watersports. Elbow Beach has plenty to offer – its own beach, air-conditioned rooms, and its restaurants, make it a great vacation spot. But Insight's all-inclusive package makes it that much better.

American Airlines FlyAAway Vacations

American Airlines have always been one of my favorites. I've traveled with them all over the world and the Caribbean and, as a former travel agent, I dealt with them on a daily basis. The service is good, the people friendly and helpful, the flight schedule is second-to-none, and their vacation packages are often the most favorably priced.

You can book through your travel agent or directly with American Airlines. Contact American at ☎ 800-433-7300 or through www.aavacations.com. Ask for their FlyAAway Vacations. A $100 deposit per person is required at the time of booking. The deposit is applied to the price of the package when you make your final payment.

American stands behind their packages with the promise that "everything will be right – if it's not, you can call us at our 800 number and we'll make it right." American Airlines FlyAAway hotels are rated under their own system, incorporating 1, 2, 3, 4 or 5 eagles. A 1-eagle hotel is in the budget class, while a 5-eagle rating is the height of luxury. There are no 1-eagle hotels available in Bermuda.

Rates quoted are for land only; airfare from the city of your choice is extra, and will be quoted at the time of booking.

The quoted vacation price includes accommodations for the number of nights indicated, hotel taxes and service charges, and some bonus features where applicable. Round-trip hotel/airport transfers are included in all-inclusive rates, but not otherwise (those transfers can purchased at the time of booking).

American offers travel protection insurance for $78 per person. This includes trip-interruption and cancellation coverage, as well as a number of other benefits: 24-hour traveler assistance, trip and baggage delay, emergency accident and sickness, emergency evacuations, etc.

American Airlines FlyAAway Vacations offer the following nine properties in Bermuda rated from 2 eagles to 5 eagles.

PALM REEF HOTEL

2 eagles – two nights from $120 excluding airfare (by special request only; call AA.)

The Palm Reef is a small, informal hotel on Hamilton Harbour with direct ferry service into Hamilton itself. The package includes complimentary afternoon tea. Waterfront rooms with balconies are available. The rooms are spacious with brightly colored decor and comfortable furniture.

GROTTO BAY BEACH CLUB

3 eagles – two nights from $123 excluding airfare

A lovely beachfront hotel with two restaurants, a pool bar, and nightly entertainment. All rooms are air-conditioned and have TVs and coffee makers.

SONESTA BAY BEACH HOTEL

3 eagles – two nights from $145 excluding airfare.

A modern luxury hotel on a 26-acre estate with ocean frontage, including three beaches. There are also tennis courts, a full European spa, scuba diving and snorkeling programs, and four nearby golf courses. Rooms are spacious, airy, and brightly decorated. Great value for the money.

ELBOW BEACH RESORT

4 eagles – two nights from $184 excluding airfare

A beachfront luxury resort on more than 50 landscaped acres with a large private beach. There's a beach bar, a games room, nightly entertainment. All guestrooms are air-conditioned and have TVs and minibars.

FAIRMONT HAMILTON PRINCESS

3 eagles – two nights from $205 excluding airfare

A luxury hotel overlooking Hamilton Harbour and just a five-minute walk from downtown Hamilton. All rooms are air-conditioned and luxuriously furnished; many have private balconies or patios. There are two pools, one freshwater, one saltwater. Facilities at the Southampton Princess are free to guests, and they include golf and tennis. Free transfers between the two hotels.

FAIRMONT SOUTHAMPTON PRINCESS

4 eagles – two nights from $292 excluding airfare

A self-contained luxury resort on 100 acres on the South Shore. All rooms are air-conditioned and feature cable TV and private balconies. There are numerous themed restaurants on the property and an 18-hole, par-3 golf course. There are several all-weather, lighted tennis courts, a spa, aquatic programs, and a dolphin center where you can enjoy a dolphin encounter. For the money, this is perhaps the best value among the nine properties in American's program.

HARMONY CLUB

3 eagles – three all-inclusive nights from $518 excluding airfare

This all-inclusive resort is just two miles from downtown Hamilton, which make it convenient for shopping, dining and sightseeing. There are tennis courts on the property, a pool, saunas, a Jacuzzi, and there's live entertainment nightly during the high season. All meals and drinks are included in the cost, as well as afternoon tea, free use of a motor scooter for the duration of your stay, and several other bonuses. All rooms are air-conditioned and have TVs, radios and coffee makers. If you're on a budget, this is the one for you.

Friendly Vacations

I don't know this company quite as well as I do the previous four, but as a travel agent I have had some pleasant encounters with them. They are an upscale, customer-oriented operator with more than 28 years in the business. They offer some 15 choices for your vacation in Bermuda. These range in price from around $225 per person per night for three nights to more than $1,000 per person for the same three nights, depending on the class of accommodations you choose. Almost all of the hotels offered by Friendly are offered by the other previously listed operators, so I won't go into detail again. I'll simply list them for you, along with the rates, and you can find the details above or in the *Accommodations* section.

Included in the quoted rate for a Friendly Vacations package are: roundtrip hotel/airport transfers, hotel taxes, resort levies, and service charges. The rates quoted are per-person, double-occupancy; airfares are not included.

There is no website, but you can obtain brochures and book a Friendly Vacation through your travel agent.

SONESTA BEACH RESORT
Three nights from $225

FAIRMONT SOUTHAMPTON PRINCESS
Three nights from $335

FAIRMONT HAMILTON PRINCESS
Three nights from $335

HARMONY CLUB ALL-INCLUSIVE RESORT
Three nights from $545

GROTTO BAY BEACH RESORT
Three nights from $195

CLEAR VIEW SUITES & VILLAS
Three nights from $325

PALMETTO HOTEL & COTTAGES
Three nights from $279

ARIEL SANDS BEACH CLUB
Three nights from $498

ROSEDON HOTEL
Three nights from $275

MERMAID BEACH CLUB
Three nights from $299

OXFORD GUEST HOUSE
Three nights from $265

POMPANO BEACH CLUB
Three nights from $451

ROSEMONT GUEST APARTMENTS
Three nights from $225

SURFSIDE BEACH CLUB
Three nights from $239

Honeymoon Packages

 Most tour operators offer some sort of honeymoon package, but these consist of little more than a honeymoon suite, flowers and a bottle of champagne. The suites do tend to be a bit better than the average, but does that justify the extra cost? Expect to pay a least $100 more for your honeymoon package vacation. Here's what I would do: take a little time to visit your local travel agent (I've found little on offer at any of the established websites, such as travelocity.com or orbitz.com) and browse through the brochures. Then get with an agent and tell him/her exactly what it is you're looking for. You'll find the agent has a lot of options that are not easily obtained elsewhere. They will make calls on dedicated lines and work directly with the providers to get you all the little extras that can make a honeymoon the ultimate romantic get-away.

Passports & Visas

 AMERICANS & CANADIANS: You'll need a round-trip or onward ticket and some proof of identification. A passport is ideal, but, if you don't have one, you can get by with an original birth certificate and a photo ID. Passports can be obtained by US citizens through your local post office; allow up to six weeks when applying.

CITIZENS OF THE UNITED KINGDOM: You'll need a valid passport for visits of up to 30 days.

> *Never pack your passport or proof of citizenship in your suitcase!*

Customs & Duties

Register cameras and electronic equipment with customs officials at your home port or airport of departure. This will eliminate any import problems you might encounter on your return.

You may take into Bermuda duty-free: 50 cigars, 200 cigarettes, one pound of tobacco, one quart of liquor and one quart of wine.

Returning home, US citizens may take up to $400 worth of goods, duty-free; Canadian citizens, $300; and citizens of the United Kingdom, £28.

US Customs pre-clearance is available for all US residents returning on scheduled flights.

You must pay a departure tax of $20 per person before leaving Bermuda.

Trip Insurance

It's prudent to be well-insured. First, medical attention is expensive and, secondly, if you have to cancel your trip or if it's canceled due to the bankruptcy or default of one or more of your operators, that can be expensive too.

Before buying extra insurance, check to see what your existing medical and homeowners insurance policies cover. Most major medical policies cover at least medical and dental emergencies. If not, ask your agent to make the necessary changes.

Traveling with Children

Bermuda has never been regarded as a family vacation destination. Activities and amenities are still very much adult-oriented. Other than the sea and the sand, there's little for children to do. Most major resorts and some of the smaller hotels now offer children's programs, and some provide baby-sitting services. The going rate for these services is around $7 per hour, and if you have to bring in someone from the outside, you'll be expected to pay round-trip transportation.

> *Be sure to check the hotel's policy before you book – some hotels do not allow children on the premises.*

Disabled Travelers

 Bermuda can challenge the physically handicapped, especially when traveling around the island. The majority of large resort hotels are accessible to handicapped visitors; most of the smaller ones are not. Many of the larger shops and stores cater to the handicapped traveler, but smaller ones do not. The Pink and Blue public buses are not equipped to handle wheelchairs, but the ferries can handle them quite easily. The **Bermuda Physically Handicapped Association** does, however, have a bus with a hydraulic lift. It's operated by volunteers, and you can make arrangements in advance by writing Box HM 08, Hamilton, Bermuda HM AX, or ☎ 441-292-5025.

Visually-impaired persons wanting to travel with a guide dog must apply for a permit prior to travel. Once this is granted, it must be carried with you at all times. Applications are available at any of the Bermuda Tourism Offices listed below.

Information Offices

The Bermuda Ministry of Tourism can be reached through its offices in the following locations:

Bermuda: Global House, 43 Church St., Hamilton, HM 12, Bermuda, ☎ 292-0023, www.bermudatourism.com.

New York: 205 E. 42nd St., New York, NY 10017, ☎ 800-223-6106 or 212-818-9800.

Atlanta: 245 Peachtree Center Avenue NE, Suite 803, Atlanta, GA 30303, ☎ 404-524-1541.

Boston: 44 School Street, Suite 1010, Boston, MA 02108, ☎ 617-742-0405.

Chicago: Randolph-Wacker Building, 150 North Wacker Drive, Suite 1070, Chicago, IL 60606, ☎ 312-782-5486.

Travel Information

Canada: 1200 Bay Street, Suite 1004, Toronto, Ontario, M5R 2A5, ☎ 800-387-1304 or 416-923-9600.

London: Bermuda Tourism, BCB Ltd., 1 Battersea Church Road, London, SW11 3LY, ☎ 020-8410-8188.

Money

 The Bermuda dollar is divided into 100 cents, and is pegged, through gold, to the American dollar. The US dollar is accepted by all merchants on the islands; change will often be given as a mixture of American and Bermudian currency.

Checks

Personal checks drawn on US banks may be used for purchases at more than 200 locations. US checks can be cashed at some hotels or at local banks by arrangement. The **Bermuda Financial Network** at ☎ 441-292-1799 will cash US checks for a 3% fee. US travelers checks are accepted island-wide.

Credit Cards

 MasterCard, Visa and American Express are accepted at virtually every store, restaurant and hotel and may be used for cash advances at all local bank branches.

ATMs are provided at locations island-wide by the Bank of Bermuda and the Bank of Butterfield. They accept Mastercard, Visa, Cirrus and Plus, and are available for advances 24 hours a day. The Bermuda Financial Network at ☎ 441-292-1799 will provide assistance to visitors who need help with American Express.

Need money from home fast? There's a **Western Union** *location in the City of Hamilton at the Gibbons Deposit Company. You can contact them at ☎ 441-296-6969.*

Costs

Although it seems that almost everything in Bermuda is expensive, you'll receive excellent value for your money. Accommodations in the summer season can run anywhere from $100 a night at a small hotel to as high as $450. During the winter, however, rates drop considerably. The low-season rates at many of the guest houses begin at around $75, and a room at a bed & breakfast might go for as little as $50 per night, including breakfast. You'll have to share a bathroom, but the personal service and friendly atmosphere can make it quite a bargain for those on a budget.

 Traveler's Tip: *Many of the island's small hotels and guest houses do not take credit cards.*

Hotel & Restaurant Prices

Throughout the book restaurant prices are indicated as follows.

RESTAURANT PRICE SCALE	
$$$	Over $50 per person
$$	$20-$50 per person
$	Under $25 per person

Following are the rates for hotels, guest houses, and cottages.

HOTEL PRICE SCALE	
$$$$	More than $250 per night
$$$	$150-$250 per night
$$	$100-$150 per night
$	Less than $100 per night

Travel Information

Some of the quoted hotel rates might be subject to an energy surcharge. All rates are subject to a 6% government tax and do not include gratuities.

Meal Plans at Hotels

Most hotels offer a choice between MAP, BP or EP rates. Guest houses usually offer a choice of BP, CP or EP.

CP (Continental Plan) provides a continental breakfast.

EP (European Plan) denotes no set meal plan, although restaurant facilities are either on the property or nearby.

BP (Bermudian Plan) offers room and full breakfast.

MAP (Modified American Plan) includes breakfast and dinner.

FAP (Full American Plan) includes all meals.

Tipping

Be sure to read your bill before you tip. Many restaurants will automatically add a 15% service charge. If you don't see it, ask before you tip. Your hotel will add a 10% service charge to the rate. This covers everything from maid service to the dining room to the hotel porter, so there's no need to leave a room tip. Porters and baggage handlers at the airport expect to receive a dollar per bag, and cab drivers usually receive 15% of the fare.

Golf & Tennis

 Green fees at the golf courses range from a low of $49 to a high of $180. During the winter, a number of "Bermuda Golf Week" packages are available, which include accommodations and entry to a tournament (see section on *Golf*).

Tennis, too, is reasonable. Most hotels allow paying guests to use their courts free of charge. Visitors, however, will be required to register and pay by the hour – anywhere from $6 to $15, depending on the establishment.

The Niceties

Bermudans are big on good manners and mutual respect. They will definitely be a little put out if approached and questioned without so much as a hello or good morning. When interacting with waiters, store clerks and anyone else in public service, always look them in the eye, pay attention to what they're saying, and talk directly to them; it's all a part of good manners. In Bermuda, gentlemen still give up their seats to ladies when traveling on a crowded bus. Remain seated while a lady has to stand, and you're sure to garner a scornful look or two.

Clothing & Dress

Bermudians are fairly stiff-jointed about what's acceptable and what's not. Bad language in public is very much frowned upon. Scanty dress is also unacceptable: those wearing bikini tops and skimpy shorts on city streets will receive a friendly warning from the local bobby. For men, shorts worn in public should not be cut much higher than an inch above the knee. A shirt should always be worn in public. Casual sportswear is accepted everywhere.

Bermuda shorts, the famous island tradition, are still worn by men in every walk of life. These "long shorts" were introduced to the islands by British military personnel around the turn of the century. Nowadays during the summer, you'll see policemen, complete with English bobby's hat and Bermuda shorts, directing traffic or ticketing speeders. The sight of a banker in a business suit – white shirt, conservative tie, "trousers" an inch above the knee, tall socks above the calf, and a pair of highly polished shoes – is a little surprising at first.

In the evenings you'll need to dress more formally. Ladies can wear a cocktail dress, and a suit and tie is required for men at most restaurants and hotel dining rooms. Winter evenings can also be a little cool so, if you like to walk, pack a light sweater or jacket.

Tennis players must dress properly on all courts. This means white shorts or white tennis shirts, and white socks and tennis shoes.

Proper attire is also required on golf courses. Shorts must be of Bermuda length, cut just above the knee, and shirts must have collars. No jeans, gym shorts or cut-offs are allowed.

Medical Services

 Unfortunately, emergency treatment is sometimes required. Fortunately, Bermuda's health care system is ranked among the best. In an emergency, dial 911 from any telephone and an ambulance will soon be on the way. If you are ambulatory, you'll go to the **King Edward VII Memorial Hospital**, 7 Point Finger Road, Paget, ☎ 441-236-2345.

If you require medical attention while in Bermuda, payment will be expected at the time of treatment. Unfortunately, they do not accept any foreign medical insurance.

Telephones

 The area code for Bermuda is 441.

Public telephones are strategically placed around the islands, and pre-paid calling cards can be purchased almost anywhere, even at dispensing machines. Local calls cost 20¢; just deposit two 10¢ coins and dial. If you don't have the necessary change, you can deposit a quarter, but the pay phones do not give change. **Telco** (Bermuda Telephone Co., ☎ 292-5272) has its office at 30 Victoria Street and you can purchase pre-paid calling cards there, or at any one of a number outlying branches.

Bermuda also has an independent long-distance carrier, **TeleBurmuda International** (TBI), whose rates are generally cheaper than those of Telco. And a neat thing about TBI cards is that if you're from the US, Canada or the UK, you can use them when you get home. They can be pre-purchased in $10, $25 and $50 denominations, or from TBI's Customer Care Centre in the Emporium Building on Front Street. ☎ 292-7283.

International Calls

As always, when in a foreign country, international calls made from a hotel can be extremely expensive. I've found one of the best strategies is to make prior arrangements with one of your home carriers, such as MCI or AT&T. Arrange before you leave to have your foreign destination added to your long distance service at very competitive rates, and when you call home (home phone number only) using your MCI or AT&T calling card, you'll get the same low rate. For instance, an MCI call from the US to Bermuda can be as low as 35¢ and the same rate will apply when you make a calling card call from Bermuda to your home phone number. Be aware that some US carriers have no service from Bermuda, so check before you go. Some carriers also charge an international connection fee; be prepared for sticker shock. And check with your hotel to see if they impose any charges over and above those of your international carrier. Some do, and you might get an unexpected surprise when you receive your bill on check-out. Also find out what your hotel's policy is regarding local calls; some charge for these, too.

To call the US and Canada using a credit card or calling card, dial 0 plus the area code and number. Otherwise, dial 011 plus the area code and number.

Cell Phones

Can you take your cell phone with you? Yes and no. If, in the US, you subscribe to AT&T Wireless, Cingular or T-Mobile, it might be possible. These systems make use of the Global System for Mobiles (GSM), a semi-seamless network that is supposed to make cross-border cellular calls possible, if you happen to have a

Travel Information

world-capable phone. If you have a Sony Ericsson, Motorola or Samsung, your phone may be world-capable. Check with your provider.

Much happier news for visitors from Europe: all of your providers use the GSM system, so you should be able to take your instruments with you. Better check on the rates, though. You might be in for a shock when you return home.

You can rent cellular phones to take with you. **InTouch USA** is a good outfit. Contact them at ☎ 800-872-7626 or visit their website at www.intouchglobal.com. Tell them where you're going and when, and they will give you rates. They will also tell you whether or not your own cell phone will work in Bermuda.

For residents and long-term visitors, cellular service is readily available on the islands, but rather more expensive than you might be used to. At the time of writing, activation is just $10. However there's also a daily access charge of $5. Peak-time minutes (7 am-7 pm) cost 60¢; off-peak minutes, 35¢. For cellular service while on the island, you'll need to contact **BTC Mobility** (Telco's cellular arm) about a week before you leave home. You can have your bill charged to Visa, MasterCard or American Express. If you're visiting Bermuda by private boat or yacht, call BTC for activation when you get within 50 miles of the islands. ☎ 292-6032, www.mobilityltd.bm/main.asp.

Postal Service

 Bermuda's post office is at 11 Queen Street in Hamilton. However, found all over the islands are red Royal Mail post boxes, called pillar-boxes (just like the ones in England) where you can deposit mail. Mail is collected from them daily. Letters and postcards take at least a week to reach the US or the UK, so be sure to mail your cards during the first day or two of your visit or else you may arrive home before they do.

Photography

Here are some tips and simple techniques.

Film is expensive in Bermuda, so take more than you think you'll need, especially if you're shooting slides, as you might not be able to find the brand you like on Bermuda. Always carry a spare set of batteries. Though they're readily available on the islands, there's nothing more annoying than to have your camera quit as you attempt to capture the "shot of a lifetime." Don't be afraid to put your film through the airport security machines. Unless its a very high speed film, the x-ray machine won't hurt it.

Use a **low-speed film**. The fine-grain film of 50- or 100-speed will produce the best results. The lower the speed of the film, the sharper the image. It's especially advised on bright, sunny days. Use a high-speed film only when low light or a telephoto lens makes it a necessity.

Shoot at the highest possible **shutter speed** to reduce camera shake. The rule is, "the longer the lens, the faster the shutter speed." You should never hand-hold a camera at a shutter speed slower than the focal length of the lens. For example, you would only hand-hold a camera fitted with a 180mm lens when the shutter speed is set to 1/250th of a second or more; never slower. Likewise, a 50mm lens could be hand-held with the shutter set to 1/60th of a second, but no slower.

The best **light** for photography is in the early morning and late afternoon. The colors are warmer and the shadows deeper. At noon, when the sun is overhead, the lighting is flat and uninteresting.

Composition: Good composition means good photographs. Dull days and skies without detail mean dull photographs. Such situations call for a little thought before you shoot. A technique called framing will eliminate large, empty areas from your pictures and thus improve them. Shoot from beneath tree branches, through doorways and windows, and include odd sections of wall and pieces of furniture in the picture. Walk around the subject until you find something to break up those large, uninteresting areas of sky. Never place a dominant point of interest in the center of your picture; move it up or down just a little, or place it a little to one side. Be sure to think it through. Frame the shot properly: don't cut the tops off heads and buildings. Finally, look around. Is there any trash lying around?

Never shoot into the sun. Ideally, sunlight should come from behind the shoulder but never – unless you're looking for silhouettes – from in front.

Take notes. There's nothing worse than getting six rolls of film back from the lab and not knowing what it is you're looking at.

Don't miss the opportunity to **shoot under water**. Even if you don't go diving, take a camera to the beach; the fish in the shallow waters are colorful and abundant. You can purchase one of those neat little ready-to-shoot underwater cameras or rent a more sophisticated one from one of the many dive shops.

Photo Opportunities

Bermuda's small size, lush scenery and unique culture and history offer many beautiful outdoor photo opportunities.

Rooftops and Windows: Bermuda's pastel-colored homes are not only aesthetically pleasing, their details are both functional and unique. The typical stepped roofs collect rainwater for the island's freshwater supply. Window shutters not only add character to the homes, they protect the windows in stormy weather. Take a moment to compose your shots. Use a long lens and group sections of several roofs or different colored corners of the cottages together. Try cropping small sections of a building, say a shutter or a door, and you'll create quite avant-garde images.

The Ribbon of Green: Over 800 acres of reserves, parks and beaches have been nurtured and protected by the National Park System through the years. These offer a wide variety of wildlife, lush landscapes and unforgettable views. Try low-angle shots such as from ground level across the flower beds in the Botanical Gardens, the sun shining through a palmetto fan or close-ups of flowers. You'll have little trouble finding subjects among the rocks and dunes.

Bermuda from the Water: The passage across the harbour into Hamilton is one of the prettiest sights you'll see. The tiny cut seems too narrow to accommodate mammoth ships, but somehow they get through. The Hamilton skyline, especially at night, with its magnificent, towering cathedral, the Royal Naval Dockyard, with its great stone structures and clock towers, the great lighthouse on Gibbs Hill, and the magnificent beaches, all seen from the water, make great shots.

The Forts and Batteries: The great stone structures are impressive and make great pictures, but you can do even better. Once again, taking time to compose the shot will make all the difference. Try to isolate sections of the buildings for an interesting look: a flight of stone steps; a view of the ocean, beach or village framed by a gun port; or use a long lens across the battlements to draw it all together.

Churches and Graveyards: Churches, headstones and tombs produce good photos, especially if you include some of the strange epitaphs in your shot.

Homes and Gardens: These are always impeccably groomed, tailored and nurtured. Whether private homes or properties belonging to the National Trust, informal or formal gardens such as the Botanical Gardens, they all provide a thousand points of color and light to capture.

Always be on the lookout for that little something with a difference. Art is in the eye of the creator as well as the beholder. Don't be afraid to take pictures in the rain; it never lasts for long and the results as the sun breaks through the clouds can often be spectacular. (Of course, you'll need to protect your camera from water, but don't let that put you off.) Taking pictures of people bustling along the crowded streets of Hamilton in the rain, umbrellas and Bermuda shorts, can be fun and productive. Good shooting!

Getting Around

Renting a car is not an option; there is no such service. Those over age 16 may rent a moped or a bicycle; a driver's license is not required. The only difficulty, depending on what part of the world you live in, is riding on the wrong (left) side of the road!

Bicycles are popular on the islands. They are cheap to rent, convenient, easy to park, and no destination is too far away. You'll find bikes to rent at most hotels and at the ubiquitous cycle shops. Touring the island by bicycle allows you to truly absorb the beauty that surrounds you. The Royal Naval Dockyard at the West End is less than two hours from Hamilton by bicycle. You can return by ferry if the ride back is more than you can handle. The daily rate for a bicycle ranges from $20 to $25.

An adventure all their own, mopeds can be rented at many of the island hotels and resorts or at nearby cycle shops, where the rates are somewhat lower. The going rate for a moped runs from about $20 to $35 a day for a single-seater, while a double-seater will cost $35 to $45 per day. Rates are much lower if you rent for several days – by the week you can expect to pay around $110. Rates are all-inclusive, offering basic instruction, a tank of gas, helmets (required by law), a lock and key, insurance, breakdown service and even pick-up and delivery. You will be required to leave a small deposit, usually $30 to $50, to cover loss of the helmet, lock and key.

Never ridden a moped before? Don't worry. It won't take more than a few minutes to learn, but even for experienced riders the adventure can be a little hazardous. The roads on Bermuda, while well-paved and without potholes, are always crowded, narrow and winding, with one blind curve after another. The best way to avoid accidents is to stay strictly within the speed limit: a sedate 20 miles per hour. Once you've become used to riding on the left, you're in for a rare treat. The island roads will take you through a dozen communities with pastel-painted houses, well-kept colorful gardens, parks full of flowers and tiny churches. The coast roads offer magnificent views of the beaches (there's one at almost every turn), little country stores, national parks and the inviting turquoise ocean. There's no need to rush.

 Gas stations are open from 7 am until 7 pm. Gas for mopeds costs around $1.15 per liter, or $4.60 per imperial gallon. Sound a lot? Maybe, but a moped runs forever on a gallon.

The Tribe Roads

There was a time back in the 1600s when parishes were known as tribes, hence the name "the tribe roads." These roads run north to south, with many of them meandering through parts of Bermuda's most desolate areas. Some are fairly well-used thoroughfares, some are little more than footpaths, and all make great walking trails. Way back when, there were more than 40 tribe roads; today there are about 30. Of those, I've been able to find only a half-dozen. Searching out the rest would be a fun and interesting exercise. Consider renting a bike or moped, packing a sack lunch from the hotel, and heading out in the early morning along one of the major east/west highways, keeping a sharp lookout along the way for these ancient and secret roads. One of these days, I intend to do just that.

Bicycles & Mopeds

Some other things you should know when riding a bike or moped around Bermuda:

- Always give way to **pedestrians** on crosswalks. Zebra crossings have white stripes on the road and pelican crossings have pedestrian-operated red lights.
- Wear appropriate **clothing**: bathing suits, bare feet and flip-flop sandals are not allowed on motorized cycles, and they're not a good idea even on a peddle cycle.
- Bermuda law requires that you wear a **helmet** when riding a moped.
- When approaching a **roundabout** – England's most notorious type of intersection – you must give way to traffic already on the roundabout approaching from the right; once you get onto the roundabout, you have right of way. Never stop on a roundabout.

Travel Information

Bicycle & Moped Rentals

All rental companies listed below accept major credit cards, supply the necessary safety gear, and require that you leave a small refundable deposit against the loan of equipment.

Astwood Cycles Ltd. is at the Belmont Golf & Country Club, Coral Beach, Horizons Palmetto Bay, The Hamilton Princess Sonesta Beach, and White Sands, ☎ 441-292-2245. Scooters with a choice of pedal or electric start from $25 to $40 per day; reduced rates for multiple days.

Bermuda Cycles, Serpentine Road, Hamilton, ☎ 441-292-5457. Single-seat mopeds from $20 per day; two-seaters from $36 per day. Reduced rates for multiple days.

Oleander Cycles, Paget, ☎ 441-236-5235. Electric-start mopeds for one person are from $31 per day; for two persons, $40 per day. Reduced rates for multiple days.

Rent a Bike, Pitts Bay Road, Pembroke, ☎ 441-295-1180. One- and two-seaters available by the day or week. Call for rates.

Others include **Wheels Ltd.**, at 13 Donald Street in Hamilton, ☎ 441-292-2245; **Devil's Hole Cycles** in Tucker's Town, ☎ 441-293-1280; **Stonington Beach Hotel**, ☎ 441-236-0505; **Concord Cycles** at the Southampton Princess Hotel, ☎ 441-238-3336; **Castletown Cycles** at the Marriott Castle Harbour, ☎ 441-293-0007; **Somer's Cycles** in St. George's, ☎ 441-293-6437. Single-seat mopeds from $15 for three hours, $23 per day; two-seat scooters $25 for three hours, $40 per day. Reduced rates for multiple days.

Buses

The modern pink and white buses are comfortable, run frequently, go just about everywhere and are almost always on time. Expect to pay, depending upon the zone, either $2.50 or $4 per ride. You can also purchase a book of 15 tickets for either $15 or $24, depending on the zone – a real saving. Better yet, buy a three- or seven-day pass, either at the bus station or the Tourist Information Office at the Ferry Dock, for $21 or $34, respectively. In the off-season, prices drop to $16 and $26. The passes allow unlimited travel during the period of validity both on buses and ferries. They even include entry to the lighthouse on Gibbs Hill. The savings offered by these all-inclusive passes over a single ticket can be staggering.

For Lost & Found on Bermuda buses, ☎ 292-3851.

Bus stops are marked by pink and blue poles. Poles with a pink section at the top indicate the stop is for inward-bound buses going to Hamilton; those with a blue section at the top are outward-bound from Hamilton.

TO STOP A BUS YOU MUST STAND BY THE POLE. In places it might seem a bit dangerous to do this, so always exercise extreme caution and be on the lookout for fast-moving traffic.

Ferries

There's nothing quite like a boat ride on a warm, sunny day. Ferries run between Hamilton and Paget, Warwick, Somerset and the Royal Naval Dockyard. You can go out on the ferry and return by bus or vice-versa. The boat ride to the Dockyard takes about 30 minutes. A round-trip to the Dockyard, then along the coast to Grey's Bridge, Watford Bridge Wharf to Somerset and back to Hamilton, takes a good hour and can be a delightful experience.

The ferry plies back and forth between Paget and Hamilton every 30 minutes or so. The fare between Paget or Warwick and Hamilton is $2 each way; between Hamilton and the Royal Naval Dockyard or Somerset, it's $3.50; bicycles go free, but $3 is charged for each moped. Bicycles and mopeds are not allowed on the smaller ferry boats between Warwick or Paget and Hamilton. The three-

or seven-day unlimited travel pass mentioned above really comes into its own when traveling by ferry. Over the course of a week, you'll probably ride the ferry a number of times; with the average round-trip costing between $4 and $7, savings can be significant.

Yes, the ferry is the way to go. You can spend hours or days just riding back and forth or around the sound. The larger boats that travel the waters between Hamilton and Somerset have snack bars that sell hot dogs, muffins, sandwiches and ice-cold drinks. Sit inside and watch the world go by through the big windows or take a breath of fresh air on the observation deck and enjoy the sun and salt-spray tickling your face. ☎ 295-4506.

Store Hours

Hours for most stores are from 9 am until 5 pm, Monday through Saturday. But you will find some stores are now staying open later, especially on and around Front Street in Hamilton. With the exception of the stores at the Royal Naval Dockyard at the West End, all shops are closed on Sunday and legal holidays. Restaurants open at 11 am on weekdays and at noon on Saturday.

St. George

Sightseeing

The Beaches

Bermuda, tiny as it is, boasts 34 of the most beautiful beaches in the world. The sand has a pink tinge to it (best seen when wet), caused by particles of sea shells mixed with native coral and calcium carbonate. The heart of the Bermudian public beach system is the **South Shore National Park**, which covers 1½ miles of coastline. The

park has more than 11 beaches that extend from Port Royal Cove to the eastern end of Warwick Long Bay. These beaches vary considerably in size and nature. Some, like the half-mile-long Warwick Long Bay, are unbroken expanses; others are tiny secluded coves separated from one another by rocky cliffs. Port Royal Cove, Peel Bay, Jobson's Cove and Horseshoe Bay offer tiny private beaches and sheltered natural pools.

The South Shore itself, with its crystal-clear water to the front and miles of nature trails behind, is a good place to sunbathe, walk, swim, snorkel or jog. It glimmers in the early morning light and glows under a spectacular evening sunset. On a cloudy day during the winter, the character of the South Shore changes to one of splendid isolation. The air is crisp and refreshing, brisk breezes blow salt spray high into the air, and the ocean is bracing.

Along the shoreline you'll see low outcrops of rock, roughly circular in shape. Created by constant wave action that hollows out the soft inner rock, these outcrops are commonly known as reefs or boilers. The scientific name for these anomalies is algal-vermetid reefs, or serpuline atolls. On calm days, the waters around the boilers are great for snorkeling as dozens of gaily colored fish

Sightseeing

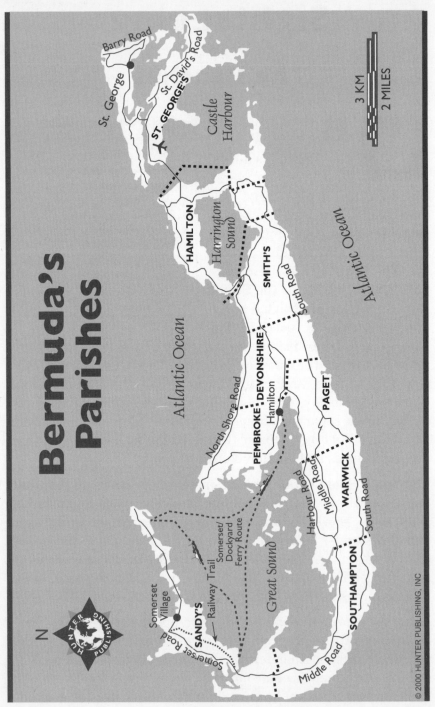

Bermuda's Parishes

3 KM
2 MILES

N

HUNTER PUBLISHING

Barry Road

St. David's Road

St. George

ST. GEORGE'S

Castle Harbour

HAMILTON

Harrington Sound

SMITH'S

Atlantic Ocean

South Road

Atlantic Ocean

North Shore Road

PEMBROKE

DEVONSHIRE

Hamilton

PAGET

Harbour Road

Middle Road

WARWICK

South Road

Great Sound

Somerset/
Dockyard
Ferry Route

Railway Trail

Somerset Village

SANDY'S

Somerset Road

SOUTHAMPTON

Middle Road

come here in search of shelter and food. You might spot an angel-fish, parrotfish, trumpet fish or even a grouper.

Starting at the west end of the island and working eastward along the South Shore, the following descriptions will give you an idea of what to expect at each beach or park.

A Word of Warning

 Snorkeling, swimming and wading are everyday activities at all of the popular beaches around Bermuda, and these activities are, for the most part, very safe. There are, however, a couple of things that you should be on the lookout for. Coral is sharp and will cut unprotected feet and hands, and any other exposed part of the body. A coral wound can be extremely painful and can lead to infection if left uncared for. Always wear shoes; better yet, stay away from coral heads altogether (coral is an endangered species). The other thing to be on the lookout for is the Portuguese man-o'war – a jelly fish. They are prevalent around the islands from March through July and are often very big. Their tentacles can trail more than 50 feet from the brilliant blue balloon that acts as a sail and propels it through the water.

Sandy's Parish

Parson's Bay (Lagoon Park, Lagoon Road)

A sheltered area of beach popular with the locals as a picnic spot. It's not near a bus stop, so you'll need to get there on your bike or moped. You'll find it on Lagoon Road just before it becomes Craddock Road. The strip has white sand and the area is usually quiet.

Mangrove Bay (Mangrove Bay Road)

Just a short distance from the shopping area in Somerset Village. It's a favorite with the locals, but is usually quiet enough during the week for a picnic, some sun and a swim. The swimming is considered safe, but it's always best to keep an eye on the young kids. It's a picturesque strip with mangroves that line the beach and follow the gentle curve of the shoreline.

Sightseeing

Somerset Long Bay Park Beach (Daniel's Head Road, Somerset Village)

One of the nicest public parks on the islands. Reminiscent of the traditional English village green, it's where the locals of Somerset Village take time out on weekends for a picnic and the eternal English game of cricket. Then there's the beach, also popular as a picnic spot, with its long, sweeping shoreline, white sand and shallow waters. The swimming here is safe for kids – at low tide the water is rarely deep enough to give concern. During the week, you can count on having most of the beach to yourself. Long walks, hot sun, snorkeling and lazy days make this the ideal spot to get away from it all. Restrooms are available in the park.

Southampton Parish

Church Bay Beach (Church Bay Park, South Road)

Here is one for the snorkelers. The reef and the potboilers (isolated rocks sticking up out of the surf) are close to shore – an easy swim and you're in the middle of more marine life than you ever imagined. Easy to recognize is the rock protruding from the ocean known to the locals as **Poodle Rock**. From a certain angle it does look exactly like a poodle. The sandy beach is a nice place to hang out, but is only incidental to the underwater delights just offshore. Where the sand meets the sea it quickly gives way to a rocky bottom.

The water gets deep very quickly at Church Bay Beach and is often quite rough, so it's not the place to let the kids loose without close supervision.

Don the flippers and mask and head out to the rocks. You can expect to see all sorts of finny inhabitants of the reef, along with some hard-shell ones as well. Look for butterfly fish, angels and parrotfish, to name but a few. Done swimming? Take a few moments to enjoy the park. There's a ruined fort on the cliff near the parking lot, some picnic tables where you can enjoy a quiet lunch, and public restrooms.

Horseshoe Bay (South Shore Park, South Road)

This is perhaps the most popular beach/park on the islands. It's certainly the most famous. Don't expect a quiet afternoon in the sun here. Even on weekdays you'll find it crowded; on weekends it can be overwhelming. But there's good reason: it's one of the most picturesque spots on the islands and the most photographed. I myself have snapped it from all angles and at all times of day, from early morning to early evening, and something new always seems to show up in the pictures. Horseshoe Bay is the first of a long line of beaches that stretches eastward for more than four miles. Yes, you can make the walk if you're the energetic type.

Horseshoe Bay is a must-see for anyone visiting Bermuda for the first time. It's on the bus route (they run every 20 minutes or so). Ask the driver to stop at Horseshoe Bay. Leave the bus stop and make your way down the driveway into the park. Once there, you'll see the beach stretching away for about a quarter-mile. The ends are enclosed by high limestone cliffs, the sand is a pale pink, and the water is clear and blue. Early morning is the best time to visit: it's less crowded then, and you can walk the sandy stretches uninterrupted by crowds of sunbathers. Snorkelers will find the waters just offshore among the rocks wonderful, but you'll need to be a strong swimmer; the swells are quite strong. Under the waves expect to see all sorts of colorful life, such as parrotfish, wrasse, angels, sergeant majors, snapper and many others. While at the beach, take time out for a light refreshment at the **Horseshoe Bay Beach House**. They serve great sandwiches and long, cool drinks. Restrooms are available and the park is wheelchair-accessible. ☎ 238-2651.

Port Royal Cove (South Shore Park off South Road)

This is one of the smaller beaches along the South Shore, hence its nickname of Baby Beach. It's extremely popular with locals and visitors alike. There's a nice, but limited, expanse of sand (that gets quite crowded at times) and a deep-water pool where you can leap from the rocks. The surrounding waters and rocky outcrops are ideal for snorkeling although the waters can get quite choppy at times. The sand is fine and pink, as is most of the sand along the South Shore; the waters are crystal clear, and the scenery surrounding the little beach is a photographer's dream. If you have small children with you, this is the ideal spot to bring them.

Warwick Parish

Chaplin's Bay (South Shore Park, South Road)

This little cove/bay is partially in Southampton Parish and partially in Warwick. It's another of those picturesque little spots that makes this area so pleasant and appealing. It's a popular spot, and is often too busy for those who like to get away from it all. But, if you get there in the early morning, you're likely to have it all to yourself.

Jobson's Cove (South Shore Park, South Road)

One of the most popular spots on the South Shore with bus service every 20 to 30 minutes. You're sure to enjoy a visit to Jobson's. It's rather tiny as beaches go – just a few square yards, in fact – but visually it's spectacular. This is another ideal spot to take the kids, for the tiny cove is completely surrounded by rocks, making the shallow waters unusually calm most of the time. The sand is fine and pink, and the beach is sheltered from even the strongest breezes. It's a great spot for a picnic. At least it would be if it weren't quite so busy. Get there early and pick your spot.

Warwick Long Bay (South Shore Park, South Road)

"Long" is the operative word, for as far as you can see eastward the great stretch of pink sand curves gently into the distance. There's room enough for everyone here – more sea and sand than you can imagine – so it's rarely crowded or even busy enough to warrant a search for a quiet spot.

Be warned, however, that Warwick Long Bay is not the ideal beach to turn the kids loose. You'll need to keep an eye on them constantly, and you shouldn't let them venture into the water on their own. The sea can turn quite rough and the sandy bottom is apt to drop off quite suddenly. Undercurrents can be a problem, too.

But this is a great place to spend the day, with or without kids. The South Shore Park, with its public services, runs almost the entire length of the bay. Hours can be spent wandering the shoreline and the park itself has cliffs, woodland trails and delightful landscaping. There's also a playground for the kids with swings, slides and ropes; all good fun. Time for something to eat? Take advantage of the concession stand just across the road above the beach for sandwiches and ice cream.

Astwood Cove (Astwood Park, South Road)

This is at the eastern end of Warwick Long Bay. Like to do a little birdwatching? Then this is the place for you. The park itself is somewhat different from South Shore Park in that there are more open spaces. Narrow footpaths thread this way and that along the cliff-tops, through fields and thicket, allowing you to get closer to nature. The inviting beach has fine sand and the sea, though a little rough at times, is ideal for snorkeling, especially among the rocks just offshore. While it's a great place for the more adventurous older kids, you'll need to keep an eye on the littler ones, and stay with them when they venture into the water.

Paget Parish

Elbow Beach (Tribe Road #4, South Road)

Elbow Beach is the jewel in Paget's crown. This magnificent stretch of pink sand is only partially open to the public; the eastern section is the private domain of the Elbow Beach Hotel and can be accessed only through the hotel grounds. The western section of the beach, however, is one of the best beaches on the islands (at least in my opinion). To reach it, take the bus or a scooter along South Road to Tribe Road #4. From there it's but a short walk along the Tribe Road to the beach. There you'll find changing facilities, beach chairs and a couple of nice cafés/restaurants where you can enjoy lunch or dinner. The $5 fee (payable as you enter the beach) entitles you to the use of all the facilities. The beach itself is a world of dunes and shore where you can relax, swim and sunbathe to your heart's content. The water is clear and inviting, ideal for a family outing, but you do need to keep an eye on the younger members; don't let them play in the water unattended.

Pembroke Parish

Clarence Cove (Admiralty House Park, Spanish Point)

Make your way to Spanish Point, on the North Shore, from Hamilton either on foot or by bus. If you decide to walk, you'll face an easy hike of about two miles.

If you have small children, it's better to take the bus either from the terminal on Washington Street or from the bus stop in front of the Tourist Information Center on Front Street.

Spanish Point was named for a Spanish sea captain whose ship was wrecked on the rocks just off the point. Admiralty House Park was named for the building in the park that once did service to the lords of the Royal Navy. Today the house is a community center. Two small beaches inside the park are reached via a footpath that leads downhill to the shore. These secluded little sandy places are considered safe for all members of the family, including small children. Most of the time, perhaps due to their location, they are quiet, without the bustling crowds sometimes the bane of the beaches on the South Shore. Only during July and August when they are the venue for summer camps do they get busy – it's then that you might consider visiting a less-crowded beach.

Smith's Parish

John Smith's Bay Park and Beach (South Road)

This is yet another South Shore local favorite, so it can get extremely busy, especially on weekends. It has acres of wide, sandy shore, clear shallow waters that make it safe for small children and, offshore, deeper waters and a reef that makes it a snorkeler's dream. Hundreds of colorful reef fish such as sergeant majors, parrotfish, jacks, blue and yellow grunts, angels, butterfly fish and wrasse casually swim by.

At times, you'll see warning flags at the beach lifeguard station indicating that water conditions may be dangerous. Check with a lifeguard (on duty during summer) before venturing into deep waters.

The park offers public toilets/restrooms, but there are no other conveniences close by. During the summer a mobile concession stand visits the park to sell soft drinks, coffee, tea and sandwiches (they're good!).

Hamilton Parish

Shelly Bay Beach (South Road)

Heading east along South Shore, you enter Hamilton Parish, where you'll find Shelly Bay Park. This is a great place to spend a day. A beach house sells snacks, soft drinks and ice cream, and there are bathrooms, changing rooms and rental lockers for stowing away those odds and ends that always seem to get lost in the sand. Rent snorkeling equipment here ($5/hour), towels ($2.50/day), loungers ($12/day) and umbrellas ($2.50/day). Like to go sailing? Try a Hobie Cat ($40/first hour, $15/each extra hour) or something slower like a peddle boat ($25/first hour, $10/each additional hour). The beach offers lots of clean sand (though somewhat gritty) and crystal-clear waters shallow enough for small children. A playground in the park has swings, slides and climbing frames galore – enough to keep even the most active kids happy for an hour or two.

St. George's Parish

Tobacco Bay Park (Coot Pond Road)

This is another popular spot with locals. The highlight is the Tobacco Bay Beach Pavilion (right on the beach), where you can rent all sorts of equipment and conveniences such as loungers ($2/hour), beach umbrellas ($5/day) and snorkeling gear ($12/two hours). Also available are fast food and soft drinks, changing rooms and bathrooms. The beach itself, although small and sometimes crowded, is considered safe for all members of the family

Sightseeing

and has lots of shallow water. Offshore, the rocks make for great snorkeling: plenty of color and life in the form of sergeant majors, parrotfish, jacks, blue and yellow grunts, angels, butterfly fish and wrasse.

Other Beaches

Several other beaches around the island are worth mentioning: **St. Catherine's Beach** on the eastern shore of St. George's; **Clearwater Beach** on Mercury Road (also in St. George's); and **Coral Beach** and **Marley Beach** on the South Shore, both located between Astwood Park and Elbow Beach.

Lifeguards & Warning Flags

During the summer months (June through October) you'll find lifeguards on duty at many public beaches from 10 am until 6 pm. A white flag at the lifeguard tower indicates an on-duty lifeguard. Also, warning flags tell beachgoers of any possible swimming hazards: a yellow flag warns that water conditions are questionable (consult a lifeguard before entering the water); a red flag means that conditions are unsafe for swimming – take heed and stay out of the water.

Touring Pembroke Parish

Although some Bermudians might argue, Pembroke Parish is not only the heart of the islands, it's also the key that opens them up. On the southern bank of Pembroke Parish is Bermuda's capital city of **Hamilton**. Everything seems to begin and end here. The government of the colony is based in the heart of the city. Buses begin and end their routes at the main terminal on Washington Street. Ferries cast off for ports on Great Sound from the dock at Front Street. And most of the fancy shops are in Hamilton.

The **Bermuda Department of Tourism**, ☎ 292-0023, is in Global House on Church Street. The staff is extremely helpful and will provide you with lots of informative material, including maps and brochures. The **Visitors Service Bureau**, ☎ 295-1480, is on Front Street at the entrance to the ferry terminal. Here, too, the staff is helpful, knowledgeable and can give suggestions for making the best of your vacation.

Hamilton

The nerve center of Pembroke Parish and the only city on the islands, Hamilton was founded in 1790 and was named for Henry Hamilton, a one-time Royal Governor of the colony. Bermuda's capital was moved from St. George's to Hamilton in 1815. Its main thoroughfare, Front Street, presents a facade of pastel-painted buildings to the cruise ships that arrive weekly at **Hamilton Harbour**. Hamilton Harbour plays host to literally hundreds of boats. Today, the three-masted British naval ships and fast sailing clippers have been replaced by giant modern cruise ships, seagoing freighters, pleasure craft of every shape and size, and public ferries. Passengers disembark directly onto Front Street, where they browse what once was known as the "Shop Window" of the British Empire. Even though the last vestiges of the British Naval presence left Bermuda in 1995, the area remains intact. Enjoy a pleasant walk along the seafront past dozens of colorful shop windows.

To the west, at the junction of Front and Queen streets, you'll find one of the few remaining police-operated traffic islands in the Caribbean (there's another in Nassau, Bahamas). Inside the painted "bird cage," a Bermudian police officer – immaculately dressed in Bermuda shorts, crisp white shirt and traditional English bobby's helmet – directs traffic with an infectious enthusiasm. It's no wonder that they're the most photographed people on the island!

If you plan to travel around the island by bus, you'll be making a number of visits to the **bus terminal** on Washington Street, ☎ 292-3854. Here you can purchase three- or seven-day travel passes. From Front Street, walk north on Queen Street, turn right onto Church Street and cross the road in front of City Hall;

Sightseeing

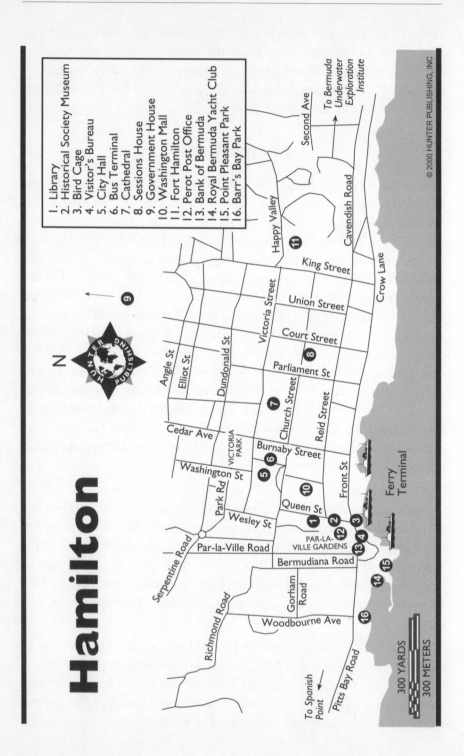

Hamilton

1. Library
2. Historical Society Museum
3. Bird Cage
4. Visitor's Bureau
5. City Hall
6. Bus Terminal
7. Cathedral
8. Sessions House
9. Government House
10. Washington Mall
11. Fort Hamilton
12. Perot Post Office
13. Bank of Bermuda
14. Royal Bermuda Yacht Club
15. Point Pleasant Park
16. Barr's Bay Park

300 YARDS

300 METERS

the bus station is next to City Hall on the left. You'll see the rows of pink and blue buses.

At the top of the hill on Church Street is Hamilton's magnificent **Anglican Cathedral of the Most Holy Trinity**, a superb example of Gothic architecture. Completed in 1991, the cathedral can accommodate a congregation of 1,000. The magnificent alter screen depicts all the saints for whom the island's parish churches are named, such as St. Andrew, St. George and St. Paul. Services are held every day and visitors are welcome. The Cathedral's tower looms 140 feet above this pastel-colored city. In the evening, the entire city becomes a fairyland of lighted buildings, capped by the cathedral. Hours: weekdays 10 am-3 pm. For services, ☎ 292-4033.

Government House, the official residence of His Excellency, The Governor of Bermuda, stands high on Langton Hill overlooking Hamilton. The immaculate grounds of the house cover more than 45 acres. Unfortunately, the House is not open to the public.

In the open country just east of the city, **Fort Hamilton** stands among beautifully landscaped gardens and offers spectacular views of Hamilton, the harbor and the sound. Go east, either on Front Street or Reid Street, turn left onto King Street and then turn right on Happy Valley Road. The fort is on your left. It's quite a walk, but a pleasant one and well worth the effort as you step back in time to the 1860s. Built upon the orders of the Duke of Wellington, Fort Hamilton was obsolete before it was completed.

The passageways beneath the fort were hewn from the solid rock by soldiers of the British Corps of Engineers. The seacoast guns that stand guard over Hamilton and the harbor never fired a shot in anger.

A stirring event held at the fort every Monday at noon, March through November, features the Bermuda Pipe Band, complete with drummers and dancers, all wearing kilts.

Watch parliamentary debates at the **Sessions House** just a block east of the cathedral on Parliament Street. It's recognizable by its singular Victoria Jubilee Clock Tower, an outstanding example of Italian-style architecture. Hours: 9:30 am-12:30 pm, 2-5 pm weekdays. The **Bermuda House of Assembly**, ☎ 292-7408, meets on the second floor and is in every way the British establishment it is meant to be. Proceedings are conducted with all the pomp and ceremony of the House of Commons in London. The Sergeant-at-Arms, bearing the Great Mace, precedes the Speaker of the House into the chamber. The Speaker then calls the house to order by banging an ancient gavel. View the proceedings from the public gallery.

Perhaps an even more enjoyable spectacle is the **Supreme Court**, ☎ 292-1350, on the lower floor of the Sessions House. Bewigged and becloaked barristers argue their cases before a panel of judges dressed in long, white wigs and bright red robes. The "Yes, me Luds," "No, me Luds," and "m'learned friends" fly around the room and provide great enjoyment to spectators. Call ahead to find out when they're in session.

Also on Church Street, a little farther west and opposite Queen Street, sits **City Hall**, a magnificent white building modeled after Stockholm's city hall. It houses a number of attractions, including the Bermuda National Gallery and a theater. To the rear of City Hall on Victoria Street is **Victoria Park**. It has lovely gardens and a Victorian bandstand, where concerts are held during the summer. The park, dedicated to Queen Victoria's Golden Jubilee, was opened in 1890. Unfortunately, it has become a gathering place for the low-life of the city; thus, it's not unusual to be accosted by beggars and other such undesirables here. Stay away from the park altogether after dark.

Opposite City Hall on Church Street is the entrance to **Washington Mall**, a large two-story shopping center that stretches the entire block from Church to Reid Street. It hosts a diversity of stores, cafés and quaint little hole-in-the-wall shops – places where you can have a cup of hot tea and a sweet roll or find unique gifts for everyone at home.

Reid Street parallels Front Street just a block away to the south. It's the second busiest shopping area in Bermuda. Just across from the Washington Mall is the **Walker Arcade**. Turn east, walk a short distance, and you'll find **Fagan's Alley**, another neat shopping center that runs from Reid Street all the way to Front Street. Turn west on Reid Street and you'll be back on Queen Street once more with the Bermuda Public Library, the Historical Society Museum, the Perot Post Office, the Par-la-Ville Gardens, and, just a short walk away on Front Street to the south, the bird cage traffic island. Before you leave Reid Street, however, be sure to stop at the **Fourways Pastry Shop** at the entrance to the Washington Mall. The pastries are a gourmet delight; bang goes the old diet, but never mind, you're on vacation!

Head south on Queen Street from Reid Street and you'll come to the **Perot Post Office**, ☎ 292-0952, a white two-story building on the right. It was here that the island's first postmaster set up shop in 1818. As it's been told, William Bennet Perot met arriving ships in the harbor, collected their mail and carried it around Hamilton inside his hat for delivery. It was Perot who introduced Bermuda's first stamp in 1848, although his motives, so it seems, were entirely selfish. Postmaster by trade and gardener by choice, Perot begrudged the time he spent hand-stamping outgoing mail. His friend, J.B. Heyl, came up with a solution. He suggested that Perot hand-stamp a whole sheet of postmarks, sign each stamp, and sell the sheet for a shilling. People could tear off a stamp, glue it to the letter and mail it, all without Perot, who was now free to pursue his gardening. His stamps? Oh boy. They are extremely rare, each worth a half-million dollars or more.

The **Par-la-Ville Gardens**, next door to the Perot Post Office, now occupy almost an entire city block from Queen Street to Par-la-Ville Road and are a favorite lunch spot for local businesspeople. The gardens are beautifully landscaped with lots of flowers and shrubs and a network of paths. Benches make ideal picnic spots to eat those sumptuous pastries you bought at the Fourways Pastry Shop.

In front of the Par-la-Ville Gardens on Queen Street is a two-story house with a balcony. The house, set back a little from the street, was the home of the Perot family. Today it houses the **Bermuda Public Library** and the **Bermuda Historical Society Museum**, ☎ 292-0952. The old house is an adventure in its own right and has a number of collections, memorabilia and artifacts. The public library, founded in 1839, moved here in 1916. Its reference

Sightseeing

Sir John Somers

section has copies of Bermudian newspapers dating back to 1784 on microfilm. Among its collection of rare books is a 1624 edition of John Smith's *Generall Historie of Virginia, New England and the Somer Isles*. Along with portraits of William Perot and his wife, you'll see magnificent portraits of Sir John Somers and his wife, which are thought to have been painted around 1605. There's also a map of Bermuda, dated 1624, that shows the division of the islands by the Bermuda Company into 25-acre shares. Other interesting exhibits include a collection of rare old English coins, furniture, fine china, a Waterford chandelier, handmade hats, clocks, and a collection of Confederate money that dates to the days of the blockade runners who ran from Bermuda into the southern ports of Charleston and Savannah. There is also a piece of lodestone that Sir George Somers used to magnetize his compass needles. Even more interesting is a letter from George Washington, written in 1775, requesting supplies of gunpowder. You'll have to request a viewing if you'd like to see it. Hours: 9:30 am-3:30 pm, Monday-Saturday. Free.

While on Queen Street, you should visit the **Bermuda Book Store**. It stands right on the corner of Front and Queen and is a quaint old place, one you might more likely find on a back street in London than on the corner of the two busiest streets of a tropical island. Space inside the store is limited, with books of every size, color and topic crammed on its shelves. A narrow staircase takes you up to more books. The wood floorboards creak as you walk around, rather like an old library. If you'd like a book about the islands of Bermuda, this is the place to find it.

From Queen Street, turn right onto Front Street, go a short way to Point Pleasant Road, and you'll see the **Bank of Bermuda** in front of you. It houses one of the finest collections of British and Spanish coins outside Europe. The coins are exhibited in glass cases and include some fine examples of "hog money," Bermuda's first official currency, introduced by the Bermuda Company in 1616. When Sir George Somers and his companions were wrecked on the islands, the only inhabitants they found were wild hogs. It seemed only fitting that the first coins should depict a wild hog and the words "Somer Ilands" (the original spelling) on one side and the image of the *Sea Venture* on the other. Hog money is the oldest British colonial coinage. Hours: Monday, 9:30 am-4 pm; Tuesday-Thursday, 8:30 am-4 pm; Friday 8:30 am-4:30 pm.

Just across the road from the Bank of Bermuda is the waterfront. The **Royal Bermuda Yacht Club**, established and given a Royal Charter in 1845, is just west of Point Pleasant Park. The Yacht Club is the hub of the Bermudian upper class. Here the elite of the islands mingles with the elite of the yachting world, international celebrities and even visiting royalty. The highlight of the Bermudian yachting calendar is, of course, the Newport to Bermuda Yacht Race.

Point Pleasant Park lives up to its name. It is, indeed, a pleasant spot to watch boats move in and out of the harbor. **Barr's Bay Park**, just west of the Yacht Club, also offers grand views of the sound and a quiet place to sit.

An agreeable walk of a couple of miles along Pitts Bay Road (the western extension of Front Street) will take you past the headquarters of the Bacardi Rum Company to the park at **Spanish Point**.

Too far to walk? Jump on a bus outside the Tourist Information Center on Front Street or at the terminal on Washington Street and ride out to the park in comfort.

Treasure Map

The park is named for a Spanish captain whose ship ran aground on the rocks off the point. With the welfare of others in mind, he erected a wooden cross with written instructions outlining where nearby drinking water could be found. His directions were misunderstood, however, as a route to buried treasure, and later English settlers later searched and dug up the entire point to no avail.

Sightseeing

Today, the area affords inspiring views across Great Sound to Somerset and the Royal Naval Dockyard. It's a good place to sit and enjoy an afternoon in the sunshine or to go swimming and snorkeling off the wide, sandy beach.

 Bermuda Underwater Exploration Institute & Ocean Discovery Centre, 40 Crow Lane, Hamilton. ☎ 441-292-7219, www.buei.org. The institute opened in 1997 to give the public an opportunity to explore the oceans around Bermuda to a depth of 12,000 feet. It's one of the most comprehensive and exciting exhibits of its type anywhere. The highlight is a simulated, seven-minute "dive" to the ocean depths, taking the plunge with all the sights and sounds you'd experience if it were the real thing. Although seen through video screens instead of windows, the creatures you'll encounter on the journey downward seem real.

Besides the dive, there are lots more exhibits to explore, many of them interactive. Some interpret the history of underwater exploration in the islands and some offer an unusual look at Bermuda's many shipwrecks. Others take a look at various types of underwater vehicles, including a full-size bathysphere as used by the indomitable Dr. Charles Beebe in 1934 while making his record-breaking dive of more than 3,000 feet. Also interesting is Jack Lightbourn's collection of more than 3,000 seashells. It is, perhaps, the most complete collection of its kind outside the great natural history museums of the world. Lightbourn began collecting seashells – like most of us do – as a child. But, unlike most of us, he didn't quit. He just kept on and on, gathering them from all corners of the world, until finally deciding to donate them to the institute.

Expect to spend two to three hours exploring the institute and museum. While there, take time out for a cup of java and a snack in the coffee bar or enjoy a great lunch at La Coquille from 11:30 am until 2:45 pm. And don't miss the gift shops – there are two – where you'll be sure to find that little something for the folks back home. The institute is wheelchair-accessible, as are the restrooms. Hours are 10 am-6 pm, Monday through Sunday, year-round (except Christmas Day). Admission is $9.75 for adults, $5 for children aged seven to 16; children six and under are free; $7.80 for seniors over 65.

Touring Sandy's Parish & the West End

 The West End is a 45-minute ferry ride from Hamilton and about 35 minutes by bus.

Sandy's Parish (pronounced SANDS) is the barb of the hook-shaped island at the extreme western end of the Bermudian archipelago. It's the location of the historic Royal Naval Dockyard, now a unique mall full of interesting shops, pubs, restaurants and cafés.

The Village of Somerset is comprised of five small islands at the extreme west end of Bermuda: Somerset, Watford, Boaz, Ireland Island North, and Ireland Island South. Somerset is the largest of the five and, consequently, is the heart of the parish.

Somerset is named for Sir George Somers who greatly favored the West End, which for a time was known as Somers' Seate. It's mostly a rural area, with small farms and open spaces, craggy coastlines, tiny inlets, coves and wonderful beaches. This sleepy little fishing village has winding lanes, old fortifications, and waves that crash against the rocks on the ocean side, yet sit tranquil in the waters of the sound on the opposite side. All the attractions are set along the main road from Somerset Bridge on the southern boundary of the parish to the Royal Naval Dockyard on Ireland North. This layout makes touring the West End extremely easy. But Sandy's is best known for the Royal Naval Dockyard, and that's all most visitors ever see of the parish.

Sandy's Parish, Somerset and the West End are much more than the Dockyard, and you'll do well to make time for a proper visit; it can all be done in a day. Take either a bus or taxi to Somerset and begin at the southern end, or else jump on a ferry and start at the Dockyard. Another option is renting a moped or bicycle. For variety, consider arriving one way and leaving by another. By bus from Hamilton (or from any stop along the way), go to Somerset Village and ask to get off at Somerset Bridge. By moped or bicycle, head east on Front Street and follow the signs. When you reach the roundabout (a quaint old English improvement on the Ameri-

Sightseeing

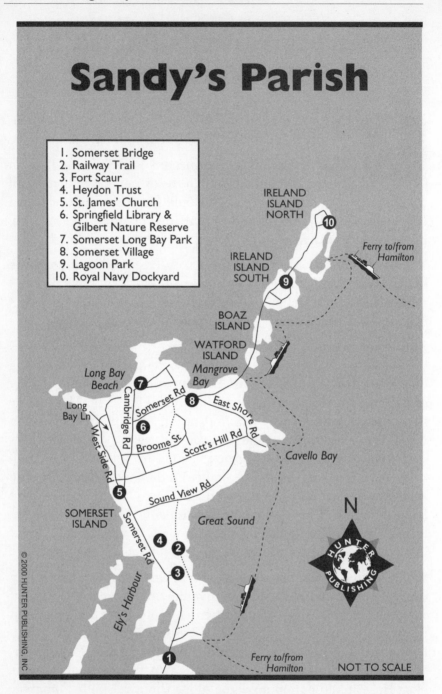

Sandy's Parish

1. Somerset Bridge
2. Railway Trail
3. Fort Scaur
4. Heydon Trust
5. St. James' Church
6. Springfield Library &
   Gilbert Nature Reserve
7. Somerset Long Bay Park
8. Somerset Village
9. Lagoon Park
10. Royal Navy Dockyard

IRELAND
ISLAND
NORTH

Ferry to/from
Hamilton

IRELAND
ISLAND
SOUTH

BOAZ
ISLAND

WATFORD
ISLAND

Long Bay
Beach

Mangrove
Bay

Long
Bay Ln

Somerset Rd

East Shore Rd

Cambridge Rd

West Side Rd

Broome St

Scott's Hill Rd

Cavello Bay

Sound View Rd

SOMERSET
ISLAND

Somerset Rd

Great Sound

N

© 2000 HUNTER PUBLISHING, INC

Ely's Harbour

Ferry to/from
Hamilton

NOT TO SCALE

can four-way stop), you can either turn west on Harbour Road, or go on to the next roundabout and turn west onto South Road, following the coastline until it joins Middle Road. From there it's just a few more scenic miles to Somerset Bridge.

Somerset Bridge is unique because it's one of Bermuda's first three bridges, built in the 17th century, and also because it's the world's smallest drawbridge. At first glance, you'll find nothing unusual about the picturesque little bridge, but look more closely and you'll see the central plank can be raised, leaving a small opening just large enough for a sailboat mast to pass through.

From Somerset Bridge continue on to the **Railway Trail** (see full description page 177). If you don't intend to hike the entire trail, simply take a stroll along the shady railway cut and enjoy splendid views of Great Sound.

Scaur Hill Fort Park is less than three-quarters of a mile down the road from Somerset Bridge. The fort was built on the highest hill on Somerset Island in the 1870s to protect Her Majesty's Royal Naval Dockyard in case of attack from the sea, ostensibly by American forces. To defend the fort and Dockyard from an attack by land from the south, an enormous dry moat was dug that effectively cut Somerset in two. Any attack from that direction would have meant crossing not only the great moat, but surviving enfilading fire from cannon and rifle.

The fort is open to the public and serves as an excellent photographic opportunity. It stands in a 22-acre park complete with trails and picnic areas. The moat heads down to the shores of Great Sound, where you can spend time fishing or swimming. The fort itself is a massive stone-wall structure with many ramparts to wander around. Stand and look out across the sound toward Hamilton and you should be able to see the Dockyard away to your left. On a clear day with a telescope or binoculars, you might see St. David's Lighthouse or Fort St. Catherine, both at the extreme eastern end of the islands. Scaur Hill Fort and Fort Park is open daily from 9 am to 4:30 pm. Admission is free.

Return to the main road and head north a short distance to the **Haydon Trust**. The old chapel is thought to have been built around 1616. Visit the church and see the original oven in a small room behind the altar, a relic of the times when the building was a private residence. The grounds are well-kept, with a large lawn and several trails. The trust is open during daylight hours. Admission is free.

Sightseeing

St. James' Church, ☎ 234-0834, stands on high ground and overlooks the ocean to the west. The church, the ocean and a magnificent sunset can provide a once-in-a-lifetime photo. Unfortunately, the original wooden church was destroyed in a hurricane in 1780. This replacement was consecrated in 1789; the iron gates were made by the Royal Engineers at the Dockyard in 1872, and the spire, added in 1880, was designed by Dr. Henry Hinson, a local physician who also designed spires for several other churches on the island. His spire was destroyed by lightening in 1937 and the one you see today is a faithful copy by Bermudian architect Will Onions. The church is open from dawn until dusk, and there's a tourist information center just a short distance away.

The **Springfield & Gilbert Nature Reserve**, ☎ 236-6483, is next. From St. James' Church stay on Somerset Road – the nature reserve is just a 10-minute walk or a two-minute moped ride away. En route, you'll pass the **Simmons Ice Cream Factory and Variety Store**. Make it a point to stop and sample some of the best ice cream on the island.

The nature reserve was once a Bermudian plantation built in the early 18th century. At the time of writing, the old house was undergoing extensive restoration, but the slave quarters, the buttery, and the mansion itself could still be viewed from the grounds. (By the time you read this, you should be able to visit inside.) A nature trail leads through more than five acres of unspoiled woodland and provides a quiet moment away from the beaches and crowds at the Dockyard. The reserve, a Bermuda National Trust property, is always open. Admission is free.

From the Springfield & Gilbert Nature Reserve, take Cambridge Road to **Somerset Long Bay Park and Nature Reserve**. The park, another one of Somerset's quiet places, has lots of appeal for the entire family. You can snorkel, swim, picnic, walk or fish from the shore. The park was established by the Bermuda Audubon Society because the mangroves and the pond attract a variety of migrating birds both in the spring and in the fall. Warblers, kingfishers, cardinals, herons, egrets and ducks all take up residence here at one time or another. The park is always open. Admission is free.

Long Bay is also where you'll find most of Somerset's nicest beaches. The gorgeous sands of the Beach Park are to the north. At the eastern end of the bay is Daniel's Head, with Daniel's Head Beach Park to the southwest and the **Sea Gardens**, an underwater world full of marine life.

One of Bermuda's best kept secrets, **Daniel's Head Beach Park**, lies along 19 acres of the Atlantic shore. It seems a wild and remote spot. In times past it was host to the Canadian military, but they are long gone, leaving only the shells of the old barracks and recreation hall behind. It's one of those places the locals like to keep to themselves, and understandably so, beautiful and inviting, where the kids can swim in warm waters that are almost always calm and shallow. It's also a great place for snorkelers as the waters teem with colorful angelfish, parrotfish, wrasse and sergeant majors. The two beaches are soft and white and ideal for the Sunday afternoon picnic – there's lots of room to cook-out and the sea on a sunny day is the color of uncut emeralds. It's a spot where lovers of the great outdoors can become one with nature, where you'll always find space to spread the blanket and just relax. Remote as Daniel's Head is, it's not devoid of the necessities. There are public telephones, bathrooms and freshwater showers you can use for free, and there is always plenty of room to park the scooter. The park is on Daniel's Head Road, off Cambridge Road.

Somerset Village itself is a quiet little town of narrow streets, flowering hedges, tiny bays and brightly painted houses. Take a little time to explore the village and enjoy a cup of tea or a spot of lunch.

To the northwest, the village is bordered by **Mangrove Bay**, named for the trees along the shoreline, to the east by Great Sound, and a little farther to the southwest by Long Bay Beach. There are several shops to browse here, many of them smaller branches of those in Hamilton, as well as several pubs and restaurants. The main beach of Mangrove Bay is a picturesque area of blue waters and small boats bobbing at anchor, but it can – because of the traffic along the coast road – be somewhat noisy and dusty.

For a boat ride or for snorkeling over the reef, you'll find the **Mangrove Bay Wharf** just a short way along Mangrove Bay Road.

The management will gladly arrange whatever trip you feel like. Back in town at the **Loyalty Inn**, enjoy a cold beer or soft drink before continuing.

Lagoon Park is on Ireland Island South. As you leave Somerset Village and travel north along the main road and shoreline across Watford and Boaz Islands, you'll eventually come to Grey's Bridge. Cross the bridge and turn right onto Lagoon Road. (Now you're on the eastern shoreline.) Lagoon Park has a number of swimming and picnic areas, walking trails and a lake with all sorts of wild birds.

An Antidote for Yellow Fever

Beyond Lagoon Park, after you rejoin the main road, you'll come to a very small bridge that spans a cut joining Great Sound to the ocean, dividing Ireland Island South from Ireland Island North. The cut was made for practical purposes. A doctor at the Royal Naval Hospital (which once stood on the hill overlooking the sound), found that he had more incidences of yellow fever at his hospital than at any other location on Bermuda. After much deliberation, he had the cut made in order to reduce the "miasmas and vapors" emanating from the sound, and so reduced the number of yellow fever cases. A figment of old-time medical myth? You might think so, but in fact the changing tides cleansed the waters of mosquito larvae and, thus, yellow fever cases at the hospital dropped dramatically.

Just past the cut bridge, on your right, you'll find the **Naval Cemetery**, which dates from the early 19th century. Inside the graveyard are a number of interesting headstones, including those of four English admirals. The main road continues northward and eventually enters the main gates of the Royal Naval Dockyard. As you pass into the Dockyard, look up and to your left. The daunting structure rising above you is the old prison, still in use today. The Dockyard is just ahead.

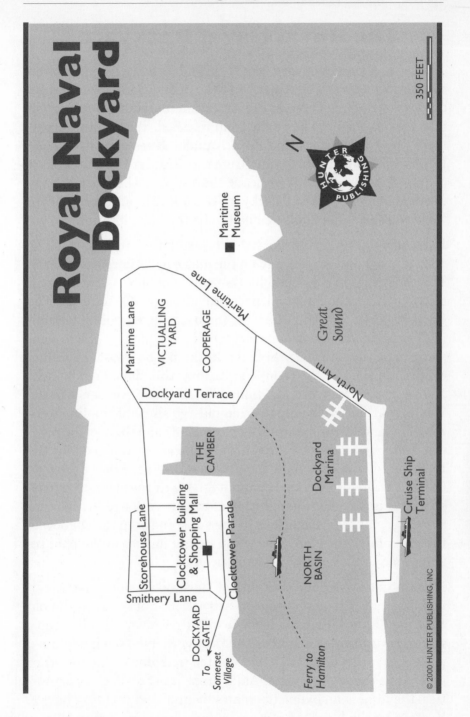

Royal Naval Dockyard

Maritime Museum

Maritime Lane

VICTUALLING YARD

COOPERAGE

Dockyard Terrace

Great Sound

North Arm

THE CAMBER

Dockyard Marina

Cruise Ship Terminal

Storehouse Lane

Clocktower Building & Shopping Mall

Smithery Lane

Clocktower Parade

DOCKYARD GATE

To Somerset Village

NORTH BASIN

Ferry to Hamilton

© 2000 HUNTER PUBLISHING, INC

350 FEET

Sightseeing

The Royal Naval Dockyard

The Royal Naval Dockyard, ☎ 234-3824, has had a long and often turbulent history. The American War of Independence brought the loss of English ports on the American mainland, but English interests in the area were far from finished. Pirates and privateers plied the waters, the French under Napoleon threatened English shipping routes to and from the West Indies, and then, of course, there were the Americans themselves. The British Navy needed a major port and a dockyard capable of handling repairs to their warships. Bermuda seemed to be the ideal location.

Extensive surveys were carried out during the latter part of the 18th century and work began on the massive port project in 1809. The construction was done by thousands of slaves and English convicts under the direction of the Royal Corps of Engineers. The great breakwaters, the wharves, the boatslip, barracks, victualing yards, and the enormous fort took many, many years to complete. The unpaid laborers, working in the most appalling conditions, died by the thousands during this time. For the next 150 years the Dockyard functioned as the British presence in the Western Atlantic. The great three-masted ships-of-the-line were replaced first by the steam-driven ironclads and then by the modern fleets we know today. Eventually, however, the need for the Dockyard dwindled and the Royal Naval Dockyard closed for good in 1951. Even so, a visit here cannot fail to stir the blood. The massive structures, where generation after generation of British seamen lived out their traditions in the sunshine or in the shadow of the great fort, are silent now. Only fading images of the past remain among the crumbling structures.

It might seem strange that one of Bermuda's oldest establishments is now its newest tourist attraction, but many of the old Dockyard buildings have been tastefully converted into shops, stores, restaurants and pubs. The Dockyard itself is a landscaped park with lawns and walks that stretch from one end to the other and along the water's edge. Aside from its shopping opportunities, the area is an extensive tourist center and yachting haven. Visitors by the hundreds arrive by bus, ferry and cruise ship to ride the tourist submarine *Enterprise*, the sightseeing helicopter, or visit the Maritime Museum housed in the nearby fortifications.

Of the buildings that remain structurally sound, the most impressive is the **Clocktower Centre**. The Clocktower Building, completed in 1856, is an exercise in architectural elegance and extravagance. The huge building has three-foot-thick walls and 100-foot-high twin towers. It was used as office space for the administration of naval stores. The clock on the south tower was cast in England in 1857 by John Moore & Sons. The matching clock on the north tower has just one hand that was set daily to indicate high-tide time (the safest time for seamen to navigate the reefs).

Today, the magnificent building has found new life as a shopping mall. The Clocktower Centre mall has 30 shops offering everything from antiques to gifts, old books to designer fashions. Even on the hottest summer days, the interior of this old building is cool – the massive walls have an insulating effect. For lunch or afternoon tea and sandwiches, try **Pirates Landing**, ☎ 234-5151. The shops in the Clocktower Centre are open daily from 10 am to 5 pm.

Beyond the center, take a short walk around the slip, where you can see boats being worked on. Farther along, you'll find the Victualling Yard and, beyond that, the old Cooperage and the Maritime Museum.

The **Victualling Yard** was the heart of naval operations within the Dockyard. It was here that food and supplies were prepared and stored. The yard is surrounded by a high, stone wall to keep supplies safe from pilferage. Today, it has become a park within a park. Where once hundreds of British seamen ran back and forth across the stone-flagged yard there are now trimmed lawns and benches surrounded by the ruins of massive stone warehouses.

Beyond the Victualling Yard is the **Cooperage**. In the days before refrigeration, the only way to preserve perishable goods like pork and biscuits was to salt them and seal them in barrels. With the many ships coming and going, a huge number of barrels were needed to handle the perishables at the Dockyard. These were made in the Cooperage, which was completed in 1831. Two large stone forges, used to make the iron hoops for the barrels, can be seen in the foyer of the cinema and at the English Pub. The old

Sightseeing

Cooperage is now home of the **Frog and Onion Pub and Restaurant**, which has to be one of the most interesting culinary experiences on the island. For sure, it's the most authentic British pub in Bermuda. Most traditional English beers are available, along with shepherd's pie, steak and kidney pie, and beef and barley pie; add some good old English-style fish and chips – all great big portions – and you're in for a special experience. Better yet, it's not expensive; expect to pay between $8 and $20 per person, and that includes the price of a pint. Do I sound biased? You bet. ☎ 441-234-1692.

The **Maritime Museum**, ☎ 234-1418, opened by Queen Elizabeth in 1975, is housed in the island's largest fortress, the onetime heart of the Dockyard's defenses. To enter the fortress, cross the wet moat by way of the drawbridge and pass under an archway in the massive stone wall. The Keep is a classic example of British military architecture. The walls are made from Bermuda limestone, the vaulted ceilings are lined with English brick, and the floors are coated with non-sparking bitumen. The massive ramparts are 30 feet high, with a water gate and an inner lagoon where small supply boats were loaded with munitions for the great ships-of-the-line. As you walk the ramparts and explore the underground storage chambers, it's not difficult to imagine life within the fort all those years ago.

The exhibits within the museum are varied and interesting. One display depicts shipwreck archaeology (there's certainly no shortage of wrecks) that includes recovered Spanish artifacts. There's also a fine collection of Bermuda boats in the Boat Loft, and "The Age of Discovery" exhibit celebrates the 500th anniversary of Christopher Columbus' discovery of the New World. Interesting, too, is the Bermuda Monetary Authority's section that traces the history of the island's currency from 1612 and the "Pillars of the Bridge" exhibit that celebrates the 50th anniversary of the establishment of the US naval bases on the island. Other displays deal with the Royal Navy, whaling, diving, navigation and shipping. Best of all, however, is to stand high upon the ramparts and let your imagination wander back to a time when the grand three-masted warships rode at anchor in the sheltered waters of Great Sound. The Maritime Museum is open daily from 9:30 am to 5 pm, May through November, and from 9:30 am to 4:30 pm, December through April. Admission is $7.50 for adults, $3 for children aged four to 16, and is free for children under four.

Bermuda Train Company

A brand new attraction, this train service takes you on a 20-minute ride from the Clock Tower at the Royal Naval Dockyard to the cruise terminal and back again, making several stops along the way. The 60-foot scaled-down train seats more than 40 passengers. For cruise ship passengers, it's a great way to come ashore; for visitors to the Dockyard, it's a fun ride. The fare is $1 per person, and the train operates daily from 8:30 am to 5 pm. ☎ 441-236-5972.

Dockyard Snorkel Park

The Snorkel Park is fun for the whole family. You snorkel over marked underwater trails to view the underwater life that inhabits the Dockyard area. Floating stations along the way allow time out for a rest. Take your own equipment and the experience will cost you only $5 per person for as long as you like on any given day. Rent their equipment, however, and the cost is $17 for the day. I don't think that's too steep, considering the experience. Lifeguards are on duty and the park, located next to the Maritime Museum, is open from 10:30 am to 6 pm, Monday through Friday, and from 11 am to 5 pm over the weekend. The park is closed November through March. ☎ 441-234-1006.

Bermuda Children's Museum

This is at the Maritime Museum in the Royal Naval Dockyard. It's an experience not just for kids, but for you as well. It has all sorts of neat stuff that kids usually can only dream about: an interactive experience where imagination and adventure stories come to life. There are play boats, guns, cannons, and all sorts of costumes they can dress up in. And, while they're having fun, they'll be learning too. Children must be accompanied by an adult. Admission is $7.50 per adult; seniors, $6; children under 15, $3.

Sound expensive? Don't panic – a family of seven (two adults and up to five children) can all get in for just $15. ☎ *441-234-1418.*

Gumba Trail & Outdoor Museum

This is yet another neat attraction at the Royal Naval Dockyard, especially where kids are concerned. But take note that it can be enjoyed only on Wednesdays during the summer months, April through July. Special tours led by a knowledgeable guide – the Gumba – explore the story behind the Caribbean Junkanoo dancers, as well as the various plants along the trail and their medicinal uses The hour-long tours are most interesting for the stories (many true), told by the Gumba. The cost is $5 per person. It's best to call ahead, too, especially if it looks like rain. ☎ 441-293-7330.

The Royal Naval Dockyard is also the place to enjoy **jet skiing**. Contact **Wet and Wild** for rates. ☎ 441-234-2426.

When you've finished at the Royal Naval Dockyard, you'll face a decision: how to get back to Hamilton. If you arrived by moped and opt for the 45-minute ferry ride home, you'll be charged $3.50 extra to take the moped on board. But the ride across Great Sound is pleasant and worth the extra money. And you'll be tired after your visit so the rest, the salt spray, and a snack from the on-board concession bar will make for a very agreeable interlude.

 The newest attraction in The Royal Naval Dockyard area is **Dolphin Quest Bermuda**. Once at what is now the Fairmont Southampton Princess Resort, Dolphin Quest has relocated to Sandy's Parish. All of the original interactive programs are still available, but there are now more members of the resident dolphin family and visitors are offered more time to get to know them. The mammals seem to be extremely happy and comfortable, and they are certainly well-treated and looked after. They perform all the usual leaps and tricks. I've done the dolphin experience many times in many different locations; the tricks and the interactive programs are much the same wherever you might be, but it's worth doing again. The animals have unique personalities and there's always something new to learn. Also, I never tire of watching the kids get down and personal with these finny creatures. The animals seem to know that kids are special and they treat them as such. The last time we did it I bought the video tape. My daughter was 16 at the time and she had a whale of a time (no pun intended). We run that video now and again: great memories. Dolphin Quest Bermuda is at the Maritime Museum at the Royal Naval Dockyard. Hours of operation are from 9:30 am until 4:30 pm daily, year-round. Wetsuits are available during the winter months. You'll need to pay the museum entrance fee of $7.50 for adults and $3 for children under 16. There's no charge for children under four. Dolphin Quest programs themselves start at around $25 per person. Give it a try; you won't be disappointed. ☎ 441-234-4464. You can make reservations online at www.dolphinquest.org.

Touring St. George's Parish

St. George is a 30-minute bus ride from Hamilton. Buses run between the town and Hamilton every 30 minutes, or every 15 minutes if you combine bus routes.

At the other end of the island – the East End – is St. George's Parish. This is where it all started and where, today, you can visit those far off days when Sir George Somers and his friends on board the *Sea Venture* first hove into view off the tip of St. Catherine's Point.

A Walking Tour of St. George

The heart of the parish is the town of St. George. Founded in 1612 by Governor Sir George Moore and named for the patron saint of England, St. George was the second English town to be established in the New World after Jamestown, Virginia. Unlike Jamestown, though, which has long been abandoned, St. George continues its quiet way of life much as it has for almost four centuries.

As I've already mentioned, St. George is the oldest town in Bermuda. Indeed, with the demise of Jamestown in Virginia, it is the oldest English colonial settlement in the New World. For many years it was the capital of Bermuda, giving up that honor to the city of Hamilton in 1815. Today, St. George is a tiny backwater at the eastern end of the island. That's not to say it's a forgotten community, far from it. The little town is a major tourist attraction in its own right.

Over the years a great deal of history has been created on the streets of St. George and in the surrounding countryside. The

Sightseeing

harbor has offered food and shelter to more than 20 generations of seafarers. Many of them saw Bermuda as no more than a small spot on the map of the journey to the New World.

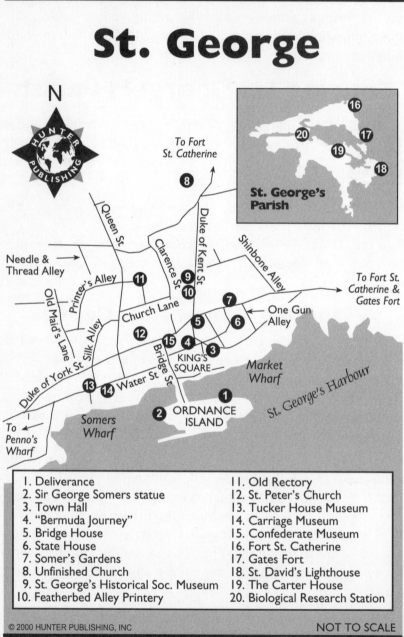

St. George

N

To Fort St. Catherine

St. George's Parish

Needle & Thread Alley

Queen St

Clarence St

Duke of Kent St

Shinbone Alley

To Fort St. Catherine & Gates Fort

Old Maid's Lane

Printer's Alley

Silk Alley

Church Lane

One Gun Alley

Duke of York St

Bridge St

Water St

KING'S SQUARE

Market Wharf

St. George's Harbour

To Penno's Wharf

Somers Wharf

ORDNANCE ISLAND

1. Deliverance
2. Sir George Somers statue
3. Town Hall
4. "Bermuda Journey"
5. Bridge House
6. State House
7. Somer's Gardens
8. Unfinished Church
9. St. George's Historical Soc. Museum
10. Featherbed Alley Printery
11. Old Rectory
12. St. Peter's Church
13. Tucker House Museum
14. Carriage Museum
15. Confederate Museum
16. Fort St. Catherine
17. Gates Fort
18. St. David's Lighthouse
19. The Carter House
20. Biological Research Station

© 2000 HUNTER PUBLISHING, INC   NOT TO SCALE

The St. George of today is a tiny community, clean and neat, with dozens of quaint shops and stores, side streets and long sloping sidewalks.

You'll need to take your time when exploring St. George. If you can, allow at least a full day, more if possible, because here you'll be treated to more old English and Bermudian tradition than anywhere else on the islands. Allow time to explore the quaint little shops and stores where the unexpected is always just around the corner, or hidden away in some dark recess waiting just for you to discover it. If you have the time and energy you should make the walk from St. George to Fort St. Catherine; it's almost a couple of miles, but the walk is fun, and the fort itself is not to be missed; just take your time. You can catch a bus from the fort back into town.

The tour of St. George I've laid out is quite comprehensive, taking in almost all the major sights of the city, and one or two spots that are not quite so obvious attractions. The tour can take as much as a full day, the fort a half-day, so allow plenty of time, and bring some extra cash to spend along the way.

Begin your tour of the parish in **King's Square**, also known over the years as the Market Square and the King's Parade. The **Visitors Service Bureau** here, ☎ 297-1642, is open 9 am to 5 pm every day except Sunday. King's Square is the hub of the town. On any given day almost every resident of St. George will pass through it or spend some time there. During the summer months it's a lively place. The Town Crier, in 17th-century costume, can often be seen ringing his bell and calling out the events of the day. As soon as you enter on the north side of the square, you'll see the town stocks, whipping posts and pillories just to your left. These offer an unusual photographic opportunity. There's also a ducking stool in the square, which once was used to punish female gossips; it was, to say the least, a harrowing experience for the lady concerned. Strange as it may seem, the men were never treated to the experience. Today, St. George's town crier, Richard Olsen, announces the punishments for the day: reenactments of those long since abandoned, including the ducking stool. King's Square is also the site of most of St. George's annual celebrations: New Years, Emancipation Day, etc., and an assortment of outdoor concerts held throughout the year. The **White Horse Tavern** is a welcoming place to enjoy a pint of beer, lunch, and a magnificent view of the harbor and *The Deliverance*. There's a visitor information center on the south side of the square at the water's edge. Here you'll find all the information you'll need about St. George and its surroundings, and more: excursions, day trips, bus schedules, pamphlets and brochures, shopping, dining, and so on. You can even buy bus tickets at the Bureau. The Bureau is open April through October from 9 am until 1 pm, and from 1:30 until 4 pm, Monday through Saturday. During the winter months, November through March, the hours are from 9 am until 2 pm, Monday through Saturday. ☎ 297-1642.

The Globe Hotel and Bermuda National Trust Museum: The old hotel was open to guests in the early to mid-19th century, but its history goes all the way back to when it was built by Bermuda's governor, Samual Day, in 1699, making it one of the oldest buildings on the islands. It hasn't seen a paying guest in many a long year. Today, however, it entertains paying guests of a different kind: it's a National Trust property housing a number of artifacts and exhibits that faithfully interpret the history of the islands in general and St. George in particular. These include a replica of the *Sea Venture* and a movie titled *Bermuda: Centre of the Atlantic*. On the upper floor you can see an exhibit called *Rogues and Runners: Bermuda and the American Civil War*. But the Globe's connections to the American Civil War go much deeper than the exhibit. During those days of blockades and gunrunners a Confederate agent actually had an office in the building. The museum is open year-round, except for public holidays, from 10 am until 4 pm, Monday through Saturday. Admission is $4. ☎ 297-1423.

From King's Square you'll naturally wander in the direction of the harbor and cross the bridge onto **Ordnance Island**. There, you'll find not only a wonderful view of King's Square and St. George, but a couple of unique points of interest. The first, and you can't fail to see it, is a full-size replica of *The Deliverance*. *The Deliverance*, along with a second ship, *The Patience*, was built from the wreckage of Sir George's flagship, *Sea Venture*. In 1610, the survivors of the wreck continued their journey to the New

World and eventually arrived safely in Jamestown. Looking at the replica of *The Deliverance*, left, it's difficult to believe that men and women set sail in such tiny vessels, often for months at a time, at the mercy of wind and weather. Would you? ☎ 297-1459.

Stop 2 on your tour is just across the way to the east. The **statue of Admiral Sir George Somers** stands in a small landscaped garden at the water's edge. It depicts a flamboyant, happy-go-lucky individual very much in keeping with what one might expect in an adventurer of his class.

Back across the bridge on the west side of King's Square is **St. George's Town Hall** (Stop 3), ☎ 297-1532. There's a small theater on the top floor where you can view an audiovisual presentation of *The Bermuda Journey* (Stop 4), the story of Bermuda and its people. The Town Hall is the meeting place for the Town Corporation, a body of three aldermen and five councilors headed by the mayor. The sedate old building has seen some exciting times, not the least of which was its siege by English soldiers, under orders from the Royal Governor to arrest the mayor, who had taken refuge inside. The Town Hall is open Monday through Saturday from 10 am until 4 pm.

Stop 5 is the **Bridge House**. Walk a short distance from King's Square up King Street; Bridge House is on the left. Built sometime around 1700, the house was home to several of Bermuda's early governors and of Virginia loyalist, Bridger Goodrich, who fled the colony during the American War of Independence. Goodrich was an adventurer of the first order. Arrogant, resourceful and ruthless, he organized a fleet of privateers and blockaded Chesapeake Bay, destroying all who traded with the American enemy. These, unfortunately, included Bermudian vessels. They fell prey to Goodrich's privateers, a fact that did not endear him to the Bermudian people. Bridge House is now an art gallery and private apartments owned by the Bermuda National Trust. The house is open Monday through Saturday from 10 am until 5 pm.

A little farther east along King Street is the **State House** (Stop 6), ☎ 297-8211. This is the oldest building in Bermuda. Built in

1620 by Governor Nathaniel Butler in the Italian style, it was the House of Assembly and the location of the principle court during the time when St. George was Bermuda's capital. Today, the house is leased to a Masonic lodge for an annual rent of one peppercorn per year. The ceremony of payment is held in April and has become one of the town's major celebrations. The State House is open to the public on most Wednesdays from 10 am until 4 pm.

North of the State House, across Duke of York Street, are the **Somers' Gardens**, Stop 7. This is where Sir George Somers' heart and entrails were buried; his body was sent back to England. When Sir George finally arrived in Jamestown he found only 60 of the colonists still alive. The winter period of 1609-1610 in Jamestown's history became known as the "Starving Time." No sooner had Somers arrived than he took a ship back to Bermuda in search of food and supplies for the starving colony. This was to be his last voyage; he died shortly after arriving in Bermuda. The gardens, opened in 1920 by the Duke of Windsor, then the Prince of Wales, feature tropical flowers, shrubs and trees. Open daily from 8 am until 4 pm.

Continue your walk through Somers' Gardens up the steps to the North Gate onto Blockade Alley. On the hill is the **Unfinished Church**, Stop 8. The church is something of an enigma. Now very much in ruins, it was designed to replace St. Peter's but, unfortunately, was never finished. Soon after construction began in the 1870s, the project was beset by financial difficulties, the work slowed, and then stopped altogether. Finally, after a storm did more damage than could easily be repaired, it was abandoned. The end of the new church, however, brought a new beginning to the old one; it's a fine building you'll visit later on your tour.

Turn south on Duke of Kent Street and walk to the corner of Featherbed Alley, where you'll find the **St. George's Historical Society Museum** (Stop 9 on our map), ☎ 297-0423. This is a fine example of 18th-century Bermudian architecture. Exhibits include the original kitchen, many examples of antique and period furniture, a collection of old documents and paintings, and a rare Bible. The museum is open on Tuesdays, Wednesdays and Thursdays from 10 am until 4 pm. Admission is $2 for adults, and 50¢ for children aged six to 16; children under the age of six are not charged.

Above: Bermuda

Below: Astwood Cove (see page 63)

Above: Abbott's Cliff, on the north side of Harrington Sound in Hamilton Parish

Below: Bermuda beach

Above: Blue hole (see page 112)

Below: Castle Island (see page 117)

Above: Clarence Cove (see page 64)

Below: The Old Rectory, built in 1705 (see page 93)

Above: The Dockyard (see page 82)

Below: Life on the reefs

Flatts Inlet (see pages 112-13)

Above: Mid-Ocean Golf Club (see page 168)

Below: Fort St. Catherine (see page 96)

Above: Hamilton Harbour (see page 67)

Below: Hawkins Island (see page 161)

Horseshoe Bay (see page 61)

Above: John Smith's Bay Park & Beach (see page 64)

Below: Clearwater Beach (see page 66)

Mangrove Bay (see page 79)

Above: South Shore cliffs, near the Reefs Hotel (see page 102)

Below: Bermuda's reefs

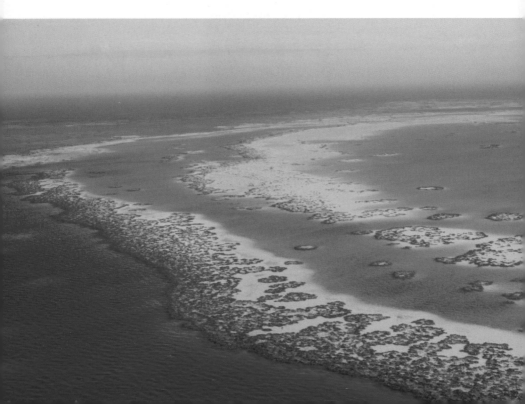

Riddells Bay Golf & Country Club (see page 169)

Above: Somerset (see page 75)

Below: Southampton (see page 101)

Above: St. David's Lighthouse (see page 97)

Below: St. George (see page 87)

Sunfish on the beach at Whale Bay (see page 102)

Just around the corner from the Historical Society Museum, on Featherbed Alley, is Stop 10, **Featherbed Alley Printery**. The little shop has a printing machine of the type invented by Johannes Gutenburg in the 1450s. This interesting place is open from 10 am until 4 pm, Monday through Saturday (closed from 11 am until 2 pm on Wednesday and Thursday).

Stop 11 is **The Old Rectory**, ☎ 236-6483. Continue on Featherbed Alley to Church Street. The Old Rectory is just to the right on Broad Alley. The house was once the home of Parson Richardson, the rector of St. Peter's from 1755 to 1805, nicknamed "The Little Bishop." It was built in 1705 by a reformed pirate. Today, the neat little house is a private residence owned by the Bermuda National Trust. It's open on Wednesday from noon until 5 pm. Admission is free.

St. Peter's Church, ☎ 297-8359, is Stop 12 on your map. From Broad Alley and the Old Rectory, you can reach it through the back entrance into the churchyard, which is opposite Broad Alley on Church Lane. The old churchyard is filled with headstones, some of which date back well over 300  years. St. Georgians and Bermudians of all walks of life are buried here. There are governors, professionals, ordinary townsfolk, pirates and, perhaps best-known, there's the grave of Midshipman Richard Dale. Dale was an American seaman who was mortally wounded during a sea battle with the English in the War of 1812. He was 20 years old when he died in 1815. The monument you see here was erected by his parents in tribute to the people of St. George because their "tender sympathy prompted the kindest attentions to their son while living and honored him when dead."

To the west of the church you'll find the graves of a number of slaves. The cedar tree you see by the back entrance is more than 500 years old and the church bell once hung from its branches.

St. Peter's is the oldest continually used Anglican church in the Western Hemisphere, and parts of it do date back to 1620, but it's not the original one; it's not even the second one. The first church was built on the site in 1612. It was a wooden affair with a palmetto thatched roof. That was replaced by a more permanent stone structure in 1619 when it was severely damaged during a storm. In turn, the second church was almost entirely replaced by the present church in 1713; the tower was added in 1814.

The church was, until the building of the State House in 1620, the new colony's only meeting place. It was here that the first assizes were held in 1616 and the Bermuda Parliament met for the first time in 1620.

There's a guide on duty during the week who will explain the history, but you can also wander around on your own.

- The altar is the oldest piece of woodwork on the island. It was carved by Richard Moore, who was a shipwright and Bermuda's first governor.

- The font is believed to be at least 500 years old and was brought to the island by the first colonists.

- The three-tier pulpit dates to the early 17th century and the galleries on either side of the church were added in 1833.

- Be sure to look at the wall memorials; some of the names are quite amusing.

- The vestry displays the fine silver collection, which includes a beautiful Charles I chalice that came over from England in 1625 and a communion set from 1697.

The church is open daily and for Sunday service. Admission is free, but donations are appreciated.

Barber's Alley

Leave St. Peter's by the front door and walk down the steps to Duke of York Street. Turn right, pass the police station in the next block and turn left onto Barber's Alley. This alley is named for a black freeman, Hayne Rainey, of South Carolina. During the American Civil War, he escaped to Bermuda on board a blockade runner. A self-educated man, he spent his time on the island barbering. When he eventually returned to America, he was elected to Congress – the first black member of the House of Representatives.

Continue down Barber's Alley to Water Street and turn right to Stop 13, **The Tucker House Museum**, ☎ 297-0545; it's just around the corner on the right side of Water Street. The house, built in 1711, is owned by the Bermuda National Trust and is an encapsulated history of the Tucker family, still an important presence on the islands. Edward "Teddy" Tucker is a diver, treasure hunter and historian of international reputation, and is something of a legend here. In days gone by members of the family have included a Governor of Bermuda, a United States Treasurer, a Confederate Navy Captain and an Episcopal Bishop.

The museum is a treasure house filled with antiques, artifacts and memorabilia, including a collection of Bermudian cedar furniture, many fine portraits, and antique silver. In addition, there's an interesting collection of items that were discovered beneath the cellar floor. The museum is open Monday through Saturday from 9:30 am until 4:30 pm, April until October, and from 10 am until 4 pm, November through March. Admission is $4.

Stop 14, **The Carriage Museum**, ☎ 297-1642, is just across Water Street from the Tucker House to the left. Remember that motor cars were not introduced to Bermuda until 1946 and, until then, the carriage was the mode of transport. As the new age of the automobile was being ushered in, it became apparent to Mrs. Bernard Wilkinson, founder of the museum, that the days of the carriage were numbered and she started her collection. Today, you can see the results of her labors. There are all sorts of carts and carriages, including a children's two-wheeler, called a dog cart; a six-passenger, enclosed Opera Bus; a magnificent Brougham; and even a surrey with a fringe on top. The museum is open Monday through Friday, and sometimes on Saturday, from 9 am until 5 pm. Admission is free, but donations are happily received.

From the Carriage Museum, turn right on Water Street and continue in the direction of King's Square. When you reach the square, turn left and go to the corner of Duke of York Street and Stop 15, **The Confederate Museum**, ☎ 297-1423. This building was erected in 1700 by Governor Samuel Day. During his administration he claimed the house as his own and initiated a court case that he was never to see the end of. Day died in prison and

Sightseeing

never knew that his claim was successful. The building served for more than half its existence as the Globe Hotel.

During the American Civil War it was the office of Confederate Agent, Major Norman Walker. Walker chose St. George because of its sympathy to the Southern cause, more for economic than ideological reasons. St. George, still trying to recover from the depression caused by the removal of the capital to Hamilton in 1815, had become the center for blockade running activities on the islands. Inside the museum you find a number of interesting Confederate artifacts, including a replica of the Great Seal of the Confederacy and an antique machine which will make a reproduction of the seal for you to take home as a souvenir. The house, owned by the Bermuda National Trust, is open Monday through Saturday, 9:30 am until 4:30 pm from April until October, and 10 am until 4 pm, November through March. Admission is $4.

That just about concludes your tour of St. George itself, but no visit would be complete without stopping at Fort St. Catherine and the much smaller, but no less interesting, Gates Fort to the south.

Fort St. Catherine, Stop 16 on the map, ☎ 297-1920, is about two miles from the town of St. George on the extreme eastern tip of the island known as St. Catherine's Point. If the walk is a little too much, you can jump on a bus. There should be one going by every 30 minutes or so. Built as part of the islands' defensive system, the fort has been restored to its original state and contains underground chambers and tunnels carved deep into the bedrock, cannon, guns, a number of military exhibits, and replicas of the Crown Jewels. There are also interesting dioramas depicting the islands' past and a video presentation that tells the history of Bermuda's forts.

The area surrounding the fort is popular for picnicking and recreation. The beaches are quiet and clean, and provide excellent opportunities for swimming and snorkeling. The fort itself, with its massive walls, ramparts, and tiny nooks and crannies, is a photographer's dream come true. It is open daily from 10 am until 4:30 pm. Admission is $5; children must be accompanied by an adult.

The last four stops on your tour of St. George's involve a bus ride.

Stop 17 is **Gates Fort**, right at the end of Cut Road on the tip on the peninsula. Take a number 3 bus outward-bound; it's a one-mile ride or an easy walk. The scenery along the way is spectacular. If you walk, take Barrack Road to the end of Cut Road, where you'll find the fort. You can visit any time you like; there are no formal hours. It's worthwhile to make the climb of the keep, if only for the view of the channel. There are also a couple of large guns up there that will provide an interesting photo opportunity.

Gates Fort is a reconstruction of a small redoubt that was built on this site in the early 1600s. At one time it was a private home. The fort itself is not much, but the sea and shore are beautiful. If you've brought along a picnic, this is the place to eat it. Gates Fort is open daily and no admission is charged.

To reach Stop 18 you'll need to return to St. George's and take a number 6 bus out to **St. David's Lighthouse**, ☎ 297-1642. You'll pass Stop 19, The Carter House, along the way, but don't worry, you'll see it on the return trip.

The small community of St. David's, apart from the naval base there, is one of the wildest and most remote spots on the islands. The locals, so islanders say, live in a world all their own. Some of the residents have supposedly never even been as far "abroad" as St. George's.

The lighthouse at St. David's is set at the highest point on the eastern coast. It stands 208 feet above sea level and was built in 1879 of Bermuda limestone. From the balcony high above St. David's Head, you'll enjoy spectacular views of the surrounding countryside, the Atlantic Ocean to the south, Ruth's Bay to the southwest, the South Shore, and St. David's and St. George's to the north. If you saw the movie *The Deep,* you'll be interested to learn that this is the lighthouse they used in the story. You'll also recall that they blew it up at the end of the movie. Well, of course, the one they destroyed was only a replica; neat! The lighthouse is open most days during the summer, but call ahead to check, ☎ 441-236-4201.

From St. David's, hop aboard another number 6 bus and head back in the direction of St. George's. Stop 19 is the **Carter House**, located inside the naval base; ask the driver to drop you off at the main gate.

The Carter House is one of the oldest homes in Bermuda. It was built in 1640 by the descendants of Christopher Carter, one of three men left behind on the islands when *The Deliverance* and *The Patience* sailed for Jamestown and the New World in 1610.

Christopher Carter

Carter was apparently something of a rogue. While waiting for the ships to return from Jamestown, he and two other men discovered a cache of ambergris – an expensive product of the sperm whale used in making perfume – washed up on the beach. The three men conspired in what became known as the "Ambergris Plot" to smuggle the stuff back to England, where they planned to sell it. But Carter got cold feet and, when the ships pulled into the harbour, he turned his co-conspirators in to Governor Moore. Carter remained on the islands and eventually settled on Cooper's Island, now a part of the naval base.

The old house built by Carter's descendants has been restored almost to its colonial condition. The interior houses antique furniture, artifacts and memorabilia, including a fine old tavern table. The Carter House is open on Wednesdays from 10 am until 3 pm and admission is free. Stop at the main gate of the naval station and show a photo ID. You might want to call ahead and double-check the opening times, ☎ 441-297-1642.

The final stop, Stop 20, is the **Bermuda Biological Station for Research**. Take a number 6 bus from the Carter House and ask the driver to drop you off at Ferry Reach, or take a number 1, 3, 10 or 11 bus inbound to Hamilton from St. George's and, again, get off at Ferry Reach.

Scientists at the research station have been studying marine life since 1903. The facilities are extensive and have been the subject of several novels, the best-known of which was *Beast* by Peter Benchley of *Jaws* fame. The story, although somewhat out of this world, gives some good insight as to the goings-on at the facility.

The station has its own deep-water ocean research ship, 13 laboratories, a 250-seat lecture hall and an extensive library. Guided tours of the facilities and grounds are conducted on Wednesdays at 10 am. There's no charge for the tour, which includes coffee and donuts, but donations are welcome. ☎ 441-297-1880.

Your tour of St. George's Parish has touched only the highlights; there's much more for you to see and do. Shopping in this little community is good and varied, but on a smaller scale than Hamilton. There are a number of restaurants and several tiny backstreet and courtyard shopping areas with flowers, trees and benches.

If you don't manage to see everything in one day, a return visit is easy enough as buses run back and forth between Hamilton and St. George from early in the morning until late in the evening.

Touring the Other Parishes

The remaining six parishes on Bermuda form a chain that runs east to west. To tour them you will need to rent a moped or a bicycle, or take advantage of the bus and ferry system. Following is a round-up, parish-by-parish, of the most interesting attractions. Be prepared to exercise a little flexibility during your tour. Who knows what you'll find around the next bend or down that tiny side road? The island is not a big one, and there's plenty of time for side trips.

It's not feasible to tour all six parishes in a single day. So I've divided the tour into three sections, each planned for a day of exploring.

If you decide to use public transport, be prepared to do a little walking. There's nothing too far off the beaten path and most of

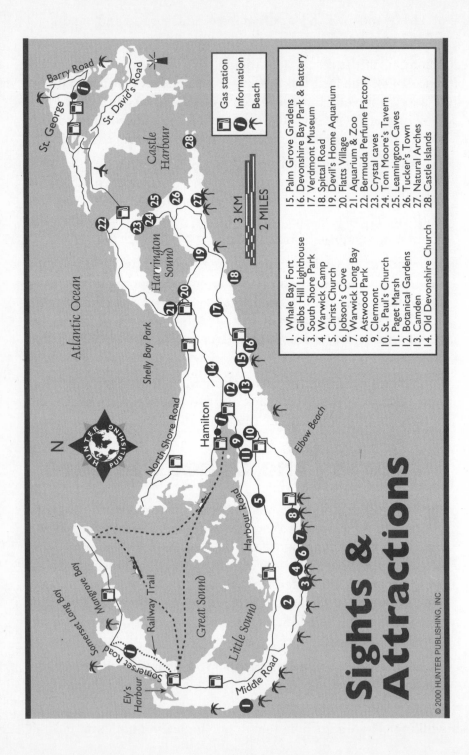

Sights & Attractions

1. Whale Bay Fort
2. Gibbs Hill Lighthouse
3. South Shore Park
4. Warwick Camp
5. Christ Church
6. Jobson's Cove
7. Warwick Long Bay
8. Astwood Park
9. Clermont
10. St. Paul's Church
11. Paget Marsh
12. Botanical Gardens
13. Camden
14. Old Devonshire Church
15. Palm Grove Gradens
16. Devonshire Bay Park & Battery
17. Verdmont Museum
18. Spittal Road
19. Devil's Home Aquarium
20. Flatts Village
21. Aquarium & Zoo
22. Bermuda Perfume Factory
23. Crystal caves
24. Tom Moore's Tavern
25. Leamington Caves
26. Tucker's Town
27. Natural Arches
28. Castle Islands

Gas station
Information
Beach

3 KM
2 MILES

Atlantic Ocean
Barry Road
St. George
St. David's Road
Castle Harbour
Harrington Sound
Shelly Bay Park
North Shore Road
Hamilton
Elbow Beach
Harbour Road
Great Sound
Little Sound
Middle Road
Railway Trail
Somerset Road
Somerset Long Bay
Mangrove Bay
Ely's Harbour

N
HUNTER PUBLISHING

© 2000 HUNTER PUBLISHING, INC

the tour stops are just a pleasant stroll away from the bus routes. As you'll be making frequent stops, it is highly recommended that you buy one of the three- or seven-day passes. A pass is convenient and will save you a great deal of money. Don't worry too much about schedules. The beauties of the Bermudian Public Transport System are its convenience, frequency and the short distances between stops. You can jump off the bus just about anywhere, secure in the knowledge that there will be another bus along in 30 minutes or less. If you decide you'd like to do the tour by moped or bicycle, the following directions will work just as well for you.

Touring Southampton Parish

 A great way to start your tour is on the ferry from Hamilton to Somerset. Ferries leave the dock in Hamilton at 9 and 10 am. The 9 am ferry goes via the Naval Dockyard and arrives at Somerset Bridge Wharf at 10:15. The later ferry goes direct to Somerset and reaches its destination in just 30 minutes. From the wharf, you can take a bus east on Middle Road into Southampton Parish. On your return trip, catch either a number 8 bus that will take you all the way back to Hamilton via Middle Road, or a number 7 that will take you to Hamilton via the scenic South Shore and the beaches.

Remember that bus stops along the routes are marked by pink and blue poles. Those poles with a pink section at the top indicate the stops for Hamilton-bound buses; those with a blue section at the top are outward-bound from Hamilton. To stop a bus you must stand by the pole. In places it might seem dangerous to do this, so always exercise extreme caution and be on the lookout for fast-moving traffic.

If you're going by moped or bicycle you can ride out to Somerset Bridge Wharf and follow the route, or you can take your rental with you on the ferry; it will cost an extra $3.50.

Sightseeing

Assuming you've arrived at Somerset Bridge Wharf by ferry, you can grab either a number 7 or number 8 bus going east to Hamilton. From Somerset Bridge Wharf, you'll travel east for about two miles to Whale Bay Road. Have the driver stop there and let you off. From Middle Road, walk down Whale Bay Road for about 700 yards. At the end you'll find a secluded, rocky little bay with a pink-tinged sandy beach and crystal-clear waters overlooked by **Whale Bay Fort**, Stop 1 on your tour (see map, page 100). The tiny fort – it's more of a battery than a fort – is overgrown now, but it's a pleasant spot where wildflowers and tropical plants grow in showy profusion. If you came by moped or bicycle you'll have to leave it behind and walk down to the beach; it's accessible only on foot. If you've brought along your swimming gear, now might be a good time to get changed and go for a dip in the ocean; you won't find a better place.

From Whale Bay Fort, walk back up Whale Bay Road, catch a number 7 bus, and continue eastward to Lighthouse Road. You'll travel about a mile to a point where the road forks and turns southward to the coast road and the beaches. Lighthouse Road is 2½ miles from Whale Bay Road. As you travel along South Road you'll pass by many of the best beaches on the islands. Stop the bus any time you feel like exploring. Leave the bus at Church Road and spend some time on the beach in the public park at Church Bay, and then stroll along the road going eastward to Lighthouse Road. It's a walk of a little more than a mile. Along the way, on the right, you'll pass by the Reefs Hotel at Christian Bay and the Sonesta Beach Hotel a little farther on. Look down from the clifftops to the sea and the beaches; the views are wonderful. Be sure to take your camera.

When you get off the bus you'll turn left onto Lighthouse Road and walk for a couple of hundred yards or so up the hill to **Gibbs Hill Lighthouse** (Stop 2), ☎ 238-8069 and 238-0524.

This magnificent lighthouse is one of the oldest of its kind in the world. Built of cast iron, its construction started in England in 1844. The plates were shipped to Bermuda and assembled on the site. At 117 feet tall, it stands on a hill 245 feet above sea level for a combined 362 feet; it's one of the highest spots on the islands.

The original lamp at Gibbs Hill was a great wick and oil affair. Today, its 1,000-watt bulb casts a beam of light that can, on a clear day, be seen by ships more than 40 miles out to sea. Aircraft can see it from more than 120 miles away. In times past it relied upon its rotating reflectors to attract the attention of ships that strayed too close to the rocks. These days the beam is locked onto wayward vessels by radar.

There's a small souvenir shop in the building at the foot of the tower where you can purchase gifts, tee-shirts and such. The grounds are well kept and a pleasant place to stroll or sit for a while.

Now, how about a trip to the top? If you decide to take it on, you'll negotiate a spiral staircase of 185 steps. Its not a climb for the faint-hearted, but the view is worth the exertion (there are stops along the way where you can rest and catch your breath). The balcony offers a spectacular all-around view of Bermuda. If you have a problem with heights, however, stay on the ground. The tower sways slightly in the wind and the balcony is narrow, with only a guard rail between you and the ground 127 feet below. After your climb to the top and back down again, a little light refreshment will definitely be welcome. If so, there's no better place to get it than in the **Lighthouse Tearoom**. Here, for less than $15, you can enjoy an old-fashioned English cream tea for two: scones, butter and clotted cream, along with a generous pot of tea. If you're an early bird, you can take breakfast in the Tearoom, and that's another culinary experience you won't want to miss. The Tearoom is open Monday through Saturday from 9 am until 5 – yes, they serve lunch as well – and on Sundays from 2 pm until 4:30. If you collect miniature lighthouses and related paraphernalia, you must drop in at the gift shop where you'll find all sorts of interesting bits and pieces, as well T-shirts and other assorted souvenirs. The lighthouse is open daily from 9 am until 4:30. Admission is $2.50. If you have a bus pass, admission is free.

Stop 3 is just a little farther along the road to the east. From the lighthouse, walk back down the hill to South Road, where you can either grab a bus or turn left and walk for about a mile to **South**

Shore Park on your right. You'll see the bays and beaches from your vantage point on the road high above. Photographers should take advantage of the far-reaching views here.

From South Road, walk down the winding road to the park and Horseshoe Bay, the first of a long line of bays and beaches that stretches eastward for more than four miles through Warwick Parish to Elbow Beach in Paget.

Before you leave the road, however, you might like to try **Tio Pepe's**, ☎ 238-1897, a neat roadside eatery close to the entrance of Horseshoe Bay. You can have lunch there and they also offer food to go. They serve good Italian cuisine and their pizza might be just what you need for a picnic on the beach.

It's very easy for a writer to get carried away when describing the South Shore. The area must be one of the most beautiful vacation spots in the world. From Horseshoe Bay, the pinkish sand and the vast turquoise ocean seems to stretch to infinity. The waves, always heavier on this side of the island, surge over the beaches and in and out of the rocky inlets and secluded coves. In one spot it might be easy to believe you are on the rocky coastline of Scotland, in another you could be on the beach in Florida. Each tiny section of the South Shore is unique.

Horseshoe Bay is perhaps the best known of the South Shore beaches. The great crescent of sand and sea stretches for several hundred yards and can, at peak periods, become extremely crowded. It's *the* place as far as Bermudians are concerned, the center of the islands' weekend social scene. Locals flock to Horseshoe for the sun, sand and sea. It's also the place where the local teenagers hang out. And it's one of two beaches on the islands where there are lifeguards on duty during the summer – the other is John Smith's Bay in Smith's Parish, way off to the east.

Even though there are lifeguards, you'll need to be careful of the undertow, which can be severe on windy days; keep a sharp eye on your youngsters.

There are public toilets and a snack bar. At either end of the bay, rocky outcrops offer a tempting opportunity to go climbing. If you do, be sure to stay on the well-worn paths. A fall from the top could put an end to your vacation.

At this point you can either go back to the road and head east (although a bus is not really necessary) or you can walk along the beach. Back on the road you'll turn right and walk for about a quarter-mile before turning left onto Camp Hill Road. Here you'll find Warwick Camp. You are now in Warwick Parish.

Touring Warwick Parish

Warwick Camp, Stop 4, was built just after the end of the Civil War. It was supposed to guard the beaches against an enemy landing. That, of course, never happened. During World War I it was used as a training ground and rifle range. Pearl White shot a movie here in the 1920s. Today, it's a quiet place where you can relax and enjoy the view.

Stop 5, **Christ Church**, is a little out of your way but, if you like old churches, it's worth a visit. Built in 1719, it's the oldest Presbyterian church in the British Commonwealth. From Camp Hill Road, turn east on South Road, go to Tribe Road 7 and make a right. Walk a half-mile or so to Middle Road then catch a bus to the Belmont Hotel; the church is just across the road.

If you decided to give Christ Church a miss, from Warwick Camp you can return to South Road, and from there to the beaches.

Stop 6, **Jobson's Cove**, is just 100 yards or so farther east. The cove is one of the most appealing spots on the island. Though secluded and often deserted during the winter, it can become a little crowded at other times, and it doesn't take many people to achieve that. If you visit when it's uncrowded, you'll be able to leave the world behind. The rocky cliffs hem in the tiny beach and, even though you're only yards away from civilization, you'll experience a feeling of total isolation, even loneliness. It's a great spot for swimming or snorkeling. Visit the cove late at night, say midnight, and don't be surprised if you find people skinny-dipping!

From Jobson's Cove, you can stay on the beach and walk east along the shoreline to Stop 7, **Warwick Long Bay**. More than a half-mile long, the pink-tinged sandy beach at Warwick Long Bay is, as the name implies, the longest and straightest continuous stretch of beach on Bermuda. In the early mornings, when there's a soft sea mist, you won't be able to see the end of it. Warwick Long Bay is protected from the big breakers by the inner reef and the sea is almost always calm. It is popular and sometimes crowded, but never uncomfortably so. There's plenty of room for all. The beach itself is backed by steep, rocky cliffs and sandy hills covered with seagrass and scrub. It's a combination, along with a huge rock that sticks up out of the ocean some 100 yards offshore, that offers photographers unique and interesting opportunities.

Stop 8 on your tour is **Astwood Park**. To reach it you can either continue your walk eastward along the beach – it's about a mile – or return to the road and take the bus. Astwood Park is a pleasant public area with flowers, shrubs, a number of picnic tables and a couple of beaches; just the place for a rest or a swim.

Touring Paget Parish

Paget Parish is a good place to start or end your day of sightseeing. You can either jump on a bus – a number 7 or 8 will get you where you want to go – or you can take the ferry from Hamilton over to one of the three docks in Paget: Lower Ferry Landing, Hodson's Ferry or Sea Kettle Wharf. Lower Ferry Landing will probably suit you best.

Paget is one of the most popular parishes in Bermuda. On one side it's bordered by the ocean, on the other by Hamilton Harbour. The view across the harbor to the city is a spectacular one. In the early evening, just after dark, the lights and the floodlit cathedral are an eye-popping sight.

The first stop of the day (Stop 9) is **Clermont**. It's just a short walk from the ferry landing on Harbour Road. This fine old house is not open to the public, but it's not out of your way and is worth stopping by to look. Once the home of Sir Brownlow Grey, the Chief Justice of Bermuda, it is noted for its fine and extensive woodwork.

Clermont is also famous as the site of Bermuda's first tennis court. Mary Outerbridge, on a visit from New York in 1874, learned to play tennis at Clermont and, on her return to the United States, she introduced the game to America.

From Clermont, walk west a short distance and turn left onto Valley Road, where you'll find Stop 10, **St. Paul's Church**. St. Paul's was built in 1796 to replace an earlier church. Its claim to fame is the ghost which was said to haunt the area for a short time around the turn of the century.

The Ghost of St. Paul's

Never seen, but often clearly heard – the soft sound of tinkling bells – the ghost was diligently hunted by locals. The hunt became something of media event, if there was such a thing in those days, with local vendors setting up refreshment stands. In the end, however, an American scientist solved the mystery by attributing the strange sounds to a rare bird: the filio. But did he solve the mystery? The bird was never seen here and the sounds continued, at least for a while. Then, one day, the ghost was gone, and it has never been heard from since.

Stop 11, **Paget Marsh**, is right next door to St. Paul's on Middle Road. Paget Marsh has been preserved by the Bermuda National Trust to show what the islands must have been like when the first settlers arrived. The 18-acre tract of unspoiled woodland reserve features many of the islands' endangered plants and shrubs, along with a variety of trees, including cedars, palmetto and mangrove. If you want to look around the marsh you'll need to give the National Trust a call before you make your visit. They are very accommodating and will be happy to make the arrangements, ☎ 441-236-6483.

From Paget Marsh, return to Valley Road and walk south to Middle Road, grab an inbound bus – stand on the left side of the road

Sightseeing

at one of the poles with a pink section at the top – and go east for about a mile to the **Botanical Gardens**, Stop 12, ☎ 236-6483. The driver will be happy to drop you off at the right spot. Alternatively, you can walk; it's quite a pleasant stroll. Walk east along Harbour Road to the roundabout, where you'll find Point Finger Road to your right, Front Street to your left, and Berry Hill Road and the Botanical Gardens opposite.

The gardens form a magnificent 36-acre landscaped park where tiny paths meander among a profusion of exotic tropical plants, flowers and trees. There's an aviary; a hibiscus garden with more than 150 varieties; and a special garden for the blind, filled with all sorts of fragrant plants and flowers – lavender, lemon, geranium, spices. The lawns are thick and green and there are a number of ruined stone buildings covered with vines; there's even a miniature forest. In the main building you'll find a visitor center where you can obtain information to guide you through the gardens, including a nature guide. There's also a tea room, a gift shop, and the offices of the Bermuda Department of Agriculture.

Be prepared to spend quite a bit of time here. The gardens are extensive and a full tour will take at least an hour and a half. You can wander around independently or you can take a guided tour, which leaves the visitor center at 10:30 in the morning on Tuesday, Wednesday and Friday through the summer months, and Tuesday and Friday only from November through March. The gardens are open daily from sunrise to sunset and admission is free.

Stop 13 is within the grounds of the Botanical Gardens. **Camden**, the official residence of Bermuda's Prime Minister, is open only on Tuesday and Friday. Even when it's not open, you can peek in the windows. Admission is free.

Touring Devonshire Parish

 Devonshire Parish, bordered by Paget, Pembroke and Smith's Parish, offers more peace and quiet than almost anywhere else on the island. There are no hotels and few restaurants. If you need a bite to eat, try the **Specialty Inn**; it's a half-mile east of Stop 16 on South Shore Road. They serve a good lunch or breakfast there, and it's not expensive.

From the Botanical Gardens go to Berry Hill Road and turn right. Walk to Tee Street, turn left and go to Middle Road. Turn right there and go a half-mile to Stop 14, **The Old Devonshire Church**. The church you see is not the original, although it stands on the site  where the first church was built in 1612. The second church, built in 1716, was destroyed in an explosion in 1970. The church you see before you is a faithful reproduction of that one. It's more like a cottage than a church, but a church it is, and a very popular one too. The pews, the communion table and the pulpit apparently came from the original church of 1612. The church silver is the oldest on the island, some pieces dating to the late 16th century. Old Devonshire is open daily from 9 am until 5:30 pm and admission is free.

From the Old Devonshire Church, turn south onto Brighton Hill Road and walk for about three-quarters of a mile to South Shore Road, where you'll find the **Palm Grove Gardens** (Stop 15).

Palm Grove is an 18-acre estate of landscaped gardens, the main feature of which is the pond, with its landscaped relief map of Bermuda. Each parish is picked out in the close-cropped map of grass. It's different and it's fun. Palm Grove is open Monday through Thursday from 9 am until 5 pm and admission is free.

From Palm Grove, return to South Shore Road and walk east for a short distance to a small side road leading off to the right. You'll see a sign pointing the way to **Devonshire Bay Park** and **Devonshire Bay Battery**, Stop 16.

Devonshire Bay is a quiet place, often deserted, always pleasant – a good spot to spend some time picnicking, swimming, or just relaxing and watching the ocean and the sea birds swooping and diving. You'll probably need a rest after all the walking you've done to get here! The battery, a small fort, was once a part of the islands' defensive system. It's now a somewhat lonely place on a site overlooking the bay. Bring your camera.

At the end of the day you can return to South Shore Road and grab a number 1 bus back to Hamilton.

Sightseeing

Touring Smith's Parish

From Hamilton, take a number 1 bus going to St. George's or Grotto Bay – there's one leaving every 30 minutes from 6:45 am onward, Monday through Friday, from 8:15 on Saturday, and every hour from 11 am on Sunday. Ask to be dropped off at the junction of Collector's Hill and Sayle Road in Smith's Parish.

Smith's has a long and interesting history dating back to the early 17th century. It's home to the islands' largest and most diverse nature reserve, and a unique aquarium. Hikers and nature lovers will feel right at home here.

Stop 17, **The Verdmont Museum**, ☎ 236-7369, is close to the junction of Collector's Hill and Sayle Road. It's the finest historic house on the island. Thought to have been built in 1710 by ship owner John Dickinson, the house very much resembles an English country manor in the classic style, with four large chimneys above an unusual roof. Over the years a number of interesting people have called this their home.

The interior of the house is filled with the memorabilia of Bermudian history covering more than 250 years. The early family portraits were painted by John Green, an American loyalist refugee who fled to Bermuda from Philadelphia at the close of the War of Independence. Green married one of John Dickinson's granddaughters and soon became a prominent member of the islands' political community, being appointed a judge of the Court of the Vice Admiralty. The last private owner of the property was a somewhat eccentric old lady who lived out her lifetime, some 75 years, surrounded by memories. When she died, her family sold the old house to the Bermuda Historic Monuments Trust, now the Bermuda National Trust, who opened it to the public in 1956.

None of the furniture you see here belonged to the original owners of the house – only the family portraits by John Green. Even so, the furniture that does fill the house provides a cross-section of Bermudian and English styles over the 18th and 19th centuries.

The handmade cedar staircase is unique; the newels have removable caps to accommodate candles. The upstairs nursery is filled with antique toys, and one has only to blink and look around to imagine small children at play dressed in the bright clothing of a bygone age.

Other items of interest at Verdmont include the two 19th-century pianos and a fine china tea service, thought to have been a gift from the Emperor Napoleon to President Madison. Unfortunately for Madison, the ship carrying it from France was set upon by privateers and the service was seized and ended up here in Bermuda. Verdmont is open every day (except Sunday) from April through October. Hours are from 9:30 am until 4:30 pm; 10 am until 4 pm, November through March. Admission is $4 for adults, $3 for senior citizens, and $1 for children and students with ID.

From Verdmont you can either catch the bus going east to St. George's or Grotto Bay, or you can hike down Collector's Hill to South Shore Road. If you walk, turn left on South Shore Road and go eastward for a mile to **Spittal Pond**, Stop 18 on your tour.

Spittal Pond, a 60-acre nature reserve, is Bermuda's showcase. Located along the shoreline overlooking the ocean, the park is interlaced with tiny paths and trails where, during the winter months, nature lovers can spend hours observing more than 25 species of waterfowl. In summer, the park is a profusion of flowers, plants and tropical trees. Be sure to check out **Spanish Rock** high on the bluff above the ocean. The rock itself, found by the early settlers and carved with the date 1543 and other markings too indistinct to decipher, was removed from the spot now marked by a plaque to prevent further erosion. It is thought, though unconfirmed, that a Portuguese ship was wrecked on the island in 1543. The crew must have found a way off the island, however, because they were long gone by the time Sir George Somers arrived in 1609. You can see a plaster cast of the original carvings at the Museum of the Bermuda Historical Society in Hamilton. The Spittal Pond reserve is open daily from sunrise to sunset and admission is free.

Stop 19 is **Devil's Hole Aquarium**, ☎ 293-2072. To reach it, you continue east along South Shore Road for a mile to Devil's Hole Hill and turn left to the Aquarium. Alternatively, take Knapton

Sightseeing

Hill to Harrington Sound Road and turn right. Both routes offer bus service; the distance is about the same. If you take a bus along South Shore Road you'll need to catch a number 1; if you go via Knapton Hill, take a number 3.

Devil's Hole Aquarium is the creation of a man named Trott, and it was Bermuda's first tourist attraction. Trott loved his fish and in 1830 he built a wall around his pond, a natural blue hole, to discourage people from fishing in it. This led to questions as to what he might be hiding behind his new wall. In order to allay any suspicions, he decided to allow people inside the wall to view the pond and, being an astute businessman, he charged admission.

Blue Holes

Blue holes are formed when an underground, underwater cave collapses, leaving a deep pool. This one is fed by sea water from underground channels and caverns, thus it stays fresh and well-stocked with fish of all shapes and sizes.

They say Devil's Hole contains more than 400 species of marine life, including giant grouper, turtles and sharks. You can fish in the pond if you like, but you can't really catch anything; the lines supplied by the staff are baited, but hookless. Still, there's nothing quite like watching a four- or five-foot shark nibbling at the end of your line; it might be the closest you'll ever get to catching one. Devil's Hole is open daily, May through October, from 9 am until 5 pm, and from 10 am until 3 pm, November through April. Admission is $5 for adults and $3 for children under 12.

To get to Stop 20, **Flatts Village**, go to the junction of Knapton Hill and take a number 3 bus westward (that's inbound toward Hamilton). A ride of about two miles brings you to the village.

Flatts Village is another neat little Bermudian community. A one-time haven for smugglers returning from the West Indies in the dead of night, it was also an occasional meeting place of the House of Assembly. Flatts is one of the oldest settlements on the islands and is very picturesque, located as it is on the shore of Harrington Sound. Today, the little town is a microcosm of Bermudian life, a collection of brightly painted cottages and houses, with tall palms and lots of flowering shrubs and plants.

Stop 21, **The Bermuda Aquarium and Zoo**, ☎ 293-2727, is in Flatts Village. This is one of Bermuda's most popular attractions. It's an aquarium in the true sense of the word: educational as well as entertaining. The large glass tanks hold examples of most of the finny inhabitants of the reefs and oceans around Bermuda, including the predators: sharks, barracudas, even a moray eel. Then there are the small aquatic habitats that house the creatures we never hear about, but that are no less important to the underwater world they live in – tiny crabs, sea urchins and corals. The strange-looking sphere you see just outside is a replica of the bathysphere which Doctor Charles Beebe used for his famous half-mile-deep dive in 1934.

Beebe's Incredible Dive

The highlight of Beebe's long career was, without doubt, his ocean dive. It was his insatiable desire to push the boundaries of the known world and his dedication to the study of sea life that led to the dive. In 1929 he built a marine laboratory and home in Bermuda on Nonesuch Island. There, with his second wife, Elswyth Thane, a novelist, he studied the sea life of the area. In 1930, in the true tradition of science fiction, he made his first descent into the ocean in a two-ton steel ball he called the bathysphere (a name derived from the Greek word bathys, meaning "deep"). In 1934, with Otis Barton, he made a dive of 3,028 feet, more than half a mile, and thus set a record for deep diving that wasn't broken until 1949.

Beebe was one of the 20th century's great adventurers, perhaps the last of a dying breed. Born in 1877, his career spanned more than 54 years and took him on explorations from the depths of the sea to the highest mountains, from Canada to South America, and from the steaming jungles of Borneo to the desolation of the Galapagos Islands.

He received a bachelor of science degree at Columbia University in 1898, remained at Columbia for another year doing postgraduate work, and then, in 1899, the New York Zoological Society named him honorary curator of birds, and director of the Society's Department of Tropical Research.

Beebe retired as director of the Department of Tropical Research in 1952, but he never stopped working. He continued his studies of jungle creatures at the New York Zoological Society's field station in Simla, in the mountains of Trinidad. He died in 1962 at the age of 85.

The Aquarium houses an exhibit that documents Beebe's epic dive. The aquarium itself contains a large collection of marine life, including reef fish, sharks and barracuda. The zoo has a fine collection of reptiles from around the world, and there's a children's discovery room where the kids can enjoy themselves working puzzles and coloring pictures. The Aquarium and Zoo are open daily from 9 am until 5 pm. Admission is $8 for adults; $4 for senior citizens and children under 12.

Touring Hamilton Parish

 From Flatts Village, take either a number 10 or 11 bus eastward along the North Shore Road toward St. George's to Stop 22, **The Bermuda Perfumery & Gardens** (☎ 293-0627, www.bermuda-perfumery.com).

The factory is set in a 200-year-old cottage near the causeway that leads over to St. George's. The staff will take you on a guided tour of the factory and gardens and explain the process used to extract natural fragrances from flowers.

The Perfume Factory began production in 1929. It seems the business grew from what the founder, William Smith, perceived to be a great waste of natural resources. Back in the early days of the 20th century, Bermuda used to ship Easter lily bulbs to the

United States. The flowers themselves were discarded, thrown into the sea. Well, one day, Smith happened to see the thousands of blooms being thrown into the sea and it didn't sit too well with him. He thought about it for a while, then came up with the idea of turning the blooms into perfume, and so it began. Smith, an engineer, designed and built all of the machinery to make the perfume; most of it is still in use. Since then it has become one of Bermuda's most popular attractions. Perhaps the most enjoyable part of the tour is walking in the gardens, which you can do on your own (complimentary maps are provided). As you walk along the tiny trails, you'll see flowers that provide the raw material for the factory: oleanders, passionflowers, jasmine, orchids and frangipani. When you've done the tour, go next door to the gift shop where you'll find a good selection of the products made here. A small bottle (one-quarter ounce) costs about $25, and from there the prices range on upward. The factory is open from 9:15 am until 5 pm, Monday through Saturday (April through October), and from 9:15 am until 4:30 pm, November through March.

 From the Perfume Factory you can walk to Stop 23. Turn right on Wilkerson Avenue and follow the road for a short distance to **Crystal Cave** and **Fantasy Cave**, the first of two cave systems along the Harrington Sound Road. Crystal Cave was discovered in 1905 by two boys playing cricket. Apparently, their ball disappeared down a hole and they went in after it. They found themselves in a vast underground cavern more than 120 feet deep, surrounded by rock formations of fantastic shapes and sizes and an underground lake. Today, the entrance to the two caves the boys found is gone, replaced by a sloping path to a wooden bridge across the lake. If you've never been underground, you should try it here. The stalactites and stalagmites are accentuated by hidden lighting that glows among the rocks and shimmers across the still waters of the lake. ☎ 293-0640.

Before you leave the area, you might enjoy a visit to the **Glass Blowing Studio**. You'll find it at 16 Blue Hole Hill; ☎ 293-2234. If you've never seen glass blowing done before, you're in for a treat. I'm not about to try to describe the process here; you have to see for yourself. Suffice it to say that it's one of the world's oldest arts, dating back more than 2,000 years. Today, it's become a fine art, and the pieces made at the studio are among the best you're ever likely to see. The products are pure Bermudian: bowls, vases, plates and ornaments, all produced in the vibrant colors of the islands. Tour the studio, see how it's done, then take a piece home with you. The studio is open from 9 am until 5 pm, Monday through Saturday, and from 10 am until 5 pm on Sundays, January through August. September through December, it's open from 10 am until 4 pm. Prices range from about $12 for a small glass ornament to more than $100 for larger, more exotic pieces. Admission is free.

Go south from Crystal Caves along Harrington Sound Road for a short distance to **Tom Moore's Tavern**, Stop 24. It's not far and is an easy walk.

The old tavern has its roots set firmly in Bermuda's history. It was built by Thomas Trott in 1652. Trott called his new home Walsingham, after Robert Walsingham, a sailor on the *Sea Venture*, and for whom the nearby bay on Castle Harbour is named. Later it became the haunt of Irish poet, Tom Moore, who arrived on Bermuda in 1804. At that time the house was still owned by the descendants of Thomas Trott. Moore befriended them and paid frequent visits to the estate. In fact, he did much of his writing there. Today, the house is a popular restaurant, still surrounded by woods and gardens as it was when first built. It has lost little of its charm over the 350 years. The restaurant is open only for dinner. You'll have to make a reservation, ☎ 441-293-8020, www.tommoores.com, and take either a taxi or a number 3 bus from Hamilton.

 Leamington Caves, Stop 25, are just a little farther south along Harrington Sound Road. Again, it's just a short walk from Stop 24, so you can stroll in the sunshine and enjoy the view along the way.

Leamington Caves are smaller and less impressive than Cahow Lake. A grotto with lots of stalactites, stalagmites and other rock formations, it's still worth time out for a visit. One of the more interesting rock formations is an amber pillar the staff has named the **Statue of Liberty**. It's a little difficult to make the connection, but you can decide that for yourself.

If you'd like a bite to eat before you visit the cave, try the **Plantation**. Lunch will cost you $15 or so per person, but that entitles you to visit the caves for free. Otherwise the entrance fee is $4 for adults and $2 for children aged 4 to 12. The caves are open from 10 am until 4 pm, Monday through Saturday from mid-February through late November. They are closed December and January.

Continue south along Harrington Sound Road for about a mile to **Tucker's Town**, Stop 26. You can take a bus if you like, but the walk is quite pleasant if time allows.

Daniel Tucker was one of the first governors of Bermuda. In 1616 he decided to move his home from St. George's to a new settlement on Castle Harbour. Work was begun on the new town. Some streets and small houses made it off the drawing board into reality, but eventually the project was abandoned. Tucker's Town became a tiny fishing community and existed as such for 300 years until after the end of the First World War in 1918. Around that time a large tract of Tucker's Town was purchased for use as a country club and steamship dock. The result of that purchase is the Mid-Ocean Club and the Marriott Castle Harbour Hotel. Soon after the club was founded, its members started building homes in the surrounding area. Today, the community is the most affluent on the islands. Only club members are allowed to purchase property here and homes sell for upwards of $2 million.

Stop 27 is below the Mid-Ocean Golf Club clubhouse on the South Shore. **Natural Arches** is one of the most beautiful and, consequently, most photographed spots on the island. Its major attractions are the two natural stone arches carved by the action of the wind and surf over many thousands of years. Walk on down to the South Shore Road, where you'll find signs pointing the way to Castle Harbour and Natural Arches.

When you've finished at Natural Arches, continue eastward to **Castle Island**, Stop 28; you either have to walk or take a taxi. The walk is one of the most beautiful on the islands. You won't see many people along the way, but you will enjoy wonderful views and the fresh salt breeze. Castle Island is one of a group of islands

Sightseeing

located at the tip of the southern peninsula that bounds Castle Harbour. The islands were fortified by the first settlers soon after they landed on Bermuda in the early 17th century; hence the name Castle Harbour. Today, the islands are a part of Bermuda's nature reserves, and you can go birdwatching, hiking and picnicking along the way.

If you've been looking frequently at your map of the islands, you can't have failed to notice one small piece of land at the entrance to Castle Harbour. Its name alone should have caught your interest. **Nonesuch Island** is not on your tour. You may, however, be able to rent a boat or pay someone to take you out there and wait while you look around. Nonesuch is another of Bermuda's nature reserves, not far from civilization, but very remote, isolated and totally unspoiled.

Nonesuch Island & David Wingate

Nonesuch Island is the home of the reclusive David Wingate, Bermuda's only conservation officer. For most of his adult life Wingate has dedicated himself to the restoration of the Bermuda that settlers found here when they arrived in 1609, and to the preservation of a small pelagic bird, the cahow, that was thought to be extinct.

Over a lifetime of living almost as a hermit on Nonesuch, David Wingate has planted more than 8,000 trees and brought back the cahow. Today, the 15-acre island is the way Bermuda must have been when Sir George Somers and his men first stepped ashore.

You can reach Nonesuch only by a short boat ride. You arrive on the island at a tiny dock flanked by a twisted, semi-submerged iron hulk. From there, make your way up the cliffs to a pathway that winds through the jungle, either to David Wingate's house high above the ocean, or off into the depths of the island jungle in the other direction.

A walk around the island will take about an hour. Allow more time if you want to stop off at one of the many tiny bays and inlets or spend some time on a pristine sandy beach. Along the way you'll see a tiny cemetery – there are only a couple of weather-worn headstones – and a healthy display of vegetation and trees, all endemic to the islands. You'll find no hibiscus on Nonesuch. They weren't here when Sir George arrived, and Wingate won't have them on the island today. Instead, you'll find samples of the Bermudian red cedar and the palmetto. From the earliest times, the red cedar was exploited almost to the point of extinction on the other islands.

The Cahow – Back From Extinction

 The cahow, a member of the petrel family of sea birds, was thought to be extinct until, at the turn of the 20th century, a single specimen was found in the rocky crevices on one of the Castle Harbour islands. It was identified as such by a comparison with fossilized bones found in the limestone caves on the islands. Three years later another specimen was found when it flew into St. David's Lighthouse and was killed. Today, after a great deal of effort, Wingate is the guardian of more than 40 pairs of nesting cahows and the island itself has become a symbol of hope for conservationists around the world.

Sightseeing

Sailing Bermuda's waters

Adventures

Boating

The Wildcat

"This aint no pussycat, baby!" How many times did I hear that phrase

and want to strangle the man who uttered it. I do know that I spent the most hair-raising couple of hours of my life on board the *Wildcat*, a 50-foot-plus, high-speed catamaran powered by two 800 horsepower, supercharged Caterpillar diesels.

It was a cool, somewhat overcast morning when I stood at the dock on Front Street waiting for the boat to arrive. I'd been told by those who know I was in for a fairly wild ride, and that seas off the South Shore were expected to be a little on the choppy side. So what? I consider myself a fairly experienced sailor – I've spent many a day deep sea fishing and had yet to experience anything I couldn't handle. Anyway, I was looking forward to a couple of hours of offshore sightseeing. The boat arrived at the dock; it looked docile enough, even taking into account the rather garish paint job – yellow with black tiger stripes. I boarded and seated myself strategically in the last row of seats against the rail – the best place, so I thought, to enjoy the views. I should have known something was afoot when I was asked to strap myself in and the tour guide, a tall Bahamian with an attitude, announced to the passengers for the first time that, "This aint no pussycat, Baby!" He then went on to give a safety talk that I felt would have been more appropriate on an airplane. Finally, the boat cruised quietly out of the Great Sound and into the ocean off the North Shore – the first leg of a ride that would take us completely around the is-

Adventures

land, more than 50 miles. The waters off the North Shore were as smooth as glass. The wind barely whispered over the bow. The sun was shining; it was going to be a beautiful day. So far, so good.

Once the boat was a half-mile off-shore the engines began to growl and the speed rose to some 20 knots, at which point the great boat rose out of the water onto its hydroplanes, and the speed continued to increase. Within a few minutes we were skimming over the emerald waters at almost 50 knots, and I have to tell you it was exhilarating, though still no indication of what was to come.

We sped eastward toward St. George, then south around the eastern end of the island, and the sea became a little choppy, throwing up clouds of spray and causing the boat to buck, but not alarmingly so. All the while the guide was giving us a running commentary over the speaker system, from the relative comfort of the enclosed bridge, I might add. The boat slowed and we pulled into the harbor at St. George to pick up more passengers.

Everyone began congratulating each other, exclaiming that it wasn't as bad as they had expected. Ten minutes later we were back on the ocean, speeding up and heading for the South Shore. We rounded the southeastern tip of the island and turned west into a sea that was running five to six feet. The guide yelled over the noise, "Hold on, folks. This ain't no pussycat, baby." At this point the boat took off for the first time. It hit a wave and rose some 10 feet into the air, and it stayed there as it traveled forward more than 50 feet before slamming down and throwing up a huge cloud of spray and a wall of almost solid water, most of which landed squarely on me! Yes, my carefully chosen seat was now the worst possible place to be on the whole boat.

For what seemed like hours, although I now know it was only about 25 minutes, I suffered shower after shower of water and spray that hit me full in the face at more than 50 miles an hour, and that's not all. The pesky boat spent more time in the air than it did on the water. We suffered bone-shattering, pounding hits as the great catamaran sailed high in the air and then crashed down again. Never once did it slow down. The cries of excited joy from the passengers as we had sped across the quiet waters off the North Shore had by now turned into screams of desperation. Everybody on board, except for that excruciatingly annoying guide and his crew, wanted the torture to end. And it did, eventually.

We rounded the western end of the island and sped back onto the quiet waters and onward toward the entrance to the Great Sound. The gentle cruise back to the dock was a definite anticlimax. Everyone was exhausted, glad it was over. At least, I was. During the 10 minutes it took to make it back to the moorings on Front Street, however, I began to hear people telling each other that "it wasn't so bad." I don't know. I staggered up the steps to Front Street where the guide was waiting to say goodbye. I shook his hand and thanked him. Yes, I thanked him for one of the most terrifying two hours I had ever experienced. Was I out of my mind? I must have been. That was my first and last trip on the *Wildcat*, and the tour guide was absolutely right: It ain't no pussycat, *Baby*. What it is is a real outdoor adventure. It's not for the faint-hearted, or those with physical or medical limitations, but if you like to experience thrills on a grand scale, this is a ride you should not miss. The price of the adventure might, at first, seem high. I assure you it's not. This is definitely one of those times when you get exactly what you pay for. It's not my kind of adventure, but, for those who enjoy this type of wild experience, it would be worth twice the price. Adults, $38; children under 12, half-price. For bookings and information, ☎ 441-293-RIDE.

Kayak Bermuda

 I was wondering when some enterprising individual would realize what wonderful opportunities for sea kayaking are available on Bermuda; well, here we are at last.

Kayak Bermuda is the brainchild of Stephen "V" and Lexie McKey. They don't have a full sea-going itinerary yet, but what they do have is something unique and extraordinarily appealing. At the moment, they are specializing in short tours, 2½ to three hours, that anyone, experienced or not, can easily manage. They start with a practice paddle along Millionaire's Row at Tucker's Town and then continue on along the coral and limestone cliffs of the Castle Island Nature Reserve. There, you can observe the longtail birds and float over the coral reefs. After 35 to 45 minutes, you have the choice of relaxing on the beach or snorkeling, or you can continue kayaking another 20 to 25 minutes to reach some faster and more exciting paddling in the waves off the South Shore. Then again, you might like to go on the evening tour, which will take you along the North Shore to observe the sunset. I've got to tell you, this sort of soft adventure really appeals to me. The company uses the safe "sit on top" kayaks that are stable and easy to use, even for first-timers; full instruction is included. Tours depart at 9:30 am, 1:30 pm and 7 pm, June through September, from Ordnance Island & Penno's Wharf, St. George. The rate is $50 per person for all ages over eight years old. Children under 16 must paddle with an able adult. Payment is at the dock by cash or credit card. It's best to make a reservation at ☎ 441-297-3862 or 235-2424; or visit the website at www.kayakbermuda.bm.

Boat Rentals

 "You can do it all with a Boston Whaler," at least that's what the brochure says, and they're "unsinkable," again according to the brochure. Seriously, though, if you love getting out and about on the water, you should consider renting one of these sturdy craft. They are available for rent at **Water Sports**, Robinson's Marina at Somerset Bridge, ☎ 441-234-0914. The boats travel at speeds up to 35 miles per hour, have center consol steering, Bimini tops to provide shade from the midday sun, and you can take along optional snorkeling gear, fishing rods and tackle, and a cooler with ice, all for a nominal extra fee. You can explore the coastline and its many secluded coves, tiny islands and beaches, or speed around the Great Sound. You can snorkel over a reef, off an island beach, or even over a shipwreck. If you want a secluded picnic, that's available too. You can even feed the fish over the shipwreck of the HMS *Vixen*. All this is possible through map orientation and advice about route selection provided by Tony Roach, the owner of Water Sports. Tony's colored map highlights the best beaches, snorkeling spots, and where to find the best fishing, as well as convenient waterside restaurants. Never driven a boat before? Don't worry Tony's staff will show you how in just a few minutes; it's that easy.

You can rent a Boston Whaler at two hours for $60; four hours for $100; six hours for $140; and eight hours for $160. Gas is extra, costing about $15 for four hours. The boats will carry up to four adults (one adult equals two children under 12 years old). Reservations are advised (no deposit is necessary) and you should plan to arrive about 30 minutes before you intend to depart. ☎ 441-234-0914.

Fishing

 Nothing beats heading out to sea in the early morning just as the sun is peeping over the horizon, when the air is crisp and cool, with the breezes blowing gently in your face. And few things compare with the feeling one gets aboard a slowly trolling boat on a calm sea under a hot summer sun, a heavy rod between your knees, and a can of something cold in your hand. The ultimate experience comes when you hook your first billfish and you find yourself involved in the fight of a lifetime as the fish does its utmost to tear rod and line from your aching fingers. In the distance, you see him hurl himself many feet into the air and drop down with a mighty splash as he tries to rid himself of the hook. And then you have him there at the side of the boat, exhausted, docile, deep blue back glistening in the sunlight, your first sailfish. And so it begins.

You don't have to be a world-class angler to take advantage of what Bermuda has to offer. In fact, it's okay if you've never fished in your life. There are plenty of skilled guides on the islands willing to take you in hand and show you how it's done. A couple of hours of instruction, a fast boat or a calm, shallow-water flat, and you're in business, as surely hooked as any wahoo or amberjack – doomed to spend the rest of your days in search of "The Big One."

In recent years the numbers of fish on the reefs and in the shallow water within the reefline have declined. This situation has caused real concern and new government regulations have already done much to restore the dwindling finny population.

The quality of sport fishing in Bermuda is high year-round, but the prime season is between May and November. There are more species of fish in the waters off Bermuda than you're ever likely to catch, and you have several options as to how you might go about it. Of course, offshore fishing is the premier version of the sport in Bermuda, but there really is something for everyone. You don't need to charter expensive deep-sea boats to enjoy a good day out. You can do it from a small rental boat all by yourself, from the beach, from a private dock or a hotel fishing pier. You're not likely to catch a trophy sailfish or marlin from the dock – you'll have to go to sea for that – but you will catch pompano, and perhaps even bonefish. The key is knowing where to fish.

The Catches

 On the reef you'll find **snapper**, **grouper**, **little tunny**, **Bermuda chub** (left), and **yellowtail** (below right), to mention only a few. In the deep waters beyond the reef are the great gamefish. Besides the **sailfish**, the king of fish is perhaps

the **blue marlin**, but they are few and far between. When you do find one, you're in for the experience of a lifetime. The "big blue" typically ranges in size from 100 to 200 pounds or more. Fish of three, four

and five hundred pounds have been caught in more southern waters and stories of "the one that got away" tell of fish in excess of 1,000 pounds.

Bluefin tuna is another exciting blue-water catch. Fish weighing in at 100 pounds or more are not uncommon, and catches between 500 and 800 pounds have been recorded in the western Atlantic. **Blackfin** and **yellowfin tuna** are smaller, but no less fun to catch.

Other excellent deep water species include the **kingfish**, or king mackerel. They can be caught year-round, although peak seasons are the spring and summer. Then there's **dolphin**. No, not Flipper; he's a mammal. This dolphin is a fish. Dolphin are usually found fairly close to the shoreline, weigh anywhere from five to 20 pounds, and are excellent to eat. **Wahoo** weigh 15 to 30 pounds and, in rare cases, as much as 60 pounds. They too make tasty dinners and are highly prized by sport fishermen. Wahoo are most often found lurking in the deep water off the edge of the reef. **Amberjack** is another prized sporting fish found most often in the cooler, deep waters just off the edge of the reef during the summer months, and closer to shore the rest of the year. Amberjack can run anywhere from 20 to 40 pounds. Other species include **white marlin, almaco jack, skipjack tuna** and **rainbow runner**.

Sharks, too, are common throughout the waters of the Bermudas and can be found in both shallow waters and deep. Makos, blues, hammerhead and tiger sharks abound. The truth is, however, that the fight usually lasts only as long as it takes for the shark's razor-like teeth to bite through the wire traces that hold him. Even so, you're sure to remember the battle for a long time.

The wily **barracuda** is found in large numbers, in shallow or deep waters, and can often be seen swimming close to the surface in the clear waters over the reefs and sandy banks. Barracuda range in size from a few pounds to about 15 or 20 pounds and, small though they might be, you're sure of a good fight if you can get one on the hook.

Grouper is a tasty fish, often found swimming lazily, close to the bottom on the reefs all around Bermuda. Catches average 15 to 25 pounds, and fish of 30 to 45 pounds are not uncommon. Likewise the **snapper**. He,
too, may be caught on the reefs throughout the islands. Most common are the red and gray variety.

Licenses & Regulations

A fishing license is not required. You are not allowed to collect sea turtles, whales, porpoises and dolphins (the mammal), or corals of any type. Nor are you allowed to take the conch, helmet shells, bonnet shells, netted olive shells, Bermuda cone shells, scallops, the Atlantic pearl oyster, calico clams or West Indian tap shells.

No spear fishing is allowed within one mile of any shore; scuba gear may not be used to spear fish. A spear gun may not be used anywhere at any time.

No more than two fish of any one species may be taken by spear fishing in any 24-hour period. Lobsters may only be taken from September 1st to March 31st, by licensed residents only.

Adventures

Basic fishing information can be obtained from the **Bermuda Department of Tourism**, ☎ 441-292-0023, or from the **Bermuda Game Fishing Association**, PO Box HM 1306, Hamilton HM FX, Bermuda, ☎ 297-8093. The association is an advisory body representing the International Game Fish Association (IGFA) affiliated clubs in Bermuda, and is the caretaker for all official local records and world records held locally. ☎ 441-238-0112.

Tournaments

Visitors are encouraged to enter their catches in the annual **Game Fishing Tournament** (January 1st to December 31st) with the Bermuda Department of Tourism, Global House, 43 Church Street, Hamilton. No license is required and there is no entry fee. Awards are presented for top catches in 26 classes of fish found in local waters. Ask your captain for an entry form and details.

Qualifications for Awards

Twenty-six species of fish are recognized for competition purposes. The table below indicates these species and also advises maximum line test that may be used. Note: maximum line test does not apply to an entry for the Award of Merit.

Awards

- The **Award of Merit** may be received by a visitor only. Entrant must use the official entry form. Any game fish caught on any test line can qualify.
- The **Citation** is made for an officially entered fish a) to a visitor catching a fish weighing at least 1½ times the test line used, and b) to a resident catching a fish weighing at least twice the test line used.
- The **Outstanding Angling Achievement Award** is a handsome silver pin that may be won by catching one of four species of fish – greater amberjack, bonefish, yellowfin tuna, and wahoo – in a variety of ways: The Heaviest Fish in each Recognized Species caught by a visitor during any one year will win an award; the High Point Fish in each Recognized Species caught by a visitor in any one year will win an award.

Where to Find the Fish

Among the most popular spots for shore fishing at the western end of the islands are **Great Sound**, **Little Sound**, and many of the rocky beaches and inlets from **Frank's Bay to the Royal Naval Dockyard**. On the outside of the islands, the beaches from Long Bay southward around **Daniel's Head**, **Ely's Harbour**, and on to **West Whale Bay** seem to offer the best opportunities.

Going east, **Castle Harbour** and **St. George's Harbour** both offer good opportunities for a day's sport. The beaches off the extreme eastern end of the island around **St. Catherine's Point**, and the rocky shores around **St. David's Head** offer great possibilities too. You might also try the South Shore around **John Smith's Bay** and **Devonshire Bay**.

You can go flyfishing for bonefish almost anywhere around the islands – in the tiny inlets, the sandy coves, and on the flats inside the reef. Bonefish are not very big. Most often they will weigh in around six to 15 pounds, with some growing to 20 pounds. Hook one, however, and you're in for a battle. Bonefish are known for fighting.

Reef & Deep-Sea Fishing

Reef fishing, or deep-sea fishing, is how you'll find "The Big One." The three major reef systems forming the tip of the extinct volcano that is Bermuda lie at varying distances from the islands. The first, **the inner system**, runs as close as a half-mile from the shore in some places and stretches outward almost five miles. The second system, the **Challenger Bank**, lies 17 miles offshore; and the third, the **Argus Bank**, is more than 25 miles out. Trolling is the most popular method of fishing over the reefs, and catches of snapper, grouper, barracuda and amberjack are common. Just off the reef in deeper waters are wahoo, tuna, dolphin, sailfish and marlin.

Charter boats are available to take you out to the fishing grounds. They come in different sizes, from 28 feet to 55 feet, and are equipped with a variety of tackle with line-test weights from 20 to 130 pounds. Most boats are also fitted with all the modern gadgets for tracking the fish, including depth sounders, sonar, and radar.

Adventures

Rental Equipment
for Shore Fishing

Fishing tackle may be rented from any of the following outfits on a daily or weekly basis. You will be required to leave a deposit (usually about $30) in case of loss or damage of the equipment. Prices range from $10 per day to $50 or $60 per week.

Four Winds Fishing Tackle Ltd.	2 Woodlands Road, Pembroke, HM 07	☎ 441-292-7466
Mangrove Marina Ltd.	End of Cambridge Road, Mangrove Bay, Somerset	☎ 441-234-0914
Harbour Road Marina	Newstead, Paget	☎ 441-236-6060
Pompano Beach Club & Waterports Centre	Pompano Beach Club, Southampton	☎ 441-234-0222, extension 212
Sea Kettle Yacht Charters Ltd. (tackle comes with boat rental only)	Sea Kettle, Paget	☎ 441-236-4863

Charter Boats for Deep-Sea
& Reef Fishing

Some charter boats are available year-round, although the best fishing and charter deals are from May through November.

All Bermudian charter boats are skippered by experienced guides and are equipped with fighting chairs and outriggers. All necessary tackle, bait, ship-to-shore telephones and lifesaving gear – rafts and life jackets – are included in the price of the charter. All you need to bring is lunch and refreshments. All vessels have toilet facilities.

Skippers operate under their own set of rules with regard to the fish that you might catch. You should, therefore, check out your prospective skipper's policy before you sign on. Does the boat retain all, or a percentage of the catch? Is there freedom of selection by the party renting the boat?

Rates & Hours

You can charter a boat by the half-day (four hours) or full day (eight hours) and rates vary according to the size of the boat and the reputation of its captain.

 A four-hour trip will limit the grounds that may be fished.

Parties of six persons are preferred. Charter rates differ from season to season, mainly due to the fluctuation of fuel prices, and the rate is often determined by the type of fishing you want to do, e.g. deep-sea, reef or bonefishing.

All Bermudian charter fishing boats are inspected annually by the Department of Marine & Ports Services and the Department of Fisheries, who then issue a license to operate. Check that current licenses are displayed when you board the boat.

Charters can be arranged privately (see the following list) or through one of the organizations listed below.

Charter Companies

The Bermuda Charter Fishing Boat Association, Box SB 145, Sandy's, Bermuda, SB BX, ☎ 441-292-6246.

The Bermuda Sport Fishing Association, Creek View House, 8 Tulo Lane, Pembroke, Bermuda, HM 02, ☎ 441-295-2370.

The St. George's Game Fishing & Cruising Association, Box 107, St. George's, Bermuda, GE BX, ☎ 441-297-8093.

Members of the above organizations are indicated on the the list of outfitters that follows by these codes:

☆ The Bermuda Charter Fishing Boat Association

☆☆ The Bermuda Sport Fishing Association

☆☆☆ the St. George's Game Fishing & Cruising Association

To book, call the individual charter captains direct or contact the member's association booking office. Independent Charter Fishermen have no stars at the beginning of their listings and must be called direct.

Adventures

Outfitters

☆ **Michael Baxter**: ☎ 441-234-2963. *Ellen B*, 28-foot Down East; 14 rods, 4 to 50 pounds test; spinning to heavy troll; two depth sounders.

Joe Bell: ☎ 441-297-0056. *Triangle*, 46-foot Hans Pederson; selection of rods and reels; 20 to 110 pounds test; three fighting chairs; Loran; depth sounder; two downriggers and two outriggers; air-conditioned.

Alan Card: ☎ 441-234-0872. *Challenger*, 45-foot Flybridge Sportsfisherman; 26 rods; 12 to 130 pounds test; three fighting chairs; Loran; depth sounder; three outriggers and two downriggers.

Eddie Dawson, Sr.: ☎ 441-295-0140. *Sea Scorpion III*, 33-foot Young Brothers Flybridge; 10 rods; 12 to 80 pounds test; one fighting chair; two downriggers; Loran; radio depth sounder.

Allen DeSilva: ☎ 441-295-2036. *Mako 4*, 53-foot Jim Smith Sportsfisherman; 24 rods; fish finders; Loran; three fighting chairs; air-conditioning.

☆☆ **David DeSilva**: Call the association booking office, ☎ 295-2370. *Miranda*, 47-foot Bermuda, custom built; 29 rods; 12 to 80 pounds test; three fighting chairs; fish recording machine; live bait well; two downriggers.

☆☆ **Eugene Dublin**: Call the association booking office, ☎ 295-4506. *Princess*, 31-foot Bertram; 10 rods; 12 to 80 pounds test; one trolling chair; fish finders; two downriggers.

Alan Edness: ☎ 441-236-3702. *Reba M*, 35-foot custom-built Nauset; outriggers and downriggers; Pompanette fighting chair; color fish finder; radar; Epirb; satellite navigation; Loran.

☆☆☆ **Albert "Peter" Fox**: ☎ 441-297-1079. *Elain S. Too*, 35-foot Bruno Stillman; 20 custom rods; 12 to 130 pounds test; two depth sounders; downriggers and outriggers.

☆☆v **Willard "Joe" Kelly**: ☎ 441-297-8093. *Messaround*, 40-foot Down East Sportsfisherman; 15 rods; 20 to 130 pounds test; fish finder; Loran; microcomputer; three fighting chairs; live well; outriggers and downriggers.

Edmund Marshall: ☎ 441-238-0704. *Striker I*, 34-foot Striker Sportsfisherman; all necessary equipment on board.

☆ **Milton Pitman**: ☎ 441-234-1086. *Marlin Too*, 35-foot Down East Sportsfisherman; 12 rods; 12 to 50 pounds test; two fighting chairs; depth finder.

☆ **Bernard Richard**s: ☎ 441-234-2378. *Traveller*, 41-foot Duffy & Duffy Downeaster; 12 rods; 30 to 80 pounds test; two downriggers; two depth sounders.

Rudolph Richardson: ☎ 441-234-1913. *Royal Blue*, 41-foot Hatteras Sportsfisherman; 26 rods; three fighting chairs; Epirb; Loran; two VHFs; color fish finder; depth sounder; two outriggers and two downriggers; live bait well plus refrigeration; air-conditioned lounge.

Robinson's Charter Boat Marina: ☎ 441-234-0709. *Ladybird*, 22-foot Cabin Cuddy Aquasport; mainly light tackle and spinning lines.

☆☆☆ **Dendrick Taylor**: ☎ 441-297-1222. *Linda Too*, 37-foot Sportsfisherman; 14 custom rods; 20 to 130 pounds test; video depth finder; outriggers and downriggers.

☆☆ **Allan Virgil**: ☎ 441-238-2655. *Lady Gina*, 35-foot Bertram Sportsfisherman; selection of rods and reels; 30 to 130 pounds test; three downriggers; centerrigger; live bait well; fighting chair; Loran; color depth and fish finder.

☆☆ **Blake West**: ☎ 441-293-0813. *Troubadour*, 42-foot Double Ender; nine rods; 12 to 80 pounds test; depth sounder; outriggers and downriggers.

☆☆☆ **John Whiting & Miles Mayall**: ☎ 441-292-2854. *Atlantic Spray*, 40-foot custom-built Sportsfisherman; 12 custom-built rods; 12 to 130 pounds test; depth sounder.

Russell Young: ☎ 441-234-1832. *Sea Wolfe*, 43-foot Torres custom-built Sportsfisherman; selection of rods; 20 to 130 pounds test; downriggers and outriggers; three fighting chairs; live well; refrigerated fish hold; color fish finder; Loran; VHF; Epirb; air-conditioned lounge.

Adventures

Diving

Bermuda offers excellent diving. There are a number of qualified dive operators on the islands, all with expert knowledge of the waters and willing to take you on scheduled dives, or to locations of your own choosing. Unless you have an extensive diving background, it's probably best to take advantage of their knowledge, especially if you want to look for shipwrecks. For the most part, the waters off Bermuda are very clear, shallow and offer an abundance of coral reefs and underwater gardens for you to enjoy and explore, as well as more than 300 known shipwrecks, modern and ancient.

Dangerous Denizens of the Deep

As always, there are dangers, natural and manmade, that you should take into consideration when stepping out of your natural environment. The following are some that you should be particularly wary of:

- **Sharks**. The most feared predator of the deep, with a bad and, for the most part, undeserved reputation. Peter Benchley's graphic movie,  *Jaws*, based upon a fantasy of his own, has done much to enhance our natural fear of the shark. The truth is, the shark, like every other life-form on earth except man, kills only when hungry and rarely will it attack a human. Shark attacks are rare, especially in Bermuda. They say you have more chance of being struck by lightning, twice, than of being attacked by a shark. Even so, especially if you are unable to identify them, it's best that you steer clear of all sharks you might see.

- **Moray eels** are nocturnal creatures and like very much to be left alone inside their chosen lair. There are a few that have become used to humans and their hand-

outs, but most morays can, if disturbed or threatened, give you a very nasty bite. Stay at a respectful distance.

- **Barracuda**. Not really dangerous, just scary-looking, especially their rather frightening, ever-present grin. The sleek, silver tiger of the ocean is curious, however, and will often follow you around. If someone is feeding the local reef fish (which they shouldn't), be on the lookout for something bigger. A barracuda after his share of the pie attacks like lightning and, although he's only after a handout, it might be a hand he takes.

- **Reef fish**, such as the Black Hamlet at right, tend to be curious and, while they're not dangerous, you might find them nipping at your fingers, toes and hair.

- **Rays**, on the whole, are not dangerous. Tread on a stingray buried in the sand, however, and you're probably in for a trip to the local hospital. The ray's first reaction is self-preserva-  tion, and its natural instinct is to lash out with that murderous tail. Unless threatened or trodden on, rays are pretty much harmless and are fascinating to observe as they flap over the sandy bottom. Watch where you put your feet.

- **Scorpionfish** can often be found lying in wait on coral heads or close to the ocean floor. The thick spines on its back can inflict a nasty sting, but this will happen only if you startle one.

- The **stonefish**, often hard to see due to excellent camouflage, can also give a nasty sting.

- **Jellyfish**, transparent and often difficult to see, are mostly harmless. There are, however, some that are not and it's best if you avoid them all.

- **Coral** is often sharp and can become dislodged in cuts and abrasions, which will leave you in pain for a couple of days. Fire coral can be a problem, but only if you're foolish enough to handle it. Try not to touch coral at all.

Not only can it be dangerous, but it's a delicate, living organism that can easily be damaged.

■ **Sea urchins** are the spiky little black balls that lie on the sandy ocean floor or in the nooks and crannies of coral heads in shallow water. Step on one with your bare feet at your peril. The spines are brittle, often barbed, and will give you a very nasty and painful experience. Fortunately, they are usually easy to see and can be avoided. Keep a sharp look out and don't touch.

If you do happen to get stung by coral, jelly-fish, or urchin, you can treat the sting first with vinegar, which will neutralize the stinging cells. You should then get ointment from the local drugstore to ease the pain.

Wreck Diving

There are said to be more than 300 shipwrecks in the waters off Bermuda. Some of these, especially those that allow access to their interiors, can be dangerous if you aren't familiar with them or don't know what you're doing. Even experienced divers should not go alone into unknown wrecks. There are plenty of guides and dive operators around who have years of experience with each wreck and know what to avoid; it's best to hire one when you embark upon your journey into the dark unknown. Many wrecks are infested with fire coral and others are home to moray eels.

It's really not that dangerous out there if you take reasonable precautions and stay alert. You'll only get into trouble if you do something you shouldn't, are neglectful, or fail to take note of the instructions you'll receive from your guide. Be careful and never dive alone.

Where & When

While the majority of dive operators conduct trips throughout most of the year, May through October offers the best water for diving and snorkeling. It's clear, warm and quiet. No prior certification for scuba diving is necessary; you can learn when you get there. The costs range from $45 for a one-tank dive to $70 for two tanks. Lessons start at around $80 for novices, and you can be out on the reef the same afternoon. Most of the larger resort hotels offer some sort of diving package, including three-hour courses of instruction for beginners. These cost about $95, and that includes the use of equipment.

Just about any underwater experience you fancy is available off Bermuda's beach reefs. The coral is honeycombed with ledges, caves and caverns, and the depth varies from just a few feet to more than a thousand beyond the drop-offs. The marine life is abundant, colorful and curious, and you can spend endless hours with just a snorkel, mask and fins, never leaving the shallows.

Shipwrecks lie in waters that vary in depth from a few feet below the surface to more than 100 feet. Of these, only 40 are in good enough condition to offer an interesting dive. The best wrecks are described in this chapter. Most of the operators know where the wrecks are and are knowledgeable about the water and conditions prevailing at each site. It is highly recommended that you go with an experienced guide.

Helmet Diving

Hartley's Underwater Wonderland, ☎ 441-292-4434, at Flatts Village opposite the Aquarium, is one of Bermuda's most unusual adventures. Reminiscent of the undersea walk depicted in the movie *20,000 Leagues Under The Sea*, the three-hour cruise is sure to be one of the highlights of any vacation. You'll leave Flatts Village aboard the *Carioca*, a 50-foot diesel-powered vessel complete with hot shower, Captain Bronson Hartley and a crew of two, and head out to the reef. There, you'll don your helmet – yes, you can keep your glasses on and you won't even get your head wet – and descend a ladder to the ocean floor, a depth of 10 to 15 feet. You walk the sandy bottom for 30 minutes or so and see the colorful coral formations and hundreds of multi-colored fish waiting for handouts. No matter what your age, from five to 85, if you can negotiate the ladder, you can enjoy the wonders of the under-

Adventures

sea world, and you don't even have to be able to swim. The entire experience is like a walk in a garden. Is it safe? You bet. Bronson Hartley is highly experienced. As a young man, he dove with Charles Beebe (see pages 71 and 110-11). **Hartley's Reef Safari**, ☎ 441-234-2861, www.hartleybermuda.com, at Watford Bridge in Somerset, offers a similar experience and is operated by Bronson's son, Greg Hartley. The cost of a dive at either location is $40; just bring your swimsuit and a towel. Hot chocolate is provided when the water temperature is below 80□. Wetsuits are available during the winter months.

Shipwrecks

Bermuda's reefs have, over the past 400 years or so, claimed hundreds of ships, and there's no doubt that they will continue to do so.

The 33 wrecks listed here are the best-known and offer the most interesting dives. Once again, regardless of experience, you should never dive the wrecks, much less enter them, without an experienced guide. You'll find a list of operators with the required experience at the end of this chapter.

Each wreck is listed by name and number.

1. The **Beaumaris Castle** lies in 25 feet of water on the outer edge of the reef some two miles east of St. Catherine's Point. She was an English steel-hulled sailing ship built in Glasgow, Scotland, in 1864. *Beaumaris Castle* was 202 feet long, 36 feet across the beam, and displaced just over 1,000 tons. She ran aground carrying a cargo of jute and linseed oil on April 24th, 1873, while en route from Calcutta, India, to New York. Within hours, a number of small boats had rushed to offer assistance. Unfortunately, they could do little for the stricken ship other than rescue the crew and salvage a little of her cargo. Coincidentally, units of the

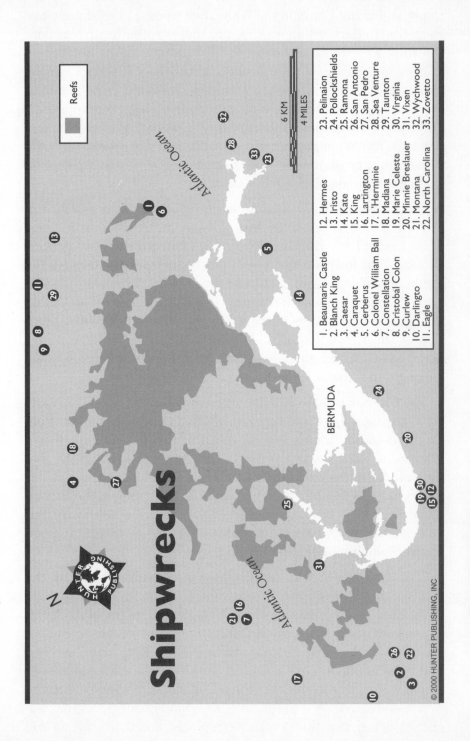

Shipwrecks

Atlantic Ocean

Atlantic Ocean

BERMUDA

Reefs

6 KM
4 MILES

N

HUNTER PUBLISHING

1. Beaumaris Castle
2. Blanch King
3. Caesar
4. Caraquet
5. Cerberus
6. Colonel William Ball
7. Constellation
8. Cristobal Colon
9. Darlington
10. Eagle
11. Eagle
12. Hermes
13. Iristo
14. Kate
15. King
16. Lartington
17. L'Herminie
18. Madiana
19. Marie Celeste
20. Minnie Breslauer
21. Montana
22. North Carolina
23. Pelinaion
24. Pollockshields
25. Ramona
26. San Antonio
27. San Pedro
28. Sea Venture
29. Taunton
30. Virginia
31. Vixen
32. Wychwood
33. Zovetto

© 2000 HUNTER PUBLISHING, INC

Adventures

Coast Wrecking Company of New York were, at the same time, operating in Bermudian waters, and they were called in to refloat the ship. The weather, however, held up operations until early June, when powerful pumps were installed in the ship's holds. The salvage operations were abandoned when a crew member, overcome by gasses while trying to clear a clogged pump, died, and three others, including the captain, were also overcome and had to be taken ashore. Slowly, over the years, the wreck deteriorated to her present condition, a scattering of bits and pieces on the northern side of Mill's Breakers.

2. The *Blanch King* was an American schooner built in Maine in 1887. Today, she lies in 35 feet of water on the reef some three miles east of Ely's Harbour. The ship, a four-masted, two-decker, was 192 feet long, 42 feet across the beam, and displaced 1,156 tons. On December 2nd, 1920, she was heading from Norfolk, Virginia, to Bermuda with a cargo of coal. She hit the reef and sank; all eight crew members managed to get off safely. The main portion of the wreckage includes some machinery and the center board box that housed a retractable keel. Bits and pieces of cable, rigging and fixtures lie scattered over the reef.

3. The *Caesar* was an English wooden sailing ship built in Durham, England, 1814. On July 3rd, 1818, *Caesar* was en route from England to Baltimore with a cargo of grindstones, medicine, glassware, clock parts and lead oxide when she fouled the reef about three miles west of Ely's Harbour and sank. Today she lies in pieces in 35 feet of water, not far from the wreck of the *Blanch King*. She's been thoroughly worked over since her discovery, but you can still see a part of her cargo of grinding wheels, and you might, if you're lucky, find an old bottle or two.

4. The *Caraquet* was an English mail packet built at the Harland & Wolfe shipyard in Belfast, Ireland, in 1894. On June 25th, 1923, while on the way from St. John to Halifax, rough seas, fog and abnormally strong currents pushed her off course and she ended up on the rocks 10 miles north of Hamilton. All of her crew and passengers made it safely off the ship before she sank in 45 feet of water, where she lies today. The massive wreck, scattered over a wide area, is a great dive. Enormous boilers, a great anchor, winches, capstans, machinery, plates, beams and all sorts of

Bermuda from the air (above)

Hamilton from the Harbour (below)

Front Street, Hamilton (above)

Church Bay (below)

Horseback riding on the South Shore (above)

Port Royal, Hole 16 (opposite)

Wreck diving (below)

Clock Tower at the Royal Naval Dockyard (above)

Bermuda street sign (below)

Overlooking Horseshoe Bay beach (above)

Tennis at Sonesta (below)

other bits and pieces provide a mighty backdrop for underwater photographers and are great for explorers.

5. **H.M.S. Cerberus**, a 32-gun English Navy ship-of-the-line built in 1779, was lost after hitting the rocks while leaving Castle Harbour sometime early in 1783. The crew tried valiantly to save the sinking ship. They threw its guns and shot overboard, cut its masts and rigging adrift, but all to no avail and, eventually, they were ordered to abandon ship. In the days that followed, further efforts were made to salvage the guns and gun carriages, and some were eventually brought ashore. *Cerberus* was 126 feet long, 36 feet across the beam, and displaced a little more than 700 tons. She lies just off King's Island, to the south of Castle Harbour.

6. The **Colonel William Ball** was a magnificent luxury yacht built in 1929 and typical of those extravagant times. Originally named *Sialia*, and then *Egeria*, she was 120 feet long with a 23-foot beam, and displaced 291 tons. In 1941 she was acquired by the U.S. Army Transportation Corps and re-named *Colonel William Ball*; she ran aground in bad weather on Mill's Breakers, two miles east of St. Catherine's Point. Today she lies in about 20 feet of water close to the wreck of the *Beaumaris Castle*.

7. The **Constellation** was made famous as the subject of the movie *The Deep*, based upon a novel by Peter Benchley. She was a four-masted sailing ship built in Maine in 1918. From the time of her launching, she enjoyed a somewhat off-beat career. At one time, plans were afoot to turn her into a floating school and, with that in mind, she was completely refitted and provided with all the modern conveniences, including electricity and refrigeration. Alas, those plans came to naught. At the outbreak of the Second World War, she was converted yet again, this time as a freighter.

In 1942, she set sail from New York with a cargo of Scotch whiskey, cement, and drugs; her destination was La Guira, Venezuela. She ran into difficulties in high seas soon after leaving New York and began to take on water. Her steam-driven pumps broke down and what little the crew could do with the hand pumps was not enough. Her captain decided to head for Bermuda to make repairs.

Adventures

On July 30th, 1942, in calm seas and while waiting for a pilot to guide her into port, she was taken by strong currents and driven hard onto the rocks five miles northwest of the entrance to Great Sound; she was a total loss. It's laughable that the U.S. Navy was able to salvage only a select amount of *Constellation*'s cargo. Seven hundred cases of Scotch whiskey were retrieved; the cement and the drugs remained in the wreck. And it was those drugs that were the inspiration for Peter Benchley's novel.

Today, *Constellation* lies where she sank all those years ago, on a sandy bottom in about 30 feet of water. She has not suffered the years underwater very well. Her remains are strewn over a wide area and her cargo of cement is easily seen – a huge pile of hardened bags on the sandy bottom. There are still quite a few pieces of cargo waiting to be found, including some of the drugs.

8: The *Cristobal Colon* was a Spanish luxury liner built in 1923. She was 500 feet long, 61 foot in the beam, and displaced almost 11,000 tons. She was one of the finest and most luxurious passenger ships of her time. On October 25th, 1936, the vessel was heading from Cardiff, Wales, to Vera Cruz, Mexico with 160 crew members aboard, but no passengers. Her captain, Cresencia Navarro Delgardo, decided to swing by Bermuda in order to check the instruments. He was steaming at 15 knots some eight miles north of the island and to the east of North Rock when he sighted a light, which he believed to be the lighthouse at St. David's. A short while later he saw a closer blinking light, which he thought must be the North Rock Beacon; it wasn't. The beacon had been out of service for more than a week, and bad weather had prevented repairs. Delgardo altered course away from what he thought was the beacon and ran hard onto North Rock itself.

The crew all managed to make it safely ashore, but their troubles weren't ended. At that time, the Spanish Civil War was still raging and many believed the *Cristobal Colon* was on her way to Mexico to pick up weapons for the Spanish government. Be that as it may, the Spanish Government seemed in no hurry for the return of the stranded crew and, believing their own government would have to pick up the tab for the crew's keep, the Bermudians put them to work. Finally, however, they embarked for Spain on

Christmas Eve, 1936. Legend has it that, upon their return, General Franco had them all executed.

For a number of years the wreck sat high in the water on the rocks eight miles from the islands. Her position made salvage an easy task. Her furniture, fittings, equipment, and art work were all taken from the ship. Many of the best pieces were stolen by looters who arrived under cover of darkness in fleets of motley boats. Even today, Bermudian homes are adorned with bits and pieces from the wreck. Of the hundreds of islanders who plundered the great ship, only 13 were caught and brought to trial; of those, 12 were convicted.

High in the water and intact as she was, the *Cristobal Colon* was a hazard to other shipping. Not that they would run into her. She looked for all the world like she was still under way. In 1937, the captain of *Iristo*, a Norwegian ship, spotted the wreck and, believing her to be negotiating the channel, he decided to follow her in. Within minutes, he, too had run afoul of North Rock. This brought some action. The *Colon* was stripped of her masts and funnels in an effort to warn other ships away.

When war broke out in Europe the once-proud ocean liner became a target for U.S. Air Force bombers. Slowly but surely she was blown apart, reduced to the waterline, and then to rubble spread over a wide area on the ocean floor.

Today, she is still the largest shipwreck in Bermuda. She lies in shallow water on both sides of the reef that caused her demise. She is, perhaps, one of the most interesting underwater sites in the islands – a photographer's dream come true. Her eight massive boilers, machinery, winches, and propellers can be seen at various depths from 15 feet to more than 70 feet.

9: The **Curlew** left Halifax on March 14th, 1856, bound for Bermuda and St. Thomas. She was a 182-foot, three-masted English sailing steamer, 22 feet across the beam and had a displacement of 528 tons. By the early morning hours of March 17th she was off the northern coast of Bermuda fighting heavy seas. Despite all efforts, she ran aground on the reef eight miles north of St. Catherine's Point, about a mile west of the *Cristobal Colon*.

The captain gave orders for the crew to abandon ship, but the seas were heavy and the weather poor; three of her four lifeboats were lost in the launching. The fourth was successfully put to sea and made it safely ashore where its crew raised the alarm. Two Navy ships were immediately dispatched to the *Curlew*'s aid and the rest of her crew, now clinging to the rigging for dear life, were taken off the ship.

Today, there's not much left to see here. A victim of the incessant pounding of the breakers, she lies scattered on the reef in 35 feet of water a mile west of North Rock.

10: The **Darlington**, while en route from New Orleans to Bremen in Germany, was lost on the rocks of the Western Reef six miles west of Ely's Harbour on February 22, 1886.

The *Darlington* was a fairly new ship, built at the massive Swan & Hunter shipyard in Newcastle, England, in 1881. She was a steamer, 285 feet long, 36 feet across the beam, and displaced 1,990 tons. On her last voyage she was carrying a cargo of cotton and grain. Her loss was blamed on her captain, Richard Ward. It seems he failed to post a lookout while sailing in unfamiliar waters. Her crew of 28 officers and men were all rescued.

The *Darlington* lies on her port side, collapsed flat, but still fairly intact. She's been under 15 to 30 feet of water now for more than 100 years.

11: The **Eagle** was wrecked on the breakers northeast of North Rock and eight miles north of St. Catherine's Point on January 12th, 1659. She was an English ship owned by the Virginia Company and was sailing from England to Jamestown when she struck the rocks. Her passengers and crew all made it safely ashore.

The wreck was discovered, quite by accident, in 1956 when the yacht, *Elda*, was wrecked on the same site. Today, what little is left of the *Eagle* lies 35 feet beneath the surface a little more than a mile east of the *Cristobal Colon*.

12: The **Hermes** was taking a cargo of used goods and gifts to the poor in the Cape Verde Islands when she broke down in Bermudian waters. For a long time she lay abandoned, too expensive to repair. Eventually the government gave her to the Bermuda Divers Association, who stripped her and then, in 1984, sank her a mile offshore, south of Horseshoe Bay.

The *Hermes* was built in Pennsylvania in 1943. She was a 165-foot freighter and displaced 254 tons. Today, she lies upright and completely intact on the ocean bottom in about 80 feet of water. She is, without doubt, the most photogenic wreck in the islands. Divers can explore the wreck, inside and out. All hatches were removed prior to sinking, allowing unobstructed access to the cargo hold, engine room, pilot house and galley. She's one of the most popular shipwreck sites in Bermuda.

13: The *Iristo*, mentioned earlier, was a Norwegian-owned steamer built in 1918 in Ohio. She was 251 feet long, almost 44 feet across the beam, and displaced more than 1,820 tons. Between the time of her construction and her passing, she changed owners and names several times, finally becoming the *Iristo* and the property of Hans F. Grann in 1936.

In March, 1937, she was en route from St. John's in Newfoundland to Bermuda with a cargo of flour, gasoline, a fire engine and a steam roller when her captain spotted the wreck of the *Cristobal Colon*. Thinking the wreck was on her way through the channel into Bermuda, Captain Christian Stephenson decided to follow the *Colon* into port. He did, in fact, follow her onto the reef.

Iristo was pulled off the reef that same afternoon by a seagoing tug out of St. George's. The damage to her hull was extensive and she sank the next day about a mile east of North Rock and seven miles north of St. Catherine's Point. Captain Stephenson was charged with negligence.

Iristo now lies in 50 feet of water. Her bow and stern sections are intact and, with her anchors, propeller, boilers and machinery, provides divers with a great underwater experience and photographic opportunities.

14: The ***Kate*** was an English, steel-hulled steamer en route from Galveston to La Havre, France, when she sank just a few hundred yards south of John Smith's Bay on December 10th, 1878. The ship, built in Whitby, England, in 1874, was some 200 feet long and displaced more than 1,400 tons. She was carrying a cargo of cotton when she went down.

Her loss, so it seems, was caused by a series of disastrous events that took place over several days. First, she struck an uncharted reef 22 miles northwest of the islands on November 30th. Then she hit Long Bar and sprang her plates. In an unsuccessful attempt to save her, she was taken under tow, but had to be grounded when she started to sink. Then, on December 10th, the weather turned nasty and the ship was blown off the sandy bottom into deeper water, where she became completely submerged. The bulk of the wreck – her boilers, engine, propeller shaft and other machinery – lie in about 45 feet of water.

15: The *King* was a diesel-powered Navy tugboat built in 1941. Toward the end of her days, she was converted into a treasure salvage boat and then into a dive boat owned by Gary Lamb. Lamb donated the old boat as a potential dive site. In 1984, she was sunk a half-mile off the South Shore by South Side Scuba, where she lies intact in 65 feet of water. The wreck offers divers all sorts of exciting underwater opportunities. The pilot house and galley, now home to colorful marine life, are easily accessible, and there are lots of sights for underwater photographers.

16: The *Lartington* left Savannah, Georgia, on December 8th, 1879, bound for Revel in Russia with a cargo of 4,000 bales of cotton. By the morning of December 10th, she was off the northwest coast of Bermuda fighting a gale and heavy seas. At eight o'clock that morning, she was struck by a massive wave that cracked her hull and she began to take on water. For the rest of the day the ship's pumps labored to keep her afloat. By the morning of the 12th her captain could see that they were fighting a losing battle and decided to head for Bermuda. She never made it. *Lartington* ran aground on the rocks five miles northwest of the Royal Naval Dockyard on the morning of the 14th of December.

Today, the old ship lies scattered across the sea bottom, close to the wreck of *Constellation*, in 15 to 30 feet of water. Her bow is still intact and divers can explore parts of her stern section, her boilers and propeller.

17: *L'Herminie* was a 60-gun wooden-hulled French frigate, 300 feet long, built and launched in 1824. She was a part of a squadron of warships sent to Mexican waters in 1837 to enforce French claims in the area. Unfortunately, a fourth of her crew came down with yellow fever and she was recalled to France. By December 3rd, 1838, she was fighting heavy seas and bad weather. Her captain, Commodore Bazoch, decided to seek shelter in Bermuda. She struck a reef and ran aground four miles west of Daniel's Head. Fortunately, her crew, almost 500 officers and men, were all taken safely ashore by local boats that came swiftly to assist.

L'Herminie lies in 30 to 35 feet of water. All that's left of the old wooden ship are a couple of her guns, some cannon balls, and a large anchor. Even so, she makes a splendid dive site, and the two guns offer a neat photographic opportunity.

18: The *Madiana* was a Canadian-owned steel-hulled passenger steamship built in Scotland in 1877. She was 345 feet long, 39 feet across the beam, and displaced a little more than 3,000 tons. She was launched as the *Balmoral Castle*, changed owners and names in 1882, was sold again just before the turn of the century and reverted back to her original name; then was purchased by the Quebec Steamship Company and renamed *Madiana*.

She was en route from New York to the West Indies when, on February 10th, 1903, negotiating the channel into Hamilton Harbour, she ran onto the reef just northwest of North Rock, 10 miles north of the Royal Naval Dockyard.

The crew fired distress rockets and tugs were sent to help. Unfortunately, bad weather and heavy seas made it impossible for them to get closer than a mile from the ship. Lifeboats were launched and the passengers and crew hauled through raging seas to the relative safety of awaiting boats.

Today, the wreck lies on the bottom where she went down, a mile west of the wreck of *Caraquet*, in about 25 feet of water.

19: The *Marie Celeste*. There's a name to conjure with. *Marie Celeste* was a Confederate Civil War blockade runner and, by all accounts, was a very successful one. Records prove that she made at least five successful trips past the Federal blockade squadrons. She was a steam-driven side-wheeler and one of the swiftest ships in her class. She left port in Bermuda on September 14th, 1864, bound for Wilmington, North Carolina, with a cargo of meat, rifles and ammunition. She made swiftly through the channel toward the open sea, but hadn't been under way long when the first officer informed the pilot, a Bermudian by the name of John Virgin, that he could see breakers ahead. Virgin informed him that he knew "every rock here as well as I know my own house." The words were barely out of his mouth when the ship smashed into the reef. She went down, bow first, in a matter of minutes. The ship's cook went down with her. He had gone down to his cabin to fetch some personal belongings and never made it back.

Marie Celeste lies in 50 feet of water just 600 yards off the south coast. Although the wreck has deteriorated over the years, it still offers a great many excellent underwater photographic opportunities. Parts of the wheelhouse are still discernible. The bow section, engine and the hubs of her paddle wheels, especially the one on her starboard side which is standing upright, are all visible.

20: The **Minnie Breslauer** was an English steamer on her maiden voyage when she was lost off the coast of Bermuda on January 1st, 1873. She was en route from Malaga to New York with a cargo of fruit, wine and lead when she hit the reef. Rescuers managed to pull the ship off the rocks and she headed to St. George's for repairs. Unfortunately, she was too severely damaged and went down a mile off the coast, south of Horseshoe Bay, where she lies in some 60 feet of water. She has been pretty well destroyed by more than 100 years under water, but parts of her stern section are still discernible, as are her boiler and propeller.

21: The *Montana* was an English blockade runner operating between London and the southern ports of the Confederacy. She was a sleek, swift, side-wheeler paddle steamer, 236 feet long, 25 feet across the beam and displaced 750 tons. Montana was powered by twin 260 horsepower engines that could push her at more than 15 knots. She operated covertly under a number of names other than *Montana. Paramount, Nola, Gloria* are but a few. On December 30th, 1863, she was heading from London to Wilmington and making for port in Bermuda to take on coal when she ran aground on the reef six miles northwest of the Royal Naval Dockyard.

Montana is in 30 feet of water, close to the wreck of *Lartington*, and within swimming distance of the wreck of *Constellation*. Her bow section is still fairly intact. The fantailed stern section lies a short distance from the main part of the wreck and is also recognizable. Her engines and paddle wheels lie near the center of the site, which is great for underwater photography.

22: The *North Carolina* was another steel-hulled, three-masted English vessel en route from Bermuda to Liverpool on January 1st, 1880. She was carrying a cargo of cotton when she ran onto the reef seven miles or so west of Ely's Harbour. She was 205 feet long and displaced 533 tons. Some attempts were made to salvage the ship, but the efforts failed and she went down.

North Carolina lies in 20 to 50 feet of water. Her bow and stern sections remain intact and provide wonderful underwater photographic opportunities.

23: The *Pelinaion* was a Greek freighter built in Glasgow, Scotland, in 1907. She was 386 feet long, almost 50 feet across the beam, and displaced almost 4,300 tons. Originally built for the Hill Steam Ship Company, she changed hands and names several times before coming under Greek ownership. In 1936 she was renamed *Pelinaion*; it was the name she died with.

She was headed from Takiradi, in West Africa, for Baltimore with a cargo of iron ore when, on December 22nd, 1939, she hit the reef a mile south of St. David's Head. The lighthouse was under blackout because of the war in Europe.

Pelinaion sits off St. David's head in 20 to 65 feet of water, fairly well strewn across the reef. Photographers should bring their cameras. The bow section sits only 20 feet below the surface, a huge engine sits upright and makes a fantastic photographic backdrop, while all around, her deck machinery, anchor and propeller provide more interesting views.

24: The *Pollockshields* was built in Hamburg in 1890. She was a steamer, originally named *Herodot*, 323 feet long, 40 feet across the beam, displaced 2,744 tons, and carried a crew of 37. At the outbreak of the First World War, she became a German supply ship and was on the way from New York to the Azores when she was overtaken and captured by the British warship *Argonaut*. The British government renamed her and set her to work.

On September 7th, 1915, she was off Elbow Beach in heavy fog with a cargo of munitions. She struck the reef there within sight of the beach. The ship's captain, Earnest Boothe, was lost while the crew were taking to the boats, swept overboard in heavy seas. The rest of the crew made it safely ashore. The wreck of *Pollockshields* was quite an event for the guests at the Elbow Beach Hotel, then the South Shore Hotel. They all turned out to watch the drama.

The wreck lies scattered in shallow water just off Elbow Beach and can easily be reached by swimmers and snorkelers. Great care should be exercised, however, as the surge of the breakers and the undertow can be dangerous, especially on windy days. The site is a good one for divers. There's lots to see and explore, including live shells and other ammunition.

25: The **Ramona** was a large Canadian yacht that went down on December 2nd, 1967. The 120-foot steel-hulled yacht ran aground on the reef at eight o'clock in the evening. Her distress signals went unnoticed and the crew of 10 abandoned ship. The wreck was spotted early the following morning and rescuers rushed to the site. Unfortunately, it was too late for some members of the crew. Only five of them survived.

The wreck of *Ramona* was raised some time later, in the hopes that she could be repaired, but the damage was too extensive and the work too costly, so she was stripped and taken to a site off the north shore of the Royal Naval Dockyard and sunk in 60 feet of water.

26: The **San Antonio** was a Portuguese merchant ship headed from Cartegena to Cadiz on September 12th, 1621, with a cargo of hides, indigo, sarsaparilla, and tobacco, as well as 5,000 pounds of gold and silver, when she ran onto the western reef about eight miles from Ely's Harbour. She displaced some 300 tons and was armed with 12 cannon. The story of the wreck tells of 120 survivors making it safely ashore, only to fall prey to wreckers on Bermuda who tortured them and made them give up the secret of the ship's treasure. Most of the gold and silver was recovered by the wreckers under the supervision of Bermuda's Governor Butler. The ship's anchors and most of her guns were also retrieved.

The wreck was found in 20 feet of water in 1960. A cannon was discovered, along with odds and ends of pottery, some coins, a gold chain and a jeweled ring. Today, there's little left of the wreck for divers to see, and no treasure at all.

27: The **San Pedro** was also on her way from Cartegena to Cadiz loaded with treasure and other goodies. The year was 1596 and the 350-ton Spanish ship was lost on the reef eight miles north of the Royal Naval Dockyard. She was discovered by Teddy Tucker in 1951 when he spotted some cannon lying in 30 feet of water. He raised the cannon and sold them to the Bermudian government, but it wasn't until five years later that Tucker was able to work the site extensively; *San Pedro* became the first major modern treasure site.

Tucker's first find was a 32-ounce gold bar, two smaller gold bars, and an emerald-studded gold cross. By the time the salvage work was finished, countless treasures and artifacts had been recovered. Much of what Tucker discovered was put on display at the Aquarium Museum (see pages 110-11). Unfortunately, the famous emerald cross was stolen from its display case; a plastic replica was left in its place. The cross is still missing.

Today, there is no treasure and no artifacts for you to discover. All that's left of the ancient Spanish ship are a few timbers and some ballast lying in 15 to 30 feet of water.

28: The **Sea Venture**. No list of Bermudian shipwrecks would be complete without an account of the one that started it all. The remains of the ship that brought Sir John Somers to the islands in 1609 were dis-covered in 1958 as a result of a carefully planned search by Edmund Dowding. Dowding's research indicated the vessel must lie somewhere within an area to the east of St. David's Head, known as Sea Venture Shoal. He began his search in June and found the wreck in October, lying in 30 feet of water. A representative of the Smithsonian was called in, along with local expert, Teddy Tucker, and the wreck was positively identified as that of the *Sea Venture*.

29: The **Taunton** was a Norwegian, steam-driven freighter built in Copenhagen in 1902. She was some 230 feet long, 33 feet across the beam, and displaced more than 1,300 tons. She was bound from Norfolk, Virginia to St. George on November 24th, 1920, with a cargo of coal, when she slammed into the reef eight miles north of St. Catherine's Point.

What's left of *Taunton* lies close to the surface and several other wrecks, including *Eagle*, in 20 feet of water. Although the ship is fairly well broken up and scattered across the reef, her engine and boilers offer spectacular backdrops for underwater photography, and the site is great fun to explore.

30: The **Virginia Merchant** was lost on March 26th, 1661. She had put into Castle Harbour to pick up supplies and fresh water on her way from Plymouth, England to Jamestown. She had just set sail again with 179 passengers when she ran aground on the rocks 250 yards off the South Shore at Sonesta Beach. All but 10 of her passengers and crew were lost. She was discovered in shallow waters on the breakers. All that's left are the anchor, some pieces of wood, and a small pile of ballast.

31: **H.M.S. Vixen** was a three-masted, steam-driven British gunboat, built and launched in England at Deptford in 1867. She was a strange craft. Her iron hull was sheathed with teak in an experimental effort to overcome the problems the new ironclad ships were having with marine organisms. She was an inside-out ironclad, and a marine disaster. Far from curing the problems, the teak sheathing added to them. It produced drag and added to her overall weight, thus making her the Royal Navy's slowest ironclad and rendering her nine-foot ram useless. The ship was basically unseaworthy, though she was the Royal Navy's first twin-screwed vessel. She was withdrawn from service in 1887 and taken to Bermuda as a part of the islands' coastal defense system. In 1896 she was stripped of her engines and fittings and scuttled in a narrow channel off Daniel's Head to block the way against possible attacks against the Royal Naval Dockyard.

The old ship lies just where the Royal Naval engineers left her. Her bow sticks up above the surface and her hull is still pretty much intact. She has been classified as a protected wreck, which means you'll need a permit to scuba dive over the wreck, though you won't need one to snorkel. For permit information, contact the Bermuda Department of Marine and Ports, ☎ 441-295-6575.

32: The **Wychwood** was an English freighter built in 1950 at the Sunderland shipyard in England. She was a little more than 300 feet long, 45 feet across the beam, and she displaced some 2,500 tons. On the evening of August 11th, 1955, while on the way from Nova Scotia to Trinidad, she ran aground on the reef 10 miles off shore from the Gibbs Hill Lighthouse. She was pulled off the reef by the United States Navy and taken under tow stern first. Her steering gear had been damaged by the rocks. She'd sprung her plates and was taking on water, but her pumps seemed to be handling the situation quite well. On August 13th, with the approach of hurricane Diana, her crew put her at anchor off Five Fathom's Hole and left her to ride out the storm on her own. On August 10th, her pumps were no longer able to cope with rising water and she sank. Later, she was deemed a hazard to navigation and was blown up. Today, the remains lie scattered across the sea bed in 50 to 60 feet of water.

33: The **Zovetto** was built and launched in Glasgow, Scotland, at the end of the First World War in 1919. She was a fairly large freighter, almost 400 feet from bow to stern, with a displacement of 5,100 tons. She was sold to the Italian shipping company, Parodi & Accame out of Genoa, and renamed the *Zorvetto*. On February 13th, 1924, she was bound for Baltimore out of the Black Sea port of Poti with a cargo of manganese ore when she ran onto the reef while being piloted through the channel of St. David's. Her crew all made it safely off the ship and her cargo was salvaged. Today, she lies in shallow waters less than a mile south of St. David's point off the eastern end of the island.

Dive Operators

There are a half-dozen professional dive operators in Bermuda; all of them can be relied upon to offer a variety of services in an efficient, safe and professional manner.

Many of the large hotels have their own watersports facilities and rental equipment for use by guests of other hotels. They will be pleased to arrange diving excursions with one or another of the

Adventures

dive operators. There is a decompression chamber at the King Edward Memorial Hospital on Point Finger Road in Paget.

All rates and packages quoted below were correct at the time of writing but are, as always, subject to change without notice.

BLUE WATER DIVERS LTD., at Robinson's Marina, Somerset Bridge, Sandy's, Bermuda, ☎ 441-234-1034, operates daily year-round (including holidays), from 7:30 in the morning until 6 pm. Dive trips and excursions begin at 9:30 am and 1:30 pm. Blue Water Divers offer the following courses:

- **Introduction to Scuba Diving**. You'll learn the basics of scuba diving and dive over a shipwreck in 10 to 20 feet of water. The cost of the half-day package of instruction and diving is $75, and includes the use of all necessary equipment.

- **Repeat Beginner Dive**. This is a repeat of the Introduction to Scuba. The cost for the half-day package is $55.

- **Scuba Dive**. This half-day package takes divers, depending upon experience, over a shipwreck in 30 to 80 feet of water. The basic cost of the excursion is $40. The use of equipment is charged as follows: regulator and gauge $5; mask, fins and snorkel $5; life vest $5. The use of all other equipment is included in the rate.

- **Two-Tank Dive**. This is a four-hour excursion, for experienced divers only, to a selection of wrecks lying in 30 to 80 feet of water. The basic cost is $55. The use of equipment is charged as above.

- **Snorkeling**. This is a service for those passengers who don't wish to scuba dive. They charge $25, which includes all snorkeling equipment.

Wet suits, when necessary, are provided at no extra charge. The location and the times of dives are subject to change according to the local weather conditions. Group rates are available for six persons or more, and night dives can also be arranged. Non-divers can accompany their partners for a fee of $12 per person.

DIVE BERMUDA, at 6 Dockyard Terrace, PO Box SB 246, Sandy's, Bermuda, SB 8X, ☎ 441-234-0225, operates daily from

March through December, and periodically in January and February, from 8 am until 6 pm, including holidays. Dive times are 10 am and 2 pm. Dive Bermuda offers the following instruction and excursions:

- **The Resort Course**. You'll learn the basics of scuba diving in shallow waters just off the beach before diving over a shipwreck or the reef in 10 to 30 feet of water. The course lasts for a half-day and costs $65, which includes the use of all necessary equipment.

- A **three-hour wreck or reef dive** costs $60 and includes the use of all equipment. A **three-hour night dive** costs $75. A **half-day, two-tank dive** also costs $75.

- The company also offers **Certification Courses** that last for three to four days. Prices are available on request.

The company sets a limit of six divers per boat. Excursions leave from the Royal Naval Dockyard, a 30-minute ferry ride from Hamilton. Pick-up is sometimes available from waterfront hotels. There is a reduction of $10 per person for divers using their own equipment.

FANTASEA, at 6 Fairylands Road, Pembroke, Bermuda HM 05, ☎ 441-236-6339, operates daily, weather permitting, year-round from 9 am until 7 pm. Excursions depart at 9 am and 12:30 pm. Fantasea offers the following:

- **Discover Scuba**. A four-hour introduction to scuba diving, with instruction taking place either in a pool or in shallow waters off the beach, then a dive over the wreck of *Constellation*. The cost is $80, which includes all equipment.

- **Reef & Wreck Dive**. a three-hour excursion and one-tank dive to the shipwreck *Constellation*. The cost of $75 includes equipment.

- **Snorkeling trip**s cost $38 per person. Passengers are collected from the Hamilton area.

Adventures

All dives are conducted from a boat with capacity for up to 10 persons, but limited to six divers per instructor. Dive sites are located off the South Shore and usually over the wreck of *Constellation*. Underwater cameras may be rented.

SCUBA LOOK, sponsored by South Side Scuba Ltd., at the Grotto Bay Beach Hotel, Hamilton Parish, Bermuda, ☎ 441-292-1717, operates daily March through November from 8:30 am until 5 pm. Excursions depart daily, weather permitting, at 9 am. The company offers a range of excursions and packages.

- The **Morning Two-Tank Dive** takes divers to two sites, usually one over a shipwreck and one over the reef. A half-day excursion costs $65 and includes equipment.

- The **Single-Tank Dive** takes participants, depending upon experience, to depths of 30 to 80 feet. The two-hour trip runs $45 and includes the use of equipment.

- **Lesson and Dive**. You'll learn the basics of scuba diving in the hotel pool and then dive to depths of 10 to 25 feet over the reef from a dive boat, all under the supervision of an instructor. The cost is $90 for the three-hour package (equipment is included).

- The **Repeat Beginners Dive** is a repeat of any single-tank dive under the close supervision of a qualified instructor. The cost is $50.

- The **Night Dive** lasts for 2½ hours and is for experienced divers only. The cost is $60; full details are available on request.

- The **Five-Dive Package** is for experienced divers only. Full details and costs are available on request.

- **Snorkeling** is available for $20 per person, which includes the use of equipment.

There is a $10 reduction in the fees listed above for divers using their own equipment. Reservations can be made in advance with a Visa or MasterCard. Cancellations must be made 24 hours prior to dive time.

NAUTILUS DIVING LTD., at the Southampton Princess Hotel, Southampton, Bermuda, ☎ 441-238-2332, operates daily April through November, including holidays, from 8:30 am until 5 pm. They offer the following choices:

- The **Resort Course** is an introduction to scuba diving. You'll learn the basics in the pool and then dive from a boat over a shallow reef under the supervision of your instructor. Courses are offered daily at 9:30 am and 2 pm, last for about three hours, and cost $75, which includes equipment.

- **Scuba Dive** is a one-tank dive in the morning to a depth of 30 feet, or an afternoon dive over a shipwreck to a depth of 50 feet. The excursion is suitable both for experienced divers and beginners. Trips leave daily at 11 am and 2 pm, last for about an hour and a half, and cost $40 per person (including equipment).

- **Shallow Reef Dive** is the same as the above listing. Trips leave daily at 3 pm and cost $55.

- The **Two-Tank Dive** departs at 9:30 am, takes you to a shipwreck, lasts for about two hours, and costs $65 (includes the use of equipment).

- **Snorkeling Trips** depart daily at 11 am for a shallow reef. They last for about an hour and a half and cost $20; use of equipment is included.

There is a reduction of $10 to the rates quoted above for divers using their own equipment. All dives are conducted from a 40-foot boat and the dive sites are about a seven-minute boat ride from the shore. Group charters and night dives are available on request. Call for details.

SOUTH SIDE SCUBA, Sonesta Beach Hotel, Southampton, Bermuda, ☎ 441-238-1833, operates daily, March through November, from 8:30 am until 5 pm. Excursions depart daily, weather permitting, at 9 am. The company offers a range of excursions and packages as follows:

- The **Morning Two-Tank Dive** takes divers to two sites, usually one dive over a shipwreck and one over the reef. The cost of the half-day excursion is $65 and includes the use of equipment.

- The **Single-Tank Dive** takes divers, depending upon experience, to depths of 30 to 80 feet. The cost for the two-hour trip is $60 and includes the use of equipment.

- **Lesson and Dive**. You'll learn the basics of scuba diving in the hotel pool and then dive to depths of 10 to 25 feet over the reef from a dive boat under the supervision of an instructor. The fee is $95 for the three-hour package (this includes all necessary equipment).

- The **Repeat Beginners Dive** is a repeat of any single-tank dive under the close supervision of a qualified instructor. The cost is $60.

- The **Night Dive** lasts for 2½ hours and is for experienced divers only. The cost is $75; full details are available on request.

- The **Five-Dive Package** is for experienced divers only. Full details and prices are available on request.

- **Snorkeling** is offered for $25 per person, which includes the use of equipment.

There is a $10 reduction to the fees listed above for divers using their own equipment. Reservations can be made in advance with a Visa or MasterCard. Cancellations must be made 24 hours prior to dive time.

Swimming & Snorkeling

 The shallow waters within the reef are renowned for their clarity. If you like to swim and snorkel, you can stop virtually anywhere on one of the coast roads, park your moped or bicycle, walk a short distance, and find yourself on a sandy beach with a vast expanse of deep blue ocean stretching into the distance.

For snorkeling, the south side of the island group is the easiest and most accessible. The beaches, bays and inlets offer numerous possibilities and the best spots are only as far away as the nearest beach. Swimming and snorkeling abound along the coast road to St. George's, the east end of the island from **Achilles Bay** to

Buildings Bay, a 12-mile line of beaches on the South Shore from **John Smith's Bay** in the east to **Church Bay** in the west, and from **Devil's Head Beach Park** to the **Mangrove Marina** at the extreme northwest tip of the island.

To the west, around St. George's, there's **Whale Bone Bay, Tobacco Bay, Achilles Beach Park**, and the beaches just south of **St. Catherine's Point**. From **West Whale Bay** all along the south coast as far as **John Smith's Bay** to the east, you can just about take your pick and you won't be disappointed. The short stretch of water from and including **Horseshoe Bay to Jobson's Cove** offers some of the most spectacular snorkeling. Go when the water is quiet and watch out for sudden surges that can wash you onto the rocks.

Church Bay on the South Shore and **Shell Bay** on the North Shore are particularly well suited to snorkeling, and the beaches there are regarded as some of the best on the islands. **Mangrove Bay, Long Bay** and the beaches just north of **Ely's Harbour** also offer splendid snorkeling, as do those off **Spanish Point**.

Snorkeling equipment is available for rent at most of the major hotels and dive shops around the island – see the *Diving* chapter as well as *Equipment Rental,* page 155. You will also find that most charter boats rent equipment.

Snorkeling Cruises

The following is a partial listing of companies that specialize in snorkeling cruises. The rates and packages quoted were correct at the time of writing, but are subject to change without notice.

BERMUDA BAREFOOT CRUISES LTD., PO Box DV 525, Devonshire, Bermuda, DV BX, ☎ 441-236-3498, operates daily between April and November from 7 am until 10 pm.

- **Snorkeling and sightseeing** cruises leave the dock at Darrell's Wharf aboard *Minnow* at 9:30 am and 1:30 pm and last for a minimum of 3½ hours. During the cruise you'll visit several beachy coves and pass through Somerset Bridge to a snorkel site that's suited to your ability. Equipment and instruction is provided, along with a complimentary soda or a freshly-made swizzle on the return trip. You can bring along a boxed lunch or the skipper will make a stop at a waterside restaurant. The cruise has a maximum capacity of 10 persons and costs $40 per person, which includes the use of snorkeling gear.

BERMUDA CRUISES LTD., PO Box HM 2236, Hamilton, Bermuda, HM JX, ☎ 441-236-2197, operates daily from May through mid-November.

- **Snorkeling** cruises depart twice daily from Albuoy's Point in Hamilton, the Princess Hotel Dock, and Darrell's Wharf aboard *Big Dipper*, a 55-foot powerboat. The skipper provides a commentary on the island and local waters, complimentary sodas and rum swizzles, and all necessary gear. Floats and buoyancy aids are provided; just bring a swimsuit and towel. The boat is air-conditioned and there are changing facilities and a cash bar on board. The price for a 3½-hour cruise is $40.

HAYWARD'S SNORKELING & GLASS BOTTOM BOAT CRUISES, PO Box 2249, Hamilton, Bermuda HM JX, ☎ 441-236-9894, operates April through October. It offers a selection of sightseeing and glass bottom boat cruises.

- The **Sea Gardens and Wreck Cruise** aboard the 54-foot *Reef Explorer* takes you from Hamilton across Great Sound, through Somerset Bridge, and then northward to the wreck of *H.M.S. Vixen*. The cost of the two-hour cruise is $20 per person and the boat leaves the dock next to the ferry terminal on Front Street twice daily at 10 am and 1:30 pm.

- The **Bermuda Island Cruise** leaves the dock at Albuoy's Point in Hamilton on Mondays, Wednesdays, Fridays and Saturdays at 10:30 am and returns at 4:30 pm. This cruise takes you around the perimeter of Great Sound to the Royal Naval Dockyard, where you can go shopping. After that you'll head eastward to St.

George for another stop, and then return along the north coast to Hamilton. A hot and cold lunch buffet is provided on board, along with live calypso music and complimentary rum swizzles. The cruise is $48 per person.

■ The **Pirate Party Night Cruise** leaves Albuoy's Point in Hamilton on Mondays, Wednesdays and Saturdays at 7 pm and returns 10:30 pm. It features a buffet dinner party on Hawkins Island. Live music for dancing is provided, along with free drinks for the entire evening. The cruise costs $58 per person.

■ The **Starlight Reef & Wreck Cruise** departs from the dock next to the ferry terminal on Front Street in Hamilton at 10 pm on Tuesdays, and from the Waterloo Inn in Southampton on Thursdays; it returns at midnight on both days. You'll be able to view Hamilton's brightly illuminated skyline, and the wonders of the coral reef at night through the specially lit glass bottom boat. The cost, $29 per person, includes drinks.

BLUE HOLE WATER SPORTS LTD. at the Grotto Bay Hotel, Hamilton Parish, Bermuda, ☎ 441-293-2915, operates May through November from 9 am until 5 pm.

■ The **Glass Bottom Snorkel Cruise** takes you out to the reef on board the 60-foot motor catamaran *Sun Deck II* to anchor in shallow waters over a sandy bottom. Once there, you can snorkel or watch the undersea life of the reef through the glass bottom. Snorkel gear and buoyancy aids are provided, along with instruction, music, showers and a cash bar. This 3½-hour cruise runs $45 per person.

BERMUDA WATER TOURS LTD., PO Box HM 1572, Hamilton, Bermuda, HM GX, ☎ 441-236-1500, operates May to November, Monday through Saturday; the booking line is open 24 hours daily.

■ This company offers a number of **sightseeing** cruises as well as their **Snorkeling and Glass Bottom Boat Cruise**, which departs twice daily Monday through

Saturday at 9:30 am and 1 pm from the dock next to the ferry terminal on Front Street in Hamilton. In the morning you'll board the 65-foot *Ovation* and cruise to the West End of Bermuda, where you'll view the Sea Gardens through the glass bottom and snorkel if you wish. The afternoon cruise takes you first to the inner reef and then on to the outer reef; you can snorkel at both sites. Complimentary sodas and rum swizzles are provided (coffee on the morning trip). There are changing facilities onboard and underwater cameras are available for rent. There's also a full cash bar, live calypso music, and you can get a hot dog and chips as well. The cost of either trip is $40 per person, and you'll be out for about 3½ hours. Other cruises include a day-long **Lunch, Shopping, Sightseeing, Glass Bottom and Snorkeling Cruise** for $59 per person. There's also a three-hour **Barbecue Dinner Cruise** for $59 per person. Call for details and times.

PITMAN'S SNORKELING, Somerset Bridge Hotel Dock, Somerset Bridge, Bermuda, SB 8X, ☎ 441-234-0700, operates May through October.

- Joffre Pittman's *Fathom* departs Somerset Bridge twice daily at 9:45 am and 1:45 pm for a four-hour **snorkeling cruise**. You'll ride out five miles to the fringe reef where you can snorkel over the coral and shipwrecks. Complimentary instruction is available; all necessary equipment is provided; and there are changing facilities and restrooms onboard. Just bring a swimsuit and a towel. No children under the age of five. The price is $45.

SALT KETTLE YACHT CHARTERS LTD., at Salt Kettle in Paget, ☎ 441-236-4863, operates from mid-May through mid-October.

- The **Snorkeling Adventure** departs twice daily aboard *Magic Carpet*, a 35-foot Flybridge cruiser, Monday through Friday at 9:30 am and 1:30 pm, and on Saturdays at 9:30 only, to cruise and snorkel the reef.

The crew provides snorkeling instruction and a guided tour of the reef. A second stop includes snorkeling over two shipwrecks. All necessary equipment is provided – just bring your swimsuit and a towel – along with complimentary soft drinks and rum swizzles. The four-hour cruise costs $45 per person.

SAND DOLLAR CRUISES, PO Box HM 534, Hamilton, Bermuda HM CX, ☎ 441-293-2040, operates May through November. Cruises depart twice daily, except Wednesdays, at 9:30 am and 1:30 pm.

■ The **Party Sail & Snorkel Cruise** departs from the Marriott Castle Harbour dock on *Sand Dollar*, a 40-foot Bristol Sloop, to cruise and snorkel over the reef. Free instruction is provided, along with all necessary gear, soft drinks and rum swizzles. Prices currently run $45 per person.

Rental Equipment

The companies listed below all rent snorkeling gear; some also offer scuba gear and equipment for other watersports. The rates include rental of snorkel, mask, and fins. Call and check the cost for scuba gear. Most of these operators will ask that you leave a deposit (refundable provided the equipment is returned on time and undamaged). Rented regulators must be used in the company of a licensed Bermuda diver. Rates quoted were correct at time of writing, but are subject to change.

Watersports Rental Sources

A & J Watersports, at the Palmetto Hotel, Flatts Village, Smith's Parish, ☎ 441-293-2323. $6 per hour, $10 per half-day.

Blue Hole Water Sports, at the Grotto Bay Hotel in Hamilton Parish, ☎ 441-293-2915, and at the Marriott Aquatic Center, ☎ 441-293-2543. $6 per hour, $20 all day.

Adventures

Blue Water Divers Ltd., c/o Robinson's Charter Boat Marina at Somerset Bridge, ☎ 441-234-1034. $20 per 24 hours, weekly rates offered. Scuba gear is also available; call for details and rates.

Mangrove Marina at the end of Cambridge Road, Mangrove Bay, Somerset, ☎ 441-234-0914. $6 per hour, $20 per 24 hours, weekly rates available. Masks with prescription lenses are available.

Harbour Road Marina at Newstead in Paget, ☎ 441-236-6060. $6 per hour, $20 per 24 hours, weekly rates available.

Pompano Marina at the Pompano Beach Club in Southampton, ☎ 441-234-0222. $6 per hour, $20 per 24 hours, weekly rates available.

Nautilus Diving Ltd. at the Southampton Princess Hotel in Southampton, ☎ 441-238-2332. $6 per hour.

Salt Kettle Yacht Charters at Salt Kettle in Paget, ☎ 441-236-4863. $20 per 24 hours.

South Side Scuba at the Sonesta Beach Hotel in Southampton, and at the Grotto Bay Beach Hotel in Hamilton Parish, ☎ 441-293-2915. $6 per hour, $20 per day.

Tobacco Bay Beach House on Tobacco Bay in St. George's Parish, ☎ 441-293-9711. Hourly rates are available for snorkeling at Tobacco Bay. If you want to take the equipment to other locations, you'll be required to leave an additional deposit. Underwater cameras may also be rented. $6 per hour, $20 per day.

Golf

 Bermuda has more golf courses to the square mile than any other country in the world. There are eight of them on a land mass of just 21 square miles.

Golf in Bermuda is always a pleasure. There's no rising before dawn to stand in line; rarely will you have long to wait

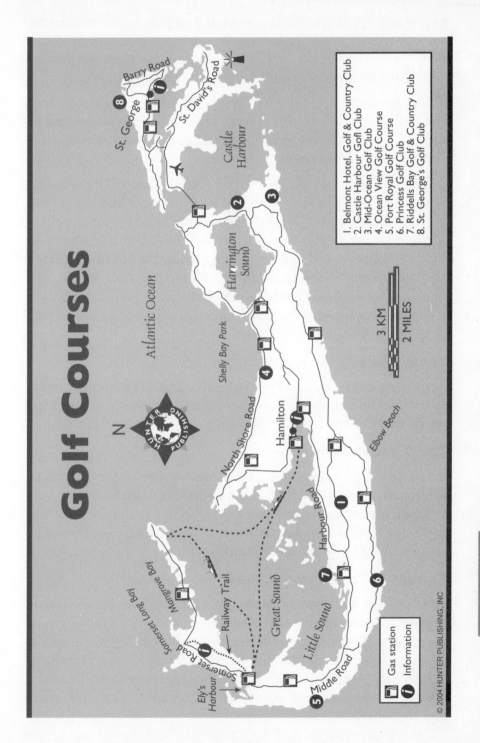

on any tee. You'll play a game at your own pace; other players do not try to rush you from behind. You'll have all the time in the world to contemplate that 40-foot put. And there are no distractions, save for the occasional song of an exotic bird.

If you stay for a week, you can play a different course every day and still have one left over. Many hotels offer special golf packages, and all stand ready to help you plan the rest of your stay around your golfing needs.

Golf can be enjoyed year-round, but there's something about the warm breezes of the early summer months that make the greens the most challenging, and the fairways the fairest. From October through March, everything is at its very best; the courses are in peak condition, tee times are readily available, and hotel rates are low. January through March, there are "Golf Weeks" in Bermuda (see below). Each month during this period, a week is set aside for a variety of tournaments tailored to golf enthusiasts of all ages and of every skill level.

Dress Code

Proper golf attire is required at all golf clubs. Shirts must have a collar and sleeves, shorts must be of Bermuda length. Jeans, gym shorts and cut-offs are not allowed.

Tee-Time Reservations

Early in 1994 the Bermuda Government Golf Courses – Port Royal, Ocean View and St. George's Golf Club – introduced a centralized, automated Tee-Time Reservation system, ☎ 441-295-6500. For private golf courses, you must book in advance. This can be done through your hotel management.

Groups & Tournament Play

Most courses will accommodate groups if the Director of Golf or golf club management is notified well in advance. Special group green fees, however, are not normally offered. If your group is playing a tournament in Bermuda, you are eligible to receive local prizes, compliments of the Bermuda Department of Tourism, provided arrangements are made in advance. The maximum group qualification is 20 players.

Golf Equipment

Golf clubs, both left- and right-handed are available at each course. Balls at most leading stores in Bermuda cost between $15 and $60 per dozen. They are priced slightly higher in the club pro shops.

Reseeding Greens

Reseeding is usually done between late September and early November, depending on weather conditions. Some courses go to temporary greens for a period of two to four weeks, others keep their greens in play. Check with your hotel or golf course during this period to determine what the local conditions might be.

Special Charges For Golfing Equipment On Airlines

Airlines differ regarding policies on golf bags. Some will include them as a part of your free baggage allowance, others charge a flat fee. Check with your airline before you make a reservation.

The Courses

1. **THE BELMONT HOTEL, GOLF & COUNTRY CLUB** in Warwick, ☎ 441-236-1301. Belmont is a par 70, 18-hole course of 5,600 yards. The green fee is $95, a cart for 18 holes, $40, handcarts $8. The pro is Cornell Bean. Belmont Hotel guests may play unlimited golf free of charge. This is a fairly short course; only one par 4 exceeds 400 yards. Elevated greens and double-tiered greens, blind second shots, tight fairways and small, narrow greens make it a challenging round. Golfers with handicaps of 10 or less should be able to shoot in 70s.... but don't bet on it!

2. **TUCKERS POINT GOLF CLUB** in Tucker's Town, ☎ 441-295-6900, is a par 70, 18-hole course of 6,440 yards. The green fee is $150, a cart for 18 holes $26 per person. The pro is Kevin Benevides. Castle Harbour offers a magnificent panorama of the surrounding countryside and the turquoise waters. It has more than 6,000 yards of undulating terrain, brought into play by architect Charles Banks. The resort-style championship course requires straight drives and well-placed second shots to heavily guarded greens, where a keen eye and a courageous spirit will help keep your score in check. Introduction by member required.

3. **MID-OCEAN GOLF CLUB** in Tucker's Town, ☎ 441-293-0330, is a par 71, 18-hole course of 6,547 yards. The green fee is $190 ($70 if you play with a member), a cart for 18 holes $40. The pro is Keith Pearman. Experts rate Mid-Ocean among the top links in the world. And, as with any great course, good shots are rewarded and bad shots are penalized. Six of the par fours exceed 400 yards, and there's even a par 3 of 238 yards. It's a very tough course, so don't expect to score well the first time out. The club features some of the most spectacular views on the islands. You'll need an introduction by a member if you want to play Mid-Ocean. Drop by the pro shop and see if you can find a willing soul.

4. **OCEAN VIEW GOLF COURSE** in Devonshire, ☎ 441-295-9093, is a par 35, nine-hole course of 2,956 yards. The green fee is $32 for 18 holes, a cart for nine holes $12. The pro is Duane Pearman. Ocean View is owned and maintained by the Government of Bermuda. Measuring less than 3,000 yards, it seems somewhat tame at first. But players soon realize that the unpredictable terrain and rambling hills and dales make it very challenging. Score well here, and you should go home satisfied.

5. **PORT ROYAL GOLF COURSE** in Southampton, ☎ 441-234-0974 and 0972, is a par 71, 18-hole course of 6,565 yards. The green fee is $75, a cart for 18 holes $34. The pro is Frank Rabain. Port Royal, also owned and operated by the government, is situated among beautiful ocean-side terrain, and is one of the most popular and difficult courses on the islands. Robert Trent Jones left his stamp all over the course: a green set on the cliffs overlooking the sea here, a graceful, winding, cliff-top fairway there. This course demands a high level of skill and concentration.

6. **THE FAIRMONT PRINCESS GOLF CLUB** in Southampton, ☎ 441-293-6952, is a par 3, 18-hole course of 2,740 yards for a total par of 54. The green fee is $66, a cart for 18 holes $28 for guests and $30 for others; hand-carts $6. The pro is Bruce Simms. The Princess is a course with a difference. Located on the grounds of the Princess Hotel, it commands one of the highest and most scenic settings on the islands. When the wind blows, the seemingly easy course becomes something of nightmare, and even on the balmiest of days it requires skillful ironwork, rather than sheer power. Playing here will reintroduce you to every club

in your bag. The par 3 Princess presents a challenge for every golfer, with elevated tees and strategically placed water and bunkers.

7. **RIDDELLS BAY GOLF & COUNTRY CLUB** in Warwick, ☎ 441-238-1060, is a par 69, 18-hole course of 5,588 yards. The green fee is $110 daily, a cart for 18 holes, $25 for one rider, $50 for two riders. The pro is Darron Swan. Riddells Bay is Bermuda's oldest golf club. For almost 80 years golfers from around the world have enjoyed this peninsula course where the fairways are tight, the greens small and narrow, the traps unforgiving, and the ocean itself is an opponent to be reckoned with. You'll need an introduction by a member or your hotel management to play at Riddells Bay.

8. **ST. GEORGE'S GOLF CLUB**, in St. George's Parish, ☎ 441-297-8353, is a par 62, 18-hole course of 4,043 yards. The green fee is $52, a cart for 18 holes, $48. The pro is Rawn Rabain. Short as it may be, Bermuda's third government-owned course offers a challenge like no other. The course was designed by the legendary Robert Trent Jones to take full advantage of the rocky terrain and the wind that blows constantly in off the ocean. Two of the par threes, for instance, depending upon the prevailing conditions, require anything from a nine-iron to a driver to reach the green. And the game becomes progressively more difficult as you proceed from one hole to the next. Correct club selection at St. George's is the requirement for a decent score.

Golf Weeks

Golf Weeks tournaments will be played at one or more of the following courses: the Belmont Golf & Country Club, Castle Harbour Golf Club, Ocean View Golf Course, Port Royal Golf Course, the Princess Golf Club (par three) and the St. George's Golf Club. The tournaments are:

- The Annual Senior Golf Classic
- The Annual Bermuda Couples Golf Tournament
- The Bermuda Amateur Golf Festival
- The Annual Easter Lily Pro-Am Invitational
- The Metropolitan Golf Association (MGA) Bermuda Mixed Pairs Championship

Adventures

Each tournament is structured so that it's fun, challenging to the player, and provides them and their non-playing companions with social activities and plenty to see and do during their spare time.

The rates and venues quoted below were correct at the time of writing, but are subject to change without notice. For complete details, information and registration, ☎ 800-223-6101, 444-238-1367, bdagolf@ibl.bm.

The **Annual Senior Golf Classic** is played in January on a number of courses, including the Ocean View Golf Course, Port Royal Golf Course, and St. George's Golf Club. The tournament format provides for a maximum handicap of 36 for women and 25 for men. Rules of the Royal and Ancient Golf Club at St. Andrews apply. The event consists of three individual tournaments, one on each course. The entry fee/deposit is $250 per person. A package, not including air fare, for a five-night stay, double occupancy, including four rounds of golf, parties, and all airport and golf transfers is available for $625 per person.

The **Annual Bermuda Couples Golf Tournament** is played in February. Featured courses include St. George's Golf Club and Port Royal Golf Course. Valentine's is a 54-hole event and each team must consist of a man and a woman. The maximum handicap for ladies is 36, for men it's 24. Each team must complete three rounds. The entry fee/deposit is $250 per person. A package, not including air fare, for a five-night stay, including MAP, double occupancy, including four rounds of golf, parties, a banquet on the final day, and all airport and golf transfers is $795 per person.

The **Bermuda Amateur Golf Festival** is held over one week in March. Featured courses include the Belmont Golf & Country Club, Castle Harbour Golf Club, Port Royal Golf Course, the Princess Golf Club (par three), and St. George's Golf Club. The tournament format provides for men's, women's and couples' tournaments. The entry fee is $75 per person. Packages, not including air fare, for a five-night stay, double occupancy, breakfast and dinner daily, golf at each of five courses, unlimited green fees, and the award cocktail reception and banquet, and all golf transfers are offered by The Belmont for $760 per golfer and

$659 for non-golfers; or at the Fairmont Southampton Princess for $859 per person, $709 for non-golfers.

For more information, you can contact the Bermuda Department of Tourism, ☎ 800-223-6106.

Golf Packages

Most operators offer some sort of golf package arrangements. Delta Airlines offers a number of options, as does Friendly Holidays and American Airlines, but if you're looking for something to meet all your needs, you can't go far wrong with Travel Impressions. Check with your travel agent for rates or go to their website at www.travelimpressions.com.

The following are Travel Impressions' golf add-ons:

Harmony Club – Bermuda's All-Inclusive Resort

- Full buffet breakfast
- Coffee, tea and sandwiches throughout the afternoon
- Traditional afternoon tea
- Daily green fees at your choice of Port Riddells Bay and Southampton Princess
- Round-trip transfer to the golf courses
- Three balls, packet of tees and one visor per person
- $30 per person per day (refund if unable to play due to weather)

Fairmont Southampton – Royal Tee Golf Package

- Club storage and 10% discount in the Hamilton Princess golf pro shop
- Unlimited tennis
- Unlimited golf at the Southampton Princess 18-hole par 3 course with a shared cart
- Two rounds of golf on choice of Port Royal or Rydell's Bay courses
- Admission to fitness center
- Ferry to Hamilton Princess

Adventures

**Fairmont Hamilton Princess –
Royal Escapade Golf Package**

- Admission to fitness center
- Unlimited tennis at Southampton Princess
- One round of golf per day at Southampton Princess (mandatory cart - extra charge)
- Ferry to Southampton Princess Beach Club
- All taxes, resort levy and gratuities related to package features

Sailing

Yacht Charters

 Nothing compares to the first-hand experience of sailing, be it out on the ocean or just on Bermuda's Great Sound. The wind stretching the sails, the deck tilted, the bow dipping and diving and banging the surf, the saltwater spraying back in your face as the boat surges onward toward a distant sandy shore. Not likely? It can happen. If you, like me, aren't a member of the yachting community, you can still enjoy a day (or half-day) under sail while visiting Bermuda; it's not as expensive as you might think. A half-day with an experienced skipper can cost from as little as $45 per hour per person, to as much as $800 for the full day, depending upon the charter company and the size of the boat. Most of the charter captains supply beer and soft drinks, and food can be arranged on request.

Allegro Charters

Captain Richard McGlynn operates two yachts, the **Allegro** and the **Artimis**. Cruises leave from Barr's Bay Park near the Royal Bermuda Yacht Club and last from three to six hours. The Allegro carries a maximum of eight passengers; a three-hour cruise costs $45 per person; six hours costs $60 per person. The larger vessel, Artimis, can carry as many as 20 passengers and the rates run from $50 per person for the three-hour cruise to $90 per person for a six-hour sail. Better yet, charter either boat for a half- or full day. *Allegro* is $250 per half-day, $400 per full day; *Artimis* is $450 per half-day, $650 per full day. Beer, soft drinks and snorkeling gear are included in the charter price. ☎ 441-235-3481.

Sail Bermuda Yacht Charters

This company provides a more popular form of charter. Half-day cruises leave Albouy's Point, Hamilton Harbour, Monday through Sunday at 10 am and 2pm, to sail around the harbor and Great Sound. It's a relaxing half-day of sightseeing, swimming and fun. You'll be treated to a complimentary rum punch, but will be required to pay for additional drinks. During the cruise you'll have the opportunity to swim or snorkel, so go prepared and wear your swimsuit under your shorts and shirt. Sail Bermuda also offers a 90-minute sunset sail, which leaves the dock about an hour before the sun goes down. Call for current rates. ☎ 441-236-9613.

Salt Kettle Yacht Charters

Captain David Ashton offers the 35-foot *Magic Carpet* for private charter snorkeling trips to the little-known best spots (coves and bays) to check out the local undersea life. If you've never snorkeled before, don't be put off. David is willing and extremely able to show you how it's done; you'll soon be swimming among the fishy folk on the reef just as if you'd been born to do it. Along with expert instruction, David can also recount the age-old stories of Bermuda's early days, along with the local lore and legends. The *Magic Carpet* can carry up to 18 people, but a lesser number makes for a more comfortable trip. Where you go is entirely at David's discretion, and depends upon the weather. The rates quoted are for eight people. If there are more in your party, simply add $22 per person. Daytime rates are as follows: three hours, $375; four hours, $450; six hours, $650; eight hours, $720. ☎ 441-296-5801.

Horseback Riding

 Horseback riding is possible throughout the year at the two commercial stables listed below. Both cater to experienced and novice riders, and all rides are accompanied by qualified instructors. Horses cannot be hired and ridden without supervision, as Bermuda has very strict laws regarding horseback riding in public areas, especially on the public beaches. Advance reservations are required at both stables.

Stables

The **Lee Bow Riding Centre**, Tribe Road #1, Devonshire, Bermuda DV O6, ☎ 441-236-4181, caters to juniors of all experience levels (to the age of 18). They offer instruction by qualified equestrian instructors throughout the day. The Centre has an outdoor arena. Lessons are available by reservation; call for hourly rates. Small groups may book ahead for trail rides.

The **Spicelands Riding Centre**, Middle Road, Warwick, ☎ 441-238-8212, is set in a rural area close to the South Shore. A bridle path leads from the Riding Center to the beach, and a full staff of qualified personnel caters to the needs of riders. They take children and adults at all levels of expertise. A number of daily trail rides are available by reservation:

- **Breakfast Rides** at 6:45 each morning head along the South Shore beaches and bridle paths. The rides last for about 1½ hours, and the price of $50 includes a continental breakfast after the ride.

- **Trail Rides** along the South Shore last for about an hour and begin at 10 am, 11:30 am and 3 pm. They run $37-50.

- **Evening Rides** are conducted Monday through Friday from May through September. Cost is $37-50.

Protective headgear is provided; hard-soled shoes or sneakers are recommended. The rates were correct at the time of writing but, as always, call ahead to verify current charges. Visa, MasterCard or American Express cards are required when making a reservation, and 24-hour's notice is required for cancellation.

Bermuda Riding for the Disabled, Windreach Recreation Village, 5 Wind Reach Lane, ☎ 238-7433. This facility has only been open for a couple of years, but it's fast gaining in popularity. Here, handicapped adults and kids can enjoy an experience they might never have the opportunity for anywhere else. All are welcome. Lessons and riding are provided free of charge – it's a charitable organization – but donations are welcome. As it's one of the more popular attractions on the islands, you should call well ahead of time to book your spot. The facility is completely wheelchair-accessible. Open Monday through Friday from 9:30 am until 3 pm, and on Saturday from 9:30 until noon.

For more information about the various equestrian opportunities on the islands, you can contact the **Bermuda Equestrian Federation**, ☎ 295-4434. They will give you all the information you need on scheduled events – show jumping and the like – throughout the year.

Hiking

 There's virtually nowhere on the islands that you can't walk. Most people take to the main roads – watch out for the traffic – and, of course, there are a great number of beaches and parks that are open to the public. In addition, many of the Tribe Roads provide access to parts of Bermuda that are rarely seen by the visitor, and the Railway Trail offers a special hiking experience that will take you from one end of the island to the other.

 Be sure to wear reflective gear if you intend to walk after dark. The main roads are often narrow and include many quick, blind curves.

For detailed walks and tours, see *Touring the Parishes*.

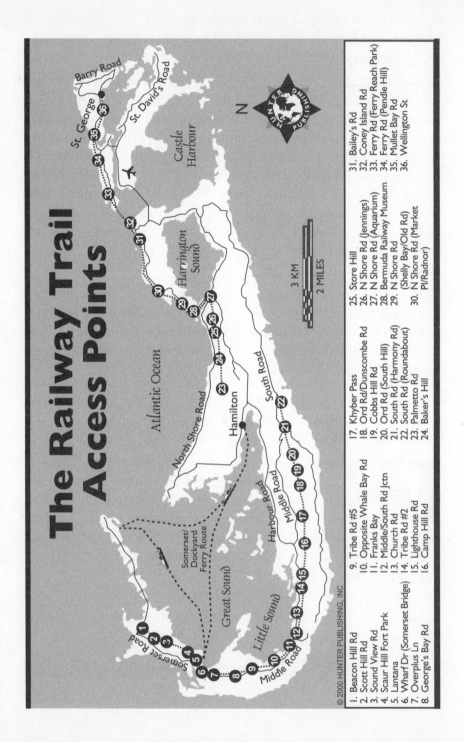

The Railway Trail
Access Points

1. Beacon Hill Rd
2. Scott Hill Rd
3. Sound View Rd
4. Scaur Hill Fort Park
5. Lantana
6. Wharf Dr (Somerset Bridge)
7. Overplus Ln
8. George's Bay Rd
9. Tribe Rd #5
10. Opposite Whale Bay Rd
11. Franks Bay
12. Middle/South Rd Jctn
13. Church Rd
14. Tribe Rd #2
15. Lighthouse Rd
16. Camp Hill Rd
17. Khyber Pass
18. Ord Rd/Dunscombe Rd
19. Cobbs Hill Rd
20. Ord Rd (South Hill)
21. South Rd (Harmony Rd)
22. South Rd (Roundabout)
23. Palmetto Rd
24. Baker's Hill
25. Store Hill
26. N Shore Rd (Jennings)
27. N Shore Rd (Aquarium)
28. Bermuda Railway Museum
29. N Shore Rd
    (Shelly Bay/Old Rd)
30. N Shore Rd (Market
    Pl/Radnor)
31. Bailey's Rd
32. Coney Island Rd
33. Ferry Rd (Ferry Reach Park)
34. Ferry Rd (Pendle Hill)
35. Mullet Bay Rd
36. Wellington St

© 2000 HUNTER PUBLISHING, INC

The Bermuda Railway Trail

Perhaps the most exciting and diverse hiking experience here is the Bermuda Railway Trail, where some of the loveliest sightseeing can be enjoyed from any number of natural vantage points. The old passenger railway offers stunning seascapes, breathtaking scenery, exotic plant and wildlife, apart from the busy roads and streets that have become the Bermuda of today.

The Bermuda Railway was established in 1931 and the track stretched 21 miles around the island, crossing water and gorges via a series of 33 trestles and bridges. It was designed to transport people around Bermuda with ease and in relative comfort. For many years it served its purpose well. The first-class section was furnished in old Colonial style, with wicker chairs, while the second class had wooden benches.

The advent of the Second World War saw the beginning of the end for the old "Rattle and Shake." By the end of the war the train was in poor shape. Faced with a repair bill in excess of a million dollars – quite a sum in those days – the Government of Bermuda decided to cut its losses and get rid of the old institution. They sold the system, lock stock and barrel, to British Guiana and, with the motor car receiving approval on the island in 1946, it was hardly missed at all.

During its 17 years of operation, the Bermuda Railway suffered not a single fatal accident and carried more than four million passengers.

When the railway left Bermuda, all that remained was 21 miles of scenic right of way and a deep feeling of nostalgia among the islanders. For 30 years the old railway track remained unused. Now it's been turned into an unofficial national park where locals and visitors alike can enjoy the rails from one end of the islands to the other.

More than 20 miles of the route are accessible to hikers, joggers, bicyclists and walkers through 35 different access points. The

Adventures

trail has been divided into seven geographical areas from east to west and, depending upon your location, you can walk from one end to the other or take it section by section. These vary in length from two to four miles, and each will take from two to four hours to complete.

Serious hikers should first visit the Visitors Information Center on the ferry dock at Front Street in Hamilton and pick up a copy of *The Bermuda Railway Trail Guide*. This free pocket-size booklet offers an interesting account of the railway's history and a detailed breakdown of the trail, section by section, with all the interesting sights along the way.

Port Royal Golf Course (see page 168)

Shopping

There are four main shopping areas in Bermuda: the **City of Hamilton**, **St. George's**, **Somerset Village** and the **Royal Naval Dockyard**. Most of them have been covered in the section on sightseeing. Despite the small size of the island, you won't be disapppointed by the high number of sophisticated, multi-story department stores, specialty shops, gift stores, jewelry outlets and perfumeries on the main streets and waterfronts of all four areas, not to mention the hidden shops tucked away all around the islands.

Service in retail stores is, for the most part, helpful and courteous. Sometimes, however, the pressures of the tourist industry will overcome even the most patient of service personnel, who tire toward the end of the day and whose tempers can become a little ragged. This doesn't happen often, but if it does, just smile and pass right along. There's always another store just down the road.

The best bargains in Bermuda are goods imported from Europe. Such items as Italian, German, English and French knitwear can often be purchased at prices far below those in the United States. Watches (Rolex, Omega, Patek Philippe), jewelry, French perfumes, Icelandic woolen goods, and fine china can be 50% cheaper than at home.

Shops not to be missed include the Scottish Wool Shop in Hamilton. On Front Street, try Constables of Bermuda for Icelandic woolens, Trimingham's (the best known department store on the islands), The Irish Linen Shop, Astwood Dickinson (fine jewelry), and Bluck's for fine china and paintings. Others are the Bridge House Straw Market in St. George's for hats and bags and the Washington Mall on Queen Street between Reid and Church Street in Hamilton.

So let's take a closer look at some of the possibilities. We'll start in Hamilton.

Perhaps the most obvious place to go shopping in the city is the **Washington Mall**. Yes, it's a mall in every sense of the American definition: long avenues of shops, stores, cafés and the like that connect one city thoroughfare to another. There are three sections: the Mall itself, then West Washington Mall and Washington Mall II. The Mall and its Western section are both entered from Reid Street. Be sure to stop in at **The Deli**: there you'll find such delicacies as cream slices (made with real cream) and sausage rolls. If you're from England, you'll know exactly what sausage rolls are. If not, you should try one. They're something of an acquired taste and not every one likes them. However, a sausage roll and a cup of hot tea always tops my list of priorities – when I can find one, that is.

Inside the Mall, you'll find a wealth of shopping opportunities, including the **Body Shop**, another English legend, **Herrington Fine Jewelers**, the **Harbourmaster** for fine leather goods, and a number of little shops where you can get those hard-to-find gifts for the folks back home.

Butterfield Place, off Front Street in Hamilton, is a unique little shopping center with all sorts or upscale goodies, including leather goods at **Voila**, Scottish woolens at the **Highlander**, fine arts at the **Michael Swann Gallery**; there's even a **Louis Vuitton** outlet.

Next to Butterfield Place, still on Front Street, is The Emporium, another unique grouping of small shops and stores. If you're a cigar aficionado, stop in at the **Tienda de Tabaco**; you might even want to take time out to enjoy a smoke with the regulars. In **The Gallery** you might just find something special for a loved one back home. The focus of The Gallery is local and African art. If you're an antique collector, philatelist or numismatist, check out **Portabello**. The ladies can drop in at **Eve's Garden** for intimate apparel. Time for lunch? Try **Kathy's Kaffee and Sushi Bar**, a neat little eatery where the food is good and you can relax over a snack and a cup of tea or coffee.

No shopping guide would be complete without a mention of **Trimingham's**, Bermuda's largest department store, with branches at the Southampton Princess, Sonesta Beach Hotel, Somerset Village and South Shore Road in Paget Parish. The main store has entrances on both Front and Reid Streets. It's the quintessential department store, carrying a range of goods from furniture to clothing, cosmetics to jewelry; if you can't find it here, you can't find it anywhere on Bermuda. ☎ 441-295-1183.

Next door to Trimmingham's on Front Street, with branches in St. George, the Southampton Princess, the Royal Naval Dockyard and the Belmont Hotel, is **H.A. & E. Smith Ltd**. One of Bermuda's oldest outfitters, Smith's is the place where Bermudians go to buy those great-looking Bermuda shorts, blazers and ties. But that's not all they stock. Looking for a cashmere sweater? You'll find a good selection here. There's also a range of Waterford crystal, and a host of other gift ideas, all at prices far below those you would expect to pay at home. ☎ 441-295-2288.

Bluck's is where to go when you're looking for fine china. The main store is on Front Street in Hamilton, and there are branches in St. George and at the Southampton Princess Hotel. Many of the designs have been commissioned from the great potteries in Europe especially for Bermuda. These include Spode, Worcester, Staffordshire and Herend. ☎ 441-295-5367.

It's difficult to describe what kind if niche **A.S. Cooper**, 59 Front Street in Hamilton, fills. I suppose it's best described as an upscale gift shop, though that hardly does it justice. Anyway, here you'll see all sorts of fine gifts to take home. These might include a bone china teapot, a unique piece of jewelry, or a bottle of exotic perfume. There are branches on Reid Street in Hamilton, on Somer's Wharf in St. George, in the Southampton Princess, the Sonesta Beach Hotel, the Elbow Beach Hotel, and at the Royal Naval Dockyard. ☎ 441-295-3961.

The **Scottish Wool Shop**, on Queen Street, is an import from Great Britain. No matter where you go in England, Scotland, or Wales, you're sure to find one of these outlets for the most famous products of the Scottish wool industry. If you're an American, the goods you can buy here will cost you up to 50% less than back home. They have elegant tweeds for the ladies, lambswool sweaters and scarves, cashmere, and fine linens. For the man, there are monogrammed golf sweaters, golf trousers and shirts. ☎ 441-295-0967.

The **Irish Linen Shop**, at Hey's Corner, 31 Front Street, in Hamilton, is another opportunity you won't want to miss. I can assure you, my wife never does. Wherever we go, she makes this outlet one of her first ports of call; yes, you can find them in Freeport and Nassau in the Bahamas, as well as on some of the islands in the Caribbean. Our dining table is always covered by a fine linen table cloth, along with napkins and placemats. The beds have Irish linen pillow cases, and the sideboard usually sports a linen mat of one sort or another. The great thing about these shops is the prices: always, you'll pay at least 40% less for your linens than you would back home. Better yet, if you happen to visit them when they're running a sale, you can walk away, loaded up, feeling as if you've just robbed the store. ☎ 441-295-4089; fax 441-295-4089.

Be sure to stop by the **Gem Cellar** and take a look at their handmade jewelry. Again, if you're looking for that one-of-a-kind gift, this old-world little jeweler's shop is where you'll probably find it. Take Old Cellar Lane from Front Street in Hamilton. ☎ 441-292-3042.

Next comes the **Royal Naval Dockyard Retail Centre** in Sandy's Parish, ☎ 444-234-3824. To me, the best thing about this place is its overpowering historical atmosphere. It's not been too long since this whole area was bustling with thousands of British seamen, and it still shows. The great Clocktower building is as intimidating today as it must have been a hundred years ago. I've spent many an hour wandering the lower and upper galleries of this great stone edifice; it borders on the hypnotic. But I can't say that I've been that impressed, with a couple of notable exceptions, by the shops therein and what they have to offer. Everything seems a little contrived, geared toward separating the visitor from his/her money. There are some 30 shops and stores in this rather strange mall that some have compared favorably with the Burlington Arcade in London. I don't agree. If you're looking for casual clothing, though, you might like to stop by the **Bermuda Railroad Company**. Their line is a quality one, though the prices might be a little on the expensive side. In fact, I found that to be true throughout the Dockyard shops. Even so, if you take into account that it's all tax-free, you're probably going to walk away with a bargain or two.

One of the places I make for when I'm in the Dockyard area is the **Ship's Inn Book Shop**. It smells as great as it looks and there's always a surprise among their rare and antique books and first editions. Another shop also has a special appeal to me. As a photographer I always like to enjoy the art of others that do what I do and, for me, there's no better place to that than at **Picturesque Bermuda**, where the name says it all. The store is always full of outstanding images of the islands, and they're all for sale. Finally, for the smokers, there's the **Humidor**. Here you can buy Cuban cigars. But, if you're an American, you'll have to smoke them while you're in Bermuda; you can't take them into the United States.

Time for lunch? You'll find several great restaurants and cafés in and around the Dockyard, including Beethoven's and the Green Frog (see the *Dining* section). While you're in Sandy's Parish, if you have time and transport, you should drop by **Dean's Bakery & Deli**, Manchester Street, Somerset Village. This is a great place to get a sandwich or something a little more sweet. Their scones are light and fluffy, turnovers filled with gooey delights, and the muffins are the best on the islands; my opinion, folks. ☎ 441-234-2918.

Just Roses, the Paget Plaza, 161 South Road, Paget, is a full-service florist where, if you're in Bermuda for a special occasion, you can buy that token of love or sympathy. If you need flowers for someone back home, that can be arranged, too, via Teleflora. ☎ 441-236-32338 or fax 441-236-9907.

Last, but not least, you'll want to know where to buy those duty-free libations. There are, of course, a large number of outlets for bottled goods, but the one that comes first to mind is **Burrows**. There are seven locations, the prime one being on Front Street in Hamilton, and there are others in St. George, Paget and Flatts Village. All offer prices significantly lower than you might expect to pay. Burrows carries a wide assortment of the finest from Scotland, Canada, France, Germany and other points around the globe. Most of the best single malt scotches are available, and they range in price from the very reasonable to the very expensive, even taking into account that all are duty-free. One point to remember: you need to know what your duty-free allowance is. For instance, travelers going home to the United States are allowed to take in only one liter of liquor per adult person, and one liter of wine. If you take in more than your allowance, you'll have to pay duty on the excess. ☎ 441-295-0176.

There are, of course, many more shopping opportunities on the islands, and half the fun is in digging them out. Take time to wander the shops in St. George; you won't be disappointed. Get out and about among the side streets in Hamilton, and don't be afraid to get off the beaten path in the parishes. There's a pleasant surprise just around almost every corner.

Tucker's Town

Where to Eat

 Dining in Bermuda can be as formal or as fancy-free as you like and you can choose a different dining style every day of the week. One day you can feast on fresh seafood served at the water's edge, another you can settle back in a plush, cosmopolitan setting and enjoy a meal of French or Italian cuisine. You might like to travel back in time and dine at a century-old Bermudian restaurant, embark on a romantic evening at sea on a starlit dinner cruise, or relax in an English-style pub where the menu is listed on a chalkboard. And then, of course, there's the old British tradition of afternoon tea. Every day, at precisely four o'clock in the afternoon, Bermudians stop for tea. They drink a variety of brews and nibble on tiny sandwiches, breads, jams, pastries and, of course, scones and clotted cream. It's a tradition most visitors enjoy, even if it does mean leaving the sun and sand for an hour or two.

The restaurants and cafés in Bermuda are as varied as they are many. When I first wrote this chapter I set out to do little more than give you a list of some of the restaurants and cafés available. Much of the list still remains just that, a list, but here and there I've added some thoughts as to value and recommendation. If I've recommended a restaurant or café, you can be sure it was worth recommending at the time of writing. If it's not up to par when you visit, I would like to know about it. Please feel free to write to me via the publisher, or you can reach me by e-mail at howardb858@aol.com.

> *Dress in restaurants is mostly casual / smart – trousers and a casual shirt for men; slacks and blouse or a dress for ladies; no shorts, tee-shirts or swimwear.*

All restaurants, unless otherwise stated, accept most major credit cards. Prices are as follows:

RESTAURANT PRICE SCALE	
$$$ (expensive)	Over $40 per person
$$ (moderate)	$20-$40 per person
$ (inexpensive)	Under $20 per person

$$ **Ascot's**, 24 Rosemont Avenue, Pembroke, ☎ 441-295-9644. A verandah restaurant open every day for dinner: seafood, chicken, steaks, homemade cheesecake, desserts and sauces.

$ **The Bombay**, Reid Street, Hamilton, ☎ 441-292-0048. A traditional Indian restaurant open for dinner, Monday through Saturday: Indian dishes and desserts. Indian furniture and music.

$$ **The Carriage House**, Somer's Wharf, St. George's, ☎ 441-297-1730. A cozy, vaulted brick dining room in historic St. George's. Open seven days a week for dinner: seafood, beef, dessert trolley.

$ **Chopsticks**, Reid Street, Hamilton, ☎ 441-292-0791. A restaurant serving Chinese and Thai dishes. Open for dinner seven days a week.

$$$ **Fourways Inn Restaurant**, Middle Road, Paget, ☎ 441-236-6517. An elegant restaurant serving classic and contemporary French cuisine. Live entertainment. Jacket and tie required. Menu changes daily.

$$ **The Freeport Restaurant and Cocktail Lounge**, Royal Naval Dockyard, Sandy's, ☎ 441-234-1692. A casual family restaurant specializing in seafood and Bermuda home cooking: fish, peas and rice, apple pie. Open for dinner seven days a week.

$-$$ **Frog & Onion**, The Cooperage, Royal Naval Dockyard, ☎ 441-234-2900. This has long been one of my favorites. A British-style pub set inside what once was the barrel-making factory for the British Royal Navy, it really does have a little of the old-English atmosphere that's hard to find now, even in the country pubs of the UK. The specialty is English beer, expensive at $4.75 a pint, but the real thing: Newcastle Brown, Watney's, Flower's, all on draft, along with that good old Irish mainstay, Guinness. I love Guinness and was surprised to find that this was one of the few establishments on Bermuda that bothers to stock it. I read a book once whose hero claimed he had only three reasons for living: the fear of death, Goldie Hawn (no, it's not Kurt Russell), and Guinness. I know what he means. The food at the Frog & Onion is your basic pub fare: pies, fish and chips and a variety of sandwiches. For dessert, you might like to try their English trifle. Open daily for lunch and dinner until midnight. Reservations not required. Take number 7 or 8 bus from Hamilton, or the ferry from all points around the Great Sound.

$ **The Green Lantern**, 9 Serpentine Road, Hamilton, ☎ 441-295-6995. Inexpensive, informal and in town. Specializes in seafood and authentic Bermudian cuisine. Open every day from 9 am to 9 pm (except Wednesdays when it opens from 9 am to 3 pm).

$$-$$$ **The Harbourfront**, 21 Front Street, Hamilton, ☎ 441-295-4207. Perhaps this restaurant's best feature is its upstairs covered patio/terrace. You'll find the place on the second floor of number 21 Front Street, accessed via a slightly off-putting, narrow stairway. Get beyond that, however, and you'll find yourself in a very pleasant dining room with a stunning view of the harbor. Due to its location and popularity, it can be a very busy restaurant at times. And this, too, might be a little off-putting. Still, if you can get in when it's not too busy, you can be sure of an excellent meal. The restaurant boasts of "the freshest fish and seafood," and I certainly won't argue with that. They also serve a variety of steaks (14 to 24 ounces), lamb and poultry; they even have a sushi and caviar bar. Gentlemen are expected to wear a jacket for dinner. Reservations are required. Open for lunch Monday through Saturday from 11:30 am until 3 pm, and for dinner from 6 until 10. You can visit their website at www.diningbermuda.com.

$$-$$$ **Henry VIII Restaurant & Bar**, South Shore Road, Southampton, ☎ 441-238-1977. This is one of those places you feel obliged to visit, and I planned to do so for many years but never quite got around to it until recently. It's advertised in all the local guide literature with lots of hype – obviously they employ a good ad agency – that portrays it as a must. It reminds me a great deal of one of those once-great local pubs in England that's been turned into a pub-and-restaurant, with none of the features that might make either one great. As a pub, it does a fair job. The beer is good and the pub-grub at lunchtime is fair. In the evenings, dinner is served in four "period" dining rooms. The dishes, often with

royal names – Royal Aylesbury Duck, for example – are also adequate but don't really live up to their exalted titles, and are often a little more expensive than I think they should be. The idea seems to be that you must pay for all this atmosphere, but English visitors will know what I mean when I say it's more than a little contrived. The Tudor theme comes off as a bit artificial. Having said all that, is it worth a visit? I think so, but with reservations, and you should be prepared to pad the budget a little, especially if there's more than two in your party. Open seven days a week for lunch and dinner. Lunch is noon until 2:30; dinner is from 6 until 10. You'll need to make reservations for dinner, and gentlemen are required to wear a jacket for dinner.

$ **The Hog Penny**, Burnaby Hill, Hamilton, ☎ 441-292-2434. Bermuda's oldest English-style pub; a fun place to eat and make merry. Open for dinner from 5:30 until 11 every day of the week.

$ **La Trattoria**, Washington Lane, Hamilton, ☎ 441-292-7059. A popular gathering place for couples and families. Italian food at reasonable prices. Open for dinner Monday through Saturday from 6 until 10:30.

$$ **Little Venice**, Bermudiana Road, Hamilton, ☎ 441-295-3503. A fine Italian restaurant with an informal atmosphere. Open every day for dinner from 6:30 until 1 am.

$$-$$$ **The Lobster Pot**, 6 Bermudiana Road, Hamilton, ☎ 441-292-6898. For more than 30 years, since it first opened in 1973, the Lobster Pot has been one of Bermuda's most popular places to dine. It's just a short bus ride from downtown Hamilton. I recommend you pay it a visit. Lobster is, of course, the specialty, and they serve both the Maine and Caribbean (spiny) varieties. They also serve a wide variety of fresh fish and shellfish, including wahoo, tuna, rockfish, and hogfish, along with shrimp, mussels and chowder (the best you'll ever eat). The lobster dishes are expensive, but lobster's expensive everywhere nowadays, except for Maine and, even there it's not so cheap anymore. Anyway, for an inexpensive treat, try a fish sandwich, or some coconut shrimp, or some Creole shrimp. Take a number 1, 2, 10 or 11 bus and ask the driver to drop you off at the Lobster Pot. If you intend to make it a dinner outing, it would be a good idea to make a reservation. Open

Warwick Long Bay (opposite)

Above: Nonesuch Island (see page 118)

Below: Snorkeling (see page 158)

Above: Bermuda's South Shore

Below: Spanish Rock (see page 111)

The Railway Trail (see page 177)

Above: Trunk Island, near the middle of Harrington Sound, Hamilton Parish

Below: Tucker's Town (see page 117)

Bermuda diving (see page 134)

Above: Communications House at the Royal Naval Dockyard

Below: Nature Reserve at Daniel's Head. (see page 79)

Above: Waterskiing

Below: Bermuda Underwater Exploration Institute & Ocean Discovery Center (see page 74)

Above: Cavello Bay, a stopping point for the City of Hamilton ferry

Below: Ely's Harbour (see pages 129, 159)

for lunch Monday through Friday from 11:30 am, and for dinner daily from 5:30 pm until 11 pm.

$$ **Monte Carlo Restaurant**, Victoria Street, Hamilton, ☎ 441-295-5453. A restaurant with a French provincial atmosphere and a Mediterranean menu. Open for dinner from 6:30 until 11, Monday through Saturday.

$ **M.R. Onions**, Par-la-Ville Road, Hamilton, ☎ 441-292-5012. Casual family dining. Breads and desserts fresh-baked in house. Open for dinner seven days from 5 until 10.

$ **New Queen Restaurant**, Par-la-Ville Road, Hamilton, ☎ 441-292-3282. Bermuda's oldest Chinese restaurant; offers both Eastern and Western dishes. Open for lunch and dinner every day.

$$$ **The Newport Room**, Southampton Princess Hotel, Southampton, ☎ 441-238-2555. An elegant restaurant with a nautical atmosphere. Gourmet dining; jacket and tie required. Open for dinner seven days from 6:30.

$$-$$$ **Palms**, at Surf Side Beach Club, South Shore Road, Warwick, ☎ 441-236-7100, www.surfside.bm. An intimate little hotel restaurant, loaded with atmosphere and good cheer. It overlooks a kidney-shaped swimming pool and the ocean beyond. The food is excellent, if a little expensive. Set menus that change daily feature a variety of American and international cuisine and there's a fairly comprehensive wine list, for fine dining on a small scale. The meals I had there were all presented with style and panache. If they happen to have rack of lamb on the menu, or lamb chops, you can order either one with confidence; mine was the best I'd had in a long time. If you have time for a drink before dinner, you'll enjoy the cozy little bar adjacent to the restaurant. It, too, overlooks the pool and ocean; very relaxing. The restaurant seats 16 to 20 people, so reservations are a must. I highly recommend it. Dress for dinner is casual smart. Open for dinner daily from 5:30 until 9:30.

$$ **Paw Paws**, 87 South Road, Warwick, ☎ 441-236-7459. A friendly European bistro with a Bermudian atmosphere; indoor and terrace dining; seafood. Open for dinner Tuesday through Sunday from 5:30 until 10.

Bobby in Birdcage, Hamilton (opposite)

$ The Porch, Front Street, Hamilton, ☎ 441-292-4737. A dockside pub with a balcony overlooking the harbor. Pub food and seafood. Open Monday through Saturday from 5:30 until 9:45.

$$ Port O'Call, 87 Front Street, Hamilton, ☎ 441-295-5373, www.portocall.bm. Just off Front Street in one of those narrow little alleyways, Port O'Call offers the chance to step out of the crowds and enjoy a little peace and quiet along with a nice meal and a drink. This small restaurant has changed over the years. The overall cozy, intimate ambience hasn't changed much, but the style of dining has evolved. Today the owners offer fine dining in the evenings and a somewhat upscale lunch at midday, obviously aimed at Bermuda's business community. Steaks, fresh fish and lobster are all specialties of the house, but for dinner you might like the rack of lamb; I can recommend it. The décor is nautical with lots of wood and brass. The service is friendly and fairly quick most of the time, but a little harried when the place is busy. It's also a good idea to make a reservation. Open for lunch Monday through Friday from noon until 2:30 pm, and daily for dinner from 6 until 11. Reservations recommended.

$-$$ Portofino, Bermudiana Road, Hamilton, ☎ 441-292-2375. A little Italian place with a happy and lively atmosphere. Just a down-to-earth pizzeria where the portions are large and the service quick and friendly. Not the most sophisticated Italian restaurant on the islands, but I can highly recommend it. The food is good, the pizzas are juicy, and the lasagna is just like mama used to make. Portofino also offers a wide variety of traditional Italian fare, including chicken cacciatore, veal parmigiana, cannelloni, and ravioli Bolognese. Open for lunch Monday through Friday from 11:30 am until 4 pm, and for dinner seven days a week from 6 until 1 am. Reservations recommended for dinner. Take a number 1, 2, 10 or 11 bus and ask the driver to drop you off at Portofino.

$$ The Red Carpet, The Atrium Building, 37 Reid Street, Hamilton, ☎ 441-292-6195. A cozy, relaxed restaurant serving seafood and Continental cuisine. Open every day from 6:30 until 10:30.

$$ Ristorante Primavera, 69 Pitts Bay Road, Hamilton, ☎ 441-295-2167. An Italian restaurant set in a villa. Surroundings are reminiscent of the fields of Tuscany. Traditional Italian cuisine in an elegant atmosphere. Open seven days from 6:30 until 10 pm.

$$ **Rockfish Grill**, Newstead Hotel, 27 Harbour Road, Paget, ☎ 441-236-6060, www.newsteadhotel.com. Aside from the excellent food served at this restaurant, the view alone makes the ferry ride across the Great Sound from Hamilton worthwhile, especially at night when the city lights are on. The cuisine features mainly steaks and seafood, flame-grilled, but with a slightly Oriental flavor. Breakfast is also a wonderful experience, served from 7 am until 10 am. It features all the ingredients of the full English "heart attack" breakfast: eggs, bacon, fried tomatoes, fried mushrooms, etc. The décor is pleasant and comfortable, the service is quick and friendly and the location is handy – a short bus or ferry ride from Hamilton (the ferry stops right on the property). Dress for dinner is smart casual. Reservations are required.

$-$$ **Swizzle Inn**, 3 Blue Hole Hill, Bailey's Bay, ☎ 441-293-1854, www.swizzelinn.com. Named for the rum swizzle drink, this is one of the oldest pubs in Bermuda and very much a down-to-earth restaurant where the food is mainly inexpensive (especially the burgers and sandwiches) and the atmosphere pleasant and relaxing. You can dine inside or out. Try the fish sandwich – it's one of the best I've ever eaten. And you should also try the bread pudding, which is out of this world. Burgers are, of course, popular with the lunchtime crowd and, though I've never tried them, they are claimed to be quite special. Dinner features more of the same, but bigger, with more of an emphasis on seafood. There's fish, shrimp and shellfish, plus there's curry as well. The Swizzle Inn is just a short bus ride from Hamilton via a number 1, 3, 10 or 11 bus. Reservations not required. Open daily from 11 am until midnight (1 am during the busy season).

$ **Rosa's Cantina**, Front Street, Hamilton, ☎ 441-295-1912. Bermuda's only Tex-Mex restaurant; Southwestern American cuisine in festive, South-of-the-Border surroundings. Open all week for lunch and dinner.

$ **Tio Pepe Restaurant**, South Road, Southampton, ☎ 441-238-1897. A homestyle restaurant offering fresh pizza and Italian dishes. Open every day for dinner from 6 until 10.

$$ Tuscany Restaurant Pizzeria & Bar, Bermuda House Lane, 95 Front Street, Hamilton, ☎ 441-292-4507. An upscale Italian restaurant with a Florentine décor. Cuisine is typically Italian with specialties from Tuscany. Nicely presented; service is quick and friendly. Prices are moderate to expensive. Handy to all the important sites in Hamilton – just a short walk away from almost anywhere. Dress should be smart casual. If you love Italian food, you will enjoy this restaurant. Open for lunch Monday to Friday from 11:30 am until 2:30 pm. Open for dinner daily from 6 until 10:30. It's best make to a reservation for dinner.

$$$ The Waterlot Inn, Fairmont Southampton Princess Hotel, Southampton, ☎ 441-238-2555. A dockside inn established in 1670. French and Continental cuisine. Elegant dining; jacket and tie required. Open for dinner seven days a week from 6:30.

$ The Wharf Tavern, 14 Water Street, St. George's, ☎ 441-297-1515. A cozy pub-style restaurant on the water's edge on Somer's Wharf in historic St. George's: seafood, prime rib, chicken, assorted desserts. Open for lunch and dinner Monday through Saturday from 10 am until 1 am.

$$ Windows on the Sound, Fairmont Southampton Princess Hotel, Southampton, ☎ 441-238-2555. This restaurant offers a grand view over Great Sound and elegant candlelit service. Jacket required. Open for dinner seven days from 6:30.

Where to Stay

Hotel accommodation, like everything else in Bermuda, is expensive. Rates, on the whole, are on a par with the very best hotels in London, Paris and New York; unfortunately the value for money is not.

Round-the-clock room service is uncommon and, when it is offered, you'll pay extra for it. Many hotels have an additional charge to rent a television (usually $5 a day). Same-day laundry service is also rare and expensive. In-house meals, when not a part of a plan, are costly, with breakfast running anywhere from $12 to $25, and dinner rarely less than $50. And that would be fine and dandy but for the fact that the service is often poor, the staff sullen and off-hand, and the guest rooms and dining rooms themselves are in need of a little freshening up. This is primarily because tourism has been taken for granted. And now, with the industry taking something of a back seat to offshore insurance and banking in the economy, little is being done to improve the situation.

If you want to save money, try to visit in the off-season between November 1st and March 31st; you'll save around 40% on your hotel room rate. A vacation during these months can offer some definite advantages. While many of the tourist-related services – the helicopter rides, charter boats, dive operators, etc. – close during winter and the water can be a little on the cool side, the weather is ideal for golf, tennis, sightseeing and shopping.

Most of the islands' accommodations are on the South Side (along with the best beaches, in Paget, Warwick and Southampton parishes), and still more are around the harbor and on the inner shores of Great Sound, served by a regularly scheduled bus and ferry service into Hamilton. It matters little where your hotel is located. The island is small and nowhere is very far from anywhere. All areas are well-served by public transportation.

Accommodations Options

Bermuda's accommodations are varied and offer visitors a choice between a casual, relaxed atmosphere and the more sophisticated, formal atmosphere of the modern luxury hotel.

The **large resort hotels** usually have their own beach or beach club and pool, and several have their own golf course. Most offer the usual luxury resort facilities, including porter, bell and room service, planned activities, sports, social desk and/or director, shops, beauty salon, bicycle livery, taxi stand, bars, restaurants, nightclubs and entertainment right on the premises.

Smaller hotels offer much less, but several do have their own beach or waterfront facilities.

The large hotels usually have their own watersports facilities that rent windsurfers, paddleboats, Sunfish and snorkeling equipment. And almost every hotel, large or small, can set you up with water-related activities from charter fishing to diving to sightseeing; many of them have access to some of the private clubs on the islands and can provide guests with special privileges.

WORD TO THE WISE

Entertainment and facilities at hotels are often cut back or not available at all from November through March. In addition, other activities may be unavailable due to renovation, maintenance or refurbishing. Be sure to check with your hotel when booking your accommodation.

The **cottage colonies** are uniquely Bermudian and feature a main clubhouse with dining room, lounge and bar. The cottages themselves are spread throughout landscaped grounds and offer both privacy and luxury. Many have kitchenettes for beverages and light snacks, but are not really equipped for full-scale cooking. All have their own beach and/or pool.

There are two **private clubs** in Bermuda. Both are in the luxury category and require an introduction by a member.

Housekeeping cottages and apartments are large properties situated in landscaped estates with their own beach and pool, much like the cottage colonies, but without the main clubhouse. Each is complete with kitchen facilities. Some are designed as wings or modern apartment-style units surrounding their own pool or have views of the ocean. The smaller locations offer less expensive accommodations with fewer amenities in less spacious surroundings. Some have a pool, all have kitchens and minimal daily maid service.

Guest houses offer bed and breakfast accommodations and are often old Bermuda homes in garden settings that have been modernized to provide comfortable guest rooms. A few have their own waterfront area and/or pool. Most offer breakfast only, all are informal. Some have kitchenette units while still others provide shared kitchen facilities.

Accommodation Plans

- **CP (Continental Plan)** includes a continental breakfast.
- **EP (European Plan)** denotes no set meal plan, although restaurant facilities are available either on the property or nearby.
- **BP (Bermudian Plan)** room and full breakfast.
- **MAP (Modified American Plan)** denotes breakfast and dinner included.
- **FAP (Full American Plan)** includes all meals.

Some of the quoted hotel rates might be subject to an energy surcharge. All rates are subject to a 6% government tax and, possibly, gratuities. Most of the hotels offer a choice of meal plans. Guest houses usually offer BP, CP or EP.

Many of the islands' hotels and guest houses do not take credit cards.

Your hotel will probably add a 10% service charge, intended to cover everything from maid service to the dining room to the hotel porter; there's no need to leave a room tip. Rates are indicated as:

HOTEL PRICE SCALE	
$$$$	More than $200 per night
$$$	$150-$200 per night
$$	$100-$150 per night
$	Less than $100 per night

I have stayed at many of the hotels listed below, and visited virtually all of them. Most of the one-time dowdy hotels have been upgraded, remodeled and renovated, some at great cost. And the surly attitudes that once were the norm have been replaced by good cheer and a willingness to help. If I've recommended a resort or hotel, you can be sure it was worth recommending at the time of writing. If it's not up to par when you visit, I would like to know about it. Please feel free to write to me via the publisher, or you can reach me directly by e-mail at howardb858@aol.com.

Resorts

$$$$ **Elbow Beach Hotel**, PO Box HM 455, Hamilton, HM BX, Bermuda, ☎ 441-236-3535, 800-344-3526, fax 441-236-8043, www.elbowbeach.com. MAP, BP. A large luxury hotel (a Wyndham Resort) on a 50-acre estate of botanical gardens overlooking the beach and the ocean. Nightly entertainment, five championship tennis courts (two lighted for night play), tennis pro and shop. Golf can be arranged at nearby courses. Private health club, beach games, and organized activities. Watersports, boating and game fishing can be arranged by the hotel staff.

$$$ **Grotto Bay Beach Hotel**, 11 Blue Hole Hill, Hamilton Parish, CR 04, Bermuda, ☎ 441-293-0188, fax 441-293-2306, www.netlinkbermuda.com/grottobay. EP, BP, MAP. Many millions of dollars have recently been spent on this now major resort hotel set on 21 acres of landscaped gardens. It sits at the water's edge in Hamilton Parish only a couple of miles from the airport. There's a private beach with two secluded coves in an enclosed bay, a deep-water dock, freshwater pool with a swim-up bar, outdoor hot tub, and two underground grottos. All rooms are air-

conditioned, have private balconies or patios with panoramic ocean views, refrigerators, hair dryers and coffee makers.

The guest rooms are situated in 11 three-story buildings spread all across the property. Some are high above the main building where the hotel reception, dining rooms and bars are located, and some are way below it on the oceanfront. At first, the complex might seem a little institutional, but you soon get used to the sprawl. The outside walls of the units are painted in a variety of pastel colors and, when the sun is low, the effect is spectacular. The best rooms are, of course, those on the lower levels, overlooking the sound. Those on the upper levels offer views over the complex and the sound beyond and are no less inspiring. All have been refurbished and redecorated and are only a little less luxurious than those of the great resort hotels on the South Shore. The ground floor rooms are all wheelchair-accessible (make sure of availability before booking).

The restaurants – there are two of them – cater for most tastes. There's the usual easy, informal dining in the **Greenhouse Restaurant**, where the food is good and nicely served – burgers and spaghetti are available for kids large and small. The **Hibiscus** dining room offers cuisine that's a little more upscale. Afternoon tea is available every day (no charge) and, best of all, there's happy hour in the bar. The service across the board is outstanding.

This is a great resort for families with children. If there's a downside to Grotto Bay (and I don't think there is) some might say it is the small beach, and it definitely can become crowded at times. The large pool, patios, and lawns, where you can seek all the sunshine you want, more than make up for the lack of sand and surf. I recommend you take advantage of the MAP dining plan. It costs only $53 per person per day and is an excellent value, even with the added 15% gratuity.

The hotel has four all-weather tennis courts, a resident tennis pro, a pro shop, and offers water-skiing, scuba diving with lessons and equipment, sailing, snorkeling, and parasailing from its own dock. Golf can be arranged on any of three nearby courses. There's a bus stop right outside the hotel.

$$$$ The Fairmont Hamilton Princess, PO Box HM 837, Hamilton, HM CX, Bermuda, ☎ 441-295-3000, fax 441-295-1914, www.fairmont.com. EP, BP, MAP. This resort hotel on the edge of Hamilton Harbour offers a full exchange with its sister hotel, the Southampton Princess. Facilities include ferry transportation to the private Southampton Beach Club, a large freshwater pool, a smaller saltwater pool and a shopping arcade. There are several restaurants, including an English pub, and guests can take advantage of exchange dining facilities at the Southampton Princess. They also have use of the Southampton Princess Golf Course, 11 all-weather tennis courts (including seven lighted courts), fishing and watersports at the deep-water dock, and a full range of nightly entertainment.

$$$$ The Sonesta Beach Hotel & Spa, PO Box HM 10170, Hamilton, HM EX, Bermuda, ☎ 441-238-8122, fax 441-238-8463, www.sonesta.com. MAP, BP, EP. This resort is set among the cliffs at the edge of the reef on Bermuda's South Shore. It has 25 acres of landscaped grounds offering, among other things, three secluded, natural bays. Facilities include a unique solar dome pool and a fully-equipped European health spa, three private beaches, shuttle bus around the property and to the top of the hill (where the bus stop is located), and a shopping center with a beauty salon. All rooms are fully air-conditioned and have a TV, phone and radio. There are three restaurants, a beach house with live entertainment during the summer, and nightly entertainment and dancing can be enjoyed at the **Palm Court Club**. Complimentary tea is served in the afternoons. There are six all-weather, floodlit tennis courts, scuba facilities with qualified instructors, fishing from the shore, golf on four nearby courses, and all watersports can be arranged by the hotel staff. There's also a full-time activities director and a selection of organized daily activities.

$$$$ Fairmont Southampton Princess, PO Box HM 1379, Hamilton, HM FX, Bermuda, ☎ 441-239-6916, 800-441-1414, fax

 441-238-8968, www.fairmont.com. MAP. An expansive resort set atop the highest point on the island offering panoramic views of the ocean and surrounding landscaped gardens and golf course. All rooms have views either of Great Sound, the South Shore or the golf course. Facilities include a secluded private beach club with an adjoining bar and restaurant, indoor pool, tennis courts and pro shop, health club, and a shopping arcade with a beauty salon. All guest rooms are air-conditioned. There's a choice of nine restaurants – six at the Southampton Princess and three at the Hamilton Princess – several bars and lounges where there's nightly entertainment, and an 18-hole golf course. Scuba diving, snorkeling, fishing and other watersports can easily be arranged.

Small Hotels

$$$ **Hamiltonian Hotel & Island Club**, PO Box HM 1783, Hamilton, HM GX, Bermuda, ☎ 441-295-5608, 800-203-3222, fax 441-295-7481. MAP, BP. On Mount Langton Hill overlooking Pembroke Parish and the City of Hamilton. There are 32 oceanview one-bedroom suites in tropical garden settings, all equipped with refrigerator, microwave, toaster and coffee maker. There's a large outdoor pool and sun deck, three tennis courts (two lighted for evening play), and golf at a nearby course.

$$$ **The Harmony Club**, PO Box 299, Paget, PG BX, Bermuda, ☎ 441-236-3500, 888-427-6684, fax 441-236-2624. A small luxury hotel in Paget Parish overlooking many acres of landscaped gardens and only five minutes by bus from Hamilton and the beaches on the South Shore. Facilities include a freshwater pool, two saunas, a whirlpool, club room, lounge, restaurant and bar. The rates include round-trip transfers between the hotel and the airport, a full American breakfast, luncheon snacks, afternoon tea, gourmet dinners and unlimited drinks, wines and spirits, scooter rentals and all taxes and gratuities. The hotel has two tennis courts.

$$$$ **The Mermaid Beach Club**, PO Box WK 250, Warwick, WK BX, Bermuda, ☎ 441-236-5031, fax 441-236-8784. MAP, BP, EP. The hotel sits on the South Shore of Warwick Parish overlooking its own private beach. All guest rooms have balconies or patios with a view of the ocean. There's a heated freshwater pool, a gift shop and a restaurant on the property. The bus stop is right outside the front entrance. The swimming and snorkeling from the beach is exceptional. Tennis, golf and all watersports, including scuba diving and charter fishing, can be arranged by the hotel.

$$$$ **Newstead**, PO Box PG 196, Paget, PG BX, Bermuda, ☎ 441-236-6060, 800-468-4111, fax 441-236-7454, www.newsteadhotel.com. MAP, BP. Newstead is right on the waterfront across the harbor from Hamilton. It is an old Bermuda mansion with modernized guest rooms and cottages set in landscaped gardens in a quiet residential area. There's a private dock, deep-water swimming in the harbor, a large swimming pool with sun deck and bar, a large lounge with a fireplace and television, and a library. Guest rooms are spacious, comfortable and air-conditioned; all have views of the gardens or harbor, but no TV. Complimentary afternoon tea is served in the lounge overlooking the harbor. Sailboats and Boston Whalers can be rented at the deep-water dock during the summer. There are two clay tennis courts, a putting green, and a game room. Golf and all watersports can be arranged. Hamilton is only a few minutes away by ferry from the dock on the hotel property. The nearest bus stop is a short walk of about five minutes.

Although I can thoroughly recommend this hotel, having spent almost a week there, I think it's more suited to the older generation and couples without children. The cuisine and service are excellent, although room service is available only during meal times; afternoon tea is served every day. The property is nicely landscaped and well-maintained, and the view over the harbor to Hamilton is exceptional, especially at night when the lights of the city are lit. Because the ferry picks up at the hotel dock, it's also an ideal spot from which to tour the islands around the Great Sound by water. Walkers too will find Newstead ideal because there are plenty of attractions and a tribe road within easy walking distance of the facility. It's an old-world property and justifiably expensive. By the way, Newstead's restaurant, the **Rockfish Grill**, is well worth a visit, even if you don't stay at the hotel. They have great steaks and seafood; live jazz for Saturday evening dining.

$$$ **Palmetto Hotel & Cottages**, PO Box FL 54, Flatts, FL BX, Bermuda, ☎ 441-293-2323, fax 441-293-8761. MAP, BP, EP. An old Bermudian mansion in Flatts Village surrounded by cottage suites on the water's edge. The main house has a comfortable lounge, a restaurant and an English-style pub. There's also a salt-water pool, sundeck and man-made beach that overlooks the beautiful Harrington Sound. The hotel is just a minute's walk from the shops in Flatts Village and a complimentary ride away from the beaches on the South Shore. Tennis, golf, water-skiing, scuba diving and most other sports can be arranged.

$$$$ **Pompano Beach Club**, 36 Pompano Beach Road, Southampton, SB 03, Bermuda, ☎ 441-234-0222, 800-343-4155, fax 441-234-1694, www.pompano.bm. MAP, BP. On the southwest shore with magnificent views overlooking the ocean, the hotel has an ocean-side freshwater pool and two Jacuzzis. The guest rooms, clubhouse, restaurant and lounge all have ocean views, and there's dancing to either a piano player or calypso band on most nights during the summer. Port Royal Golf Course is right next door; the hotel has its own paddleboats, windsurfers and Sunfish for guests and the staff can arrange other watersports, including diving and charter fishing.

$$$$ **The Reefs**, 56 South Road, Southampton, SN 02, Bermuda, ☎ 800-742-2008, fax 441-238-8372, www.thereefs.com. MAP, BP. This hotel sits high on the cliffs overlooking its own private beach on Christian Bay. You have to visit this one-of-a-kind resort to really appreciate it. It has an atmosphere all its own, but it's hard to define exactly where it stems from. Maybe it's

the sometimes misty views overlooking the ocean and beach from the terraced rooms and cottages. Maybe it's the people who work there; they certainly seem to be happier than most hotel staff, at the least the ones I've run into over the past years. Maybe it's the South Shore – everything is special on the South Shore.

The facilities at the Reefs are outstanding, as they should be for a resort of this class and the amount of money that's been spent on it. Much smaller than its glitzier neighbors and competitors, it comprises only 67 units, making for a quieter, more intimate hotel. Small as it is, it boasts three restaurants, catering to tastes as varied as you can imagine. There's also a fitness center, two all-weather tennis courts, complimentary kayaking (a great feature, considering its location on the South Shore), and you can rent snorkeling equipment and mountain bikes on the property. Watersports and golf can be arranged by the hotel staff; just give them a little advance notice. The resort comes highly recommended, by me, but it's expensive. Rates start at around $240 for a double off-season and go up from there, but they do include a MAP dining plan, and you get exactly what you pay for: a quality vacation to remember.

$$$ **Rosedon**, PO Box 290, Hamilton, HM AX, Bermuda, ☎ 441-295-1640, 800-742-5008, fax 441-295-5904, www.rosedonbermuda.com. BP, EP. On the outskirts of Hamilton in Pembroke County. The main house has Colonial rooms in modern wings and wide verandahs overlooking magnificent gardens. All the guest rooms are air-conditioned, have coffee makers, refrigerators, radio, TV, telephones and safety deposit boxes. Rosedon reminds me of one of the great antebellum mansions of the Old South. A great white house with a columned front porch that stretches the entire width of the house, where a traditional English breakfast is served with pride and flair. The gardens are spectacular, awash with the colors of giant hibiscus blooms, birds of paradise, and banana plants. There are two large, antique-filled lounges, with TVs and self-service bars – the honor system prevails – and there's a heated freshwater pool and sun deck. Unfortunately, there isn't a restaurant on the property – there are several nearby and just down the road in Hamilton – but break-

fast is included in the rate. Afternoon tea is a tradition at Rosedon and worth hurrying back for. Hamilton is a 10-minute walk away (five minutes by bus or the hotel's free shuttle service) and tennis is available by arrangement with South Shore Beach and Tennis Club or at Stonington Beach, both served by the hotel's free shuttle service. Not really a hotel for families with small children, but ideal for older couples and business travelers. It's a bit on the expensive side, but not prohibitively so.

$$ **The Royal Palms Hotel**, PO Box HM 499, Hamilton, HM CX, Bermuda, ☎ 441-292-1854, 800-678-0785, fax 441-292-1946, www.royalpalms.bm. CP. Royal Palms is a turn-of-the-century private home converted into a small exclusive hotel in a quiet residential area a short walk from downtown Hamilton. There are 12 comfortable guest rooms, lovely landscaped gardens, and an elegant restaurant and cocktail lounge. Outdoor dining is available during the summer months.

$$$$ **Stonington Beach Hotel**, PO Box HM 523, Hamilton, HM CX, Bermuda, ☎ 441-236-5416, 800-457-4000, www.stoningtonbeach.com. MAP, BP. The hotel overlooks the South Shore in Paget Parish. It has 64 comfortable rooms, all overlooking the ocean and private beach, a sunken bar, library, freshwater pool and a sundeck. Perhaps one of Bermuda's best kept secrets, this rather unusual smaller hotel has plenty to offer. A little too clinical, perhaps, for the more discerning adventurer, but it's comfortable, neat, modern and manned by a permanent staff that seems to have a flair for the off-beat; no small wonder, because the hotel is owned and operated by the Bermuda College, which means there are always a number of students-in-training at work during the holiday season. They are friendly, quick to respond, and most of them seem to be embued with a sense of humor that's rare on these islands.

The rooms are generally larger than you might expect in a small hotel, and they are tastefully furnished. Each has a balcony or patio, a ceiling fan, air-conditioning, a tub or shower or both, depending upon the size of the room, and all the usual amenities one might need for a comfortable stay – hairdryer, irons and ironing boards, and coffee makers.

Where to Stay

The beach is one of the best on the South Shore and is reached by a flight of stone steps, at the end of which you'll find a bar where you can order lunch and a drink. Afternoon tea is, of course, part of the Stonington tradition, and is served every day at 4 pm; very nice too. Highly recommended, though a little on the expensive side. The rates do, however, include breakfast and dinner.

Hamilton is just 10 minutes away by bus or taxi. There are two all-weather tennis courts, a golf course nearby, snorkeling from the hotel's beach and other sports can be arranged.

 **$$$ Waterloo House**, PO Box HM 333, Hamilton, HM BX, Bermuda, ☎ 441-295-4480, 800-468-4100, fax 441-295-2585. MAP, BP. A small hotel on the harbor with a secluded courtyard and gardens and a wonderful view of the Great Sound. The hotel, only a three-minute walk from downtown Hamilton, has an elegant dining room, a bar, a library, a small freshwater pool and a sun deck. Rooms are all air-conditioned and meals are served either in the dining room or on the Harbour Front Terrace.

Once a private home, the old house has been enlarged and extensively remodeled. The addition of five cottages, bringing the total number of guest units up to 30, and its close proximity to Hamilton, has turned it into the ideal business hotel. But it's a great vacation destination, if you are not bothered about its lack of beach.

The guest rooms are furnished mainly with English antiques that impart a somewhat old-world atmosphere. There are terraced gardens that descend to the harbor wall, and there's a lawn with tables and beach umbrellas where you can sit, take it easy, and enjoy the view and a drink before dinner. The main dining room is adjacent to the lawn and also offers views across the Great Sound. Warm and charming; could become a habit. Many people book again and again.

$$ White Sands & Cottages, PO Box PG 174, Paget, PG BX, Bermuda, ☎ 441-236-2032, 800-548-0547, fax 441-236-2486, www.white-sands-bermuda.com. MAP, BP, EP. A small, deluxe hotel set in landscaped gardens close to the beach on the South Shore. There's a large freshwater pool with a snack bar, a sun terrace and a pub-style bar, all within easy reach of Hamilton and nearby golf courses.

$ **Willow Bank**, PO Box MA 296, Sandy's, MA BX, Bermuda, ☎ 441-234-1616. MAP. An old Bermudian manor house surrounded by modern vacation cottages set in six acres of landscaped gardens. There are two private beaches and a small rocky peninsula ideal for swimming and snorkeling. Breakfast and dinner are served in the dining room, but there is no lounge or bar.

Cottage Colonies

$$$ **Arial Sands Beach Club**, PO Box HM 334, Hamilton, HM BX, Bermuda, ☎ 441-236-1010, 800-255-4245, fax 441-236-0087, www.arialsands,com. MAP, BP. A secluded cottage colony on the edge of the ocean. There's a clubhouse, freshwater pool, large lounge, cocktail bar, dining room and a terrace. All cottages are fully air-conditioned. The hotel has three all-weather floodlit tennis courts, a putting green with sand trap, and you can snorkel from the beach. Watersports and golf are available.

$$$$ **Cambridge Beaches**, Somerset, MA 02, Bermuda, ☎ 441-234-0331, 800-468-7300, fax 441-234-3352, www.cambridgebeaches.com. MAP. An exclusive cottage colony overlooking Mangrove and Long bays, set on 25 acres of landscaped gardens with five private beaches and a bay with a boat dock and marina. The clubhouse houses a formal restaurant and cocktail bar, a reading room, tea room, and has a scenic outdoor terrace. There's a European-style health and beauty spa on the premises offering a wide range of treatments. Mopeds available on the property and a private shuttle runs into Hamilton. Sailboats, motor boats, windsurfers, scuba diving, fishing and canoeing are all available at the marina. Cambridge Beaches is a member of all Bermuda golf courses.

This exclusive property is now more resort than cottage colony. Millions of dollars have recently been spent on major renovations, remodeling and refurnishing. Many of the guest units offer the ultimate in luxury, exceeding even those at the most expensive resorts on the islands. Terraced, glass-fronted bedrooms look out over uninterrupted views of the bay or gardens. The bathrooms are exquisitely designed and furnished.

The dining experience is one-of-a-kind and very expensive; the **Tamarisk Dining Room** is world famous. More down-to-earth is the **Port O' Call Pub**. The service is excellent.

There are five beaches on the property, two heated swimming pools, and a full-service marina. If you have small children (under five) you must travel with a nanny, and that, I think, says volumes about Cambridge Beaches. Exclusive and very expensive.

$$$$ The Pink Beach Club & Cottages, PO Box HM 1017, Hamilton, HM DX, Bermuda, ☎ 441-293-1666, 800-355-6161, www.pinkbeach.com. MAP, BP. On the South Beach Road at Smith's Bay, the colony features two private pink sandy beaches with guest cottages nestled in clusters around 18 acres of natural gardens. Dinner is served overlooking the ocean and breakfast can be enjoyed on the cottage patios. There are two all-weather tennis courts under the direction of a resident tennis pro; golf is offered at the nearby Mid-Ocean Club. The beaches are ideal for swimming and snorkeling.

$$$$ The St. George's Club, PO Box GE 92, St. George's GE BX, Bermuda, ☎ 441-297-1200, fax 441-297-8003, www.stgeorgesclub. com. EP. The club, on Rose Hill in St. George's, is a full-service cottage colony with 18 acres of landscaped gardens, a three-floor clubhouse, a gourmet restaurant, lounge, English-style pub and a convenience store. All of the cottages overlook either the harbor or the Robert Trent Jones golf course. They are all fully equipped with a kitchen, living room and dining room, have TVs and are air-conditioned. The resort has three freshwater swimming pools, three all-weather tennis courts, a beach club, and the golf course. The staff will arrange a variety of watersports from charter fishing to scuba diving.

Private Clubs

$$$$ Coral Beach & Tennis Club, 34 South Road, Paget, PG 04, Bermuda, ☎ 441-236-2233, fax 441-236-1876. BP. This facility features traditional Bermuda cottages, suites and rooms with private terraces on a big ocean-front estate. The main clubhouse has a large lounge, several bars and dining rooms, and the terrace and bar overlook the beach. The club has eight clay tennis courts, a resident tennis pro, and three squash courts. Some of the cottages have private pools. Fishing, swimming and snorkeling are available on the private beach. An introduction by a CBC member or from a reciprocal club is needed.

$$$$ The Mid-Ocean Club, PO Box HM 1728, Hamilton, HM GX, Bermuda, ☎ 441-293-0330, fax 441-293-8837. Rates are disclosed by the management only after introduction by a member. A large private club located on South Road in Tucker's Town on the ocean's edge. Compact efficiency units all have balconies and overlook Castle Harbour. There are three private stretches of beach with small coves and inlets. Units are air-conditioned and have phones and televisions. The club has its own 18-hole championship golf course, two all-weather tennis courts, and watersports can be arranged upon request. An introduction by a member is needed for accommodation and golf.

Housekeeping Cottages & Apartments

$ Angel's Grotto, PO Box HS 81, Smith's, HS BX, Bermuda, ☎ 441-293-1986, fax 441-293-4164, www.angelsgrotto.com. EP. Self-contained housekeeping units in Smith's Parish overlooking Harrington Sound with private access for swimming and snorkeling. Close to the beach and sightseeing attractions in the Flatts Village area. All units are air-conditioned.

$ Astwood Cove, 49 South Road, Warwick, WK 07, Bermuda, ☎ 441-236-0948, 800-637-4116. EP. Modern, bright studio apartments and suites overlooking a natural park with glimpses of the ocean. All units are attractively furnished with modern kitchens and air-conditioning. There's also a freshwater pool and a sundeck.

$ Clear View Suites, Sandy Lane, Hamilton Parish, CR 02, Bermuda, ☎ 441-293-0484, 800-468-9600, www.bermuda-online.org/clearview.htm. EP. Waterfront suites and villas in a quiet residential area near many of the sightseeing attractions. Secluded grounds, spacious rooms, ocean views, a tennis court, two pools and barbecue grills. Swimming and snorkeling on the property.

$$ Marley Beach Cottages, PO Box PG 278, Paget, PG BX, Bermuda, ☎ 441-236-1143, 800-637-4116. EP. Spacious housekeeping units and studio apartments with views of the beaches and the South Shore. Each unit has a kitchen, TV, private terrace, and all are heated and air-conditioned. There's a secluded private beach for swimming and snorkeling, as well as a heated freshwater pool. The bus stops right outside the main gate and there are lots of restaurants nearby.

$$ Rosemont, PO Box HM 37, Hamilton, HM A, Bermuda, ☎ 441-292-1055, 800-367-0040. EP. A family-owned resort on a hillside with views over the harbor. Self-contained units with cable TV and air-conditioning. Large landscaped gardens, pool and sundeck. Rosemont is a five-minute walk from downtown Hamilton.

$$$$ Surf Side Beach Club, PO Box WK 101, Warwick, WK BX, Bermuda, ☎ 441-236-7100, 800-553-9990, www.surfside.bm. EP. An extensive renovation and remodeling program has lifted this once average cottage colony to a new and better level. The accommodations consist of terraced, cottage-style suites and apartments, all oceanfront, with fully equipped kitchens and air-conditioning. Six years ago Surf Side was definitely somewhat rundown. Today, it can compete favorably with all but the most luxurious resorts of the island. The rooms are spacious, comfortable and tastefully decorated. The kitchens are stocked with the basics – coffee, tea, sugar, etc. – and more is available at the office. There's a grocery store just a short walk away where all you need can be purchased at reasonable prices.

I highly recommend the resort's Palm Restaurant. It's small, intimate and loaded with atmosphere. It overlooks a kidney-shaped swimming pool and the ocean beyond. The food is excellent, if a little expensive. Time for a drink before dinner? The bar is adjacent to the restaurant and it, too, overlooks the pool and ocean; very relaxing.

Surf Side also has its own mini-spa – be sure to book ahead – and a beauty salon. The complex also boasts of a beach, perhaps a bit of stretch – it all but disappears when the tides are high – but it's well worth the long ramble down the cliffs to the water's edge. The landscaped gardens along the way are outstanding. All this is within three miles of Hamilton. The bus runs every 15 minutes. Rates are EP, but there is a breakfast plan available at $18.50 per person per day, and a breakfast and dinner plan for $65 per person per day.

Guest Houses

$$ **Aunt Nea's Inn at Hillcrest**, 1 Nea's Alley, Old Maid's Lane, St. George, Bermuda. ☎ 441-297-1630, fax 441-297-1908, www.auntneas.com. This is an old house in the Colonial style, built sometime around 1750. It sits on a hill overlooking the Harbour. A very pleasant place to stay, this is one of Bermuda's best-kept secrets, though the word is getting around and things can sometimes get quite busy. There are 10 guest rooms; most of them have bathrooms with showers and five have Jacuzzies. The guest rooms all feature four-poster beds, some of unusual design. All rooms are air-conditioned; none have TVs, although there is one in the sitting room. Continental breakfast is included in the rate, and tea or coffee is available throughout the day at no charge. The Town of St. George is just a short distance away and the local beaches are also within easy reach, either on foot or by bus.

$ **Canada Villa**, 123 St. John's Road, Pembroke Parish, Bermuda. ☎ 441-292-0419. This inviting guest house is less than 10 minutes away, on foot, from downtown Hamilton. There are five guest rooms; two have bathrooms, while the others share a bathroom, which I can assure you is no big problem, especially considering the low nightly rate. There are TVs in the rooms, but they do have clock radios. You can watch TV in the sitting room, if you like. All rooms are air-conditioned and have ceiling fans. Continental breakfast is served throughout the morning, and you can cook meals for yourself in the kitchen, which is fully equipped with pots, pans and dishes. There's a swimming pool complete with loungers and tables.

$ **Fordham Hall**, PO Box HM 692, Hamilton, HM CX, Bermuda, ☎ 441-295-1551, fax 441-295-3906. CP. An informal guest house on Pitt's Bay Road in Pembroke Parish with a lounge and a large window-enclosed verandah where continental breakfast is served. The terrace overlooks Hamilton Harbour. Bright, airy bedrooms. Within walking distance of Hamilton, the shops and the harbor.

$ **Edgehill Manor**, PO Box 1048, Hamilton, HM EX, Bermuda, ☎ 441-295-7124, fax 441-295-3850. CP. An old Bermuda home in a quiet residential area within easy walking distance of Hamilton's shops and the harbor. Most of the spacious rooms have private balconies. Continental buffet-style breakfast with lots of home-baked goods and preserves. Semi-tropical gardens and a freshwater swimming pool. No credit cards.

$ **Green's Guest House**, PO Box SN 295, Southampton, SN BX, Bermuda, ☎ 441-238-0834, fax 441-238-8980. BP, EP. A large Bermuda home in Southampton Parish overlooking Great Sound. All rooms have private baths, air-conditioning, refrigerators, TV, VCR and radios. There's a lounge, dining room, swimming pool and sun terrace. No credit cards.

$ **Hi-Roy**, 22 Princess Estate Road, Pembroke, HM 04, Bermuda, ☎ 441-292-0808. MAP, BP. A small, modern guest house just off North Shore Road with a view of the ocean. Large lounge, enclosed sun porch. All rooms are air-conditioned and have TVs with satellite reception. Family atmosphere and home-cooked meals. No credit cards.

$ **Hillcrest Guest House**, PO Box GE 96, St. George's, GE BX, Bermuda, ☎ 441-297-1630. EP. A large home set in the streets of historic St. George's. All rooms are fully air-conditioned. The grounds are landscaped and the house is only a short walk away from the shops and restaurants.

$ Little Pomander Guest House, PO Box HM 384, Hamilton, HM BX, Bermuda, ☎ 441-236-7635, fax 441-236-8332. CP, BP. This house is really two charming waterfront Bermuda cottages on Hamilton Harbour. All rooms are air-conditioned, have TVs, refrigerators and microwaves. Close to the shops; golf courses are only a short bus ride away.

$ Loughlands, 79 South Road, Paget, PG 03, Bermuda, ☎ 441-236-1253. CP. A stately Bermudian mansion on nine acres of landscaped gardens in the middle of the islands and close to the beaches on the South Shore. All bedrooms have air-conditioning, with private bathrooms and coffee makers. There's also a large swimming pool, a sun patio and a tennis court. No credit cards.

$ Oxford House, PO Box HM 374, Hamilton, HM BX, Bermuda, ☎ 441-295-0503, fax 441-295-0250, www.oxfordhouse.com. CP. Conveniently located for Hamilton's restaurants, shops and entertainment, with the bus terminal just an easy stroll from the front entrance. Rooms are large, well-furnished, have private baths and are air-conditioned. Family-owned and -operated.

$ Que Sera, 28 Astwood Road, Paget Parish, Bermuda. ☎ 441-236-1998. This is a neat little guest house in a pleasant section of Paget, opposite the King Edward VII Memorial Hospital. There's an apartment and a couple of double guest rooms. The apartment has its own bathroom, though the two guest rooms in the main house have to share a bathroom. I've never found this caused any inconvenience. All rooms have coffeemakers and electric kettles. No meals are included in the rate, but you can head over to the hospital and take advantange of the café there. There's a swimming pool where you can relax after a hard day at the shops. If you're on a budget, this is the place to book. Small as it is, though, you'll need to reserve well in advance. No credit cards.

$ Royal Heights, PO Box SN 144, Southampton, SN BX, Bermuda, ☎ 441-238-0043, fax 441-238-8445. CP. A small, modern guest house on Lighthouse Hill in Southampton Parish with gardens and terraces overlooking Great Sound. All bedrooms are air-conditioned. There's a pool and a sun patio, and the house is only minutes away from the South Shore beaches.

$ **Salt Kettle House**, 10 Salt Kettle Road, Paget, PG 01, Bermuda, ☎ 441-236-0407, fax 441-236-8639. BP. A small, informal guest house and cottages on the harbor in picturesque Salt Kettle. Some units have kitchen facilities. Just a two-minute walk from the ferry landing. No credit cards.

$ **The White House**, 6 Southlyn Lane, Paget Parish, Bermuda, ☎ 441-236-4957. If you have children, you'll want to steer clear of this one; it's for adults only. But if you want to get away from the small ones, this is definitely a good place to consider. There are three guest rooms, a pleasant lounge and a dining room. All rooms have private baths. There's no air-conditioning, but you might only find this a problem in the hottest part of the season. There's a freshwater pool with loungers, where you can relax after a long day sightseeing or shopping, and there's an ice machine on the upper floor. Breakfast is included in the rate. The house is just a short walk from the bus stop, and there's a restaurant and a grocery store close at hand. No credit cards.

$ **Woodbourne Guest House**, PO Box 977, Hamilton, HM DX, Bermuda, ☎ 441-295-3737. CP. An informal, owner-managed guest house minutes away from the ferry, shops and restaurants in downtown Hamilton. All guest rooms are air-conditioned, have private baths, mini-fridges, radios and cable TV. Breakfast is served in the lounge/dining room.

Addenda
Ferry Information

BLUE ROUTE (Hamilton - West End - Dockyard)

Monday to Friday

Leave Hamilton	Leave Dockyard	Boaz Island	Waterford Bridge	Cavello Bay	Somerset Bridge	Rockaway	Arrive Hamilton
6:25 am	6:55	7:10	7:15	7:25	7:40		8:10
7:30	7:55	8:10	8:15	8:25			8:50
9	9:30						9:50
9:45		10:45	10:40	10:30	10:15		11:30
10	10:30						10:50
11	11:30						11:50
11:45	1	12.45	12:40	12:30	12:15		1:30
12 pm	12:30						12:50
1	1:30						1:50
1:45	3	2:45	2:40	2:30	2:15		3:30
2	2:30						2:50
3	3:30						3:50
4	4:30						4:50
4	5:30	5:15	5:10	5	4:45	4:30	6
5:30	6:35	6:20	6:15	6:05	5:55		7:05
6:15	6:45	7	7:05	7:15	7:30		8
7:15	7:45			8	8:15		8:45
9:45	10:50			10:35	10:20		11:20

Saturday

Leave Hamilton	Leave Dockyard	Boaz Island	Waterford Bridge	Cavello Bay	Somerset Bridge	Rockaway	Arrive Hamilton
9	9:30						9:50
9:45		10:45	10:40	10:30	10:15		11:30
10	10:30						10:50
11	11:30						11:50
11:45	1	12.45	12:40	12:30	12:15		1:30
12 pm	12:30						12:50
1	1:30						1:50
1:45	3	2:45	2:40	2:30	2:15		3:30
2	2:30						2:50
3	3:30						3:50
4	4:30						4:50
4	5:30	5:15	5:10	5	4:45	4:30	6
5:30	6:35	6:20	6:15	6:05	5:55		7:05
6:15	6:45	7	7:05	7:15	7:30		8
7:15	7:45			8	8:15		8:45
9:45	10:50			10:35	10:20		11:20

Sunday and holiday runs are less frequent, with the first ferry leaving Hamilton at 10:10 am and the last at 7 pm. *Note that bikes are allowed on the Blue Route.*

PINK ROUTE (Hamilton - Paget - Warwick)

Leave Hamilton	Lower Ferry	Hodson's Ferry	Salt Kettle	Darrell's Wharf	Belmont Ferry	Arrive Hamilton
7:15 am				7:35	7:30	7:45
7:20	7:24	7:28	7:32			7:38
7:45				8:05	8	8:14
7:50	7:54	7:58	8:02			8:08
8:15				8:35	8:30	8:44
8:20	8:24	8:28	8:32			8:38
8:45				9:05	9	9:14
8:50	8:54	8:58	9:02			9:08
9:15	9:47	9:43	9:39	9:35	9:30	9:51
10	10:04	10:08	10:12	10:16	10:21	10:36
10:45	11:17	11:13	11:09	11:05	11	11:21
11:30				11:40		11:50
12:15 pm	12:47	12:43	12:39	12:35	12:30	12:51
1	1:04	1:08	1:12	1:16	1:21	1:36
1:45	1:49	1:53	1:57	2:01	2:06	2:21
2:30	3:02	2:48	2:54	2:50	2:45	3:06
3:45	3:49	3:53	3:57	4:01	4:06	4:20
4:15				4:25	4:30	4:45
4:20	4:34	4:30	4:26			4:39
4:45				4:55	5	5:15
4:50	5:04	5	4:56			5:09
5:20				5:30	5:35	5:50
5:20	5:34	5:30	5:26			5:39
5:45				5:55	6	6:14
5:50	6:04	6	5:56			6:08
6:15	6:19	6:23	6:27	6:31	6:36	6:51
6:55	7:27	7:23	7:19	7:15	7:10	7:32
7:40		7:44	7:48	7:52	7:57	8:12
8:20		8:48	8:44	8:40	8:35	8:52
9		9:04	9:08	9:12		9:25
9:45		9:49	9:53	9:57		11:20

On Saturdays the first ferry leaves Hamilton at 8:15 am and the last at 9:45 pm. Sundays & holidays, the first ferry leaves at 10:10, the last at 7 pm. *Note that bikes are not allowed on the Pink Route.*

ORANGE ROUTE (Hamilton - Dockyard - St. George's)

Leave Hamilton	Arrive Dockyard	Leave Dockyard	Arrive St. George's	Leave St. George's	Arrive Dockyard	Leave Dockyard	Arrive Hamilton
9:30 am	9:50	10	11	11:15	12:10	12:30	12:50
12 pm	12:20	12:25	1:20	1:30	2:25	2:30	2:50
2	2:20	2:45	3:40	3:45	4:45	4:55	5:15
Monday to Friday. Bikes allowed to Dockyard; not to St. George's.							

GREEN ROUTE (Hamilton - Rockaway Express)

	Leave Hamilton	Arrive Rockaway	Leave Rockaway	Arrive Hamilton
Monday to Friday	6:55 am	7:20	7:25	7:45
	7:30	7:50	7:55	8:15
	7:55	8:15	8:25	8:45
	8:25	8:45	8:55	9:15
	9:15	9:50	10	10:35
	10:45	11:20	11:30	12:05
	1 pm	1:35	1:45	2:20
	2:30	3:05	3:15	3:50
	4	4:30	4:30	6
	5	5:20	5:30	5:50
	5:30	5:50	6	6:20
	6	6:20	6:30	6:50
	6:30	6:50	7	7:20
	7	7:20	7:30	7:50

Bikes not allowed on ferries leaving Hamilton from 9:15 to 2:30. Restricted schedule on Saturday, with first ferry leaving Hamilton at 7:55 am and last leaving at 5:30 pm.

Bus Information

BUS FARES

FARE CATEGORY	3 ZONE	14 ZONE
Cash*	$3	$4.50
Tokens	$2.50	$4
Tickets**	$16	$25.50
3-Day Pass (all zones)	$23	$23
7-Day Pass (all zones)	$36	$36
Monthly Pass (all zones)	$45	$45
3-Month Pass (all zones)	$120	$120

* Exact change only. Dollar bills not accepted.
**Tickets sold in booklets of 15.
Tokens and passes honored on both buses and ferries.

Ferry Schedules

QUICK REFERENCE BUS CHART		
DESTINATION	ROUTE NUMBER	FARE ZONE *
Airport	1, 3, 10, 11	14
Aquarium	10, 11	3
Belmont Hotel	8	3
Botanical Gardens	1, 2, 7	3
Caves (Crystal and Leamington)	1, 3	14
Dockyard	7, 8	14
Elbow Beach	2, 7	3
Gibbs Hill Lighthouse	7	3
Grotto Bay Hotel	1, 3, 10, 11	14
Horseshoe Bay Beach	7	3
Hospital	1, 2, 7	3
Mangrove Bay (Somerset)	7, 8	14
Maritime Museum	7, 8	14
Marriott Castle Harbour	1	14
Perfume factory	10, 11	14
John Smith's Bay Beach	1	3
Sonesta Beach Hotel	7	3
Southampton Princess Hotel	7, 8	3
St. George's	1, 3, 10, 11	14
* See Bus Fare Information for additional details on 3 and 14 Zone fares		

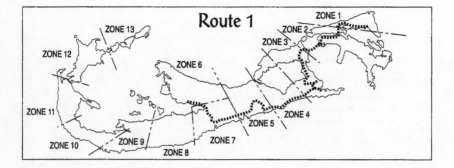

BUS ROUTE #1 (HAMILTON - ST. GEORGE'S)
via Marriott Castle Harbour, The Caves and Grotto Bay

MON TO FRI		SATURDAY		SUNDAY	
Leave Hamilton	Leave St. George's	Leave Hamilton	Leave St. George's	Leave Hamilton	Leave St. George's
		8:15	8:52		
9:15	9:52	9:15	9:52	11:00	11:00
10:15	10:52	10:15	10:52	12:00	12:00
11:15	11:52	11:15	11:52	1:00	1:00
12:15	12:52	12:15	12:52	2:00	2:00
1:15	1:52	1:15	1:52	3:00	3:00
2:15	2:52*	2:15	2:52	4:00	4:00
4:15	3:52	3:15	3:52	5:00	5:00
	4:52	4:15	4:52		

Running time fom Hamilton to St. George's is approx. 65 mins.
* Trip oprates via Harrington Sound School; does not serve South Road between Devil's Hole and Collectors Hill.

BUS ROUTE #1 (HAMILTON - GROTTO BAY)
via Marriott Castle Harbour and The Caves

MON TO FRI		SATURDAY		SUNDAY	
Leave Hamilton	Leave Grotto Bay	Leave Hamilton	Leave Grotto Bay	Leave Hamilton	Leave Grotto Bay
	7:10				
6:45	7:40				
7:15	8:10		8:10		
7:45	8:40	7:45	8:40		
8:10*	9:10	8:15	9:10		
8:45	9:40	8:45	9:40		
9:15	10:10	9:15	10:10	11:00	11:18
Every 30 mins. until				Every hour until	
4:45	5:40	4:45	5:40	4:00	4:18
5:15	6:40	5:15		5:00	5:18
5:45		5:45			
6:15		6:15			

Running time from Hamilton to Grotto Bay is approx. 45 mins.
* Trip operates via Harrington Sound School; does not serve South Rd between Devil's Hole and Collectors Hill.

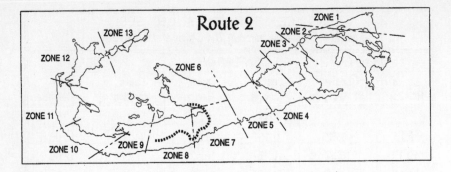

Route 2

ZONE 13	ZONE 1
ZONE 12	ZONE 2
ZONE 6	ZONE 3
ZONE 11	ZONE 4
ZONE 10	ZONE 5
ZONE 9	ZONE 7
ZONE 8	

BUS ROUTE #2 (HAMILTON - ORD ROAD)
via Botanical Gardens and Elbow Beach

MON TO FRI		SATURDAY	
Leave Hamilton	Leave Ord Road	Leave Hamilton	Leave Ord Road
	7:15		
	7:35		
7:45	7:55	7:15	7:45
8:15	8:15	8:15	8:45
9:15	8:40	9:15	9:45
10:15	9:45	10:15	10:45
11:15	10:45	11:15	11:45
12:15	11:45	12:15	
Every hour until			
4:15	3:40	4:15	4:45
4:45	4:40	5:15	5:45
5:05	5:15	5:45	6:15
5:25	5:45		
5:45	6:15		
Running time from Hamilton to Ord Road is approx. 25 mins.			

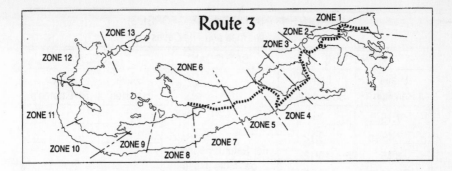

Route 3

ROUTE #3 (HAMILTON - GROTTO BAY)					
via Middle Road and The Caves					
MON TO FRI		SATURDAY		SUNDAY	
Leave Hamilton	Leave Grotto Bay	Leave Hamilton	Leave Grotto Bay	Leave Hamilton	Leave Grotto Bay
	7:00		7:00		
	7:30		8:00		
7:15	8:05 fl	8:15	9:00		
7:45	8:00	9:15	10:00		
8:15	8:35 fl	10:15	11:00	9:15	10:00
8:45	8:30	11:15	12:00	11:30	11:48
9:15	9:00				
9:45	9:30	12:15	1:00	12:30	12:48
Every hour until		1:15	2:00	1:30	1:48
3:45	4:00	2:15	3:00	2:30	2:48
4:15	4:30	3:15	4:00	3:30	3:48
4:45	5:00	4:15	5:00	4:30	4:48
5:05 fl	5:30	4:45	6:00	5:30	5:48
5:15	6:00	5:15			
5:30 fl		6:15			
5:45					
6:15					
Running time from Hamilton to Grotto Bay is approx. 40 mins.					
fl - Trip operates only as far as Flatts					

ROUTE #3 (HAMILTON - ST. GEORGE'S)
via Middle Road and The Caves

MON TO FRI		SATURDAY	SUNDAY	
Leave Hamilton	Leave St. George's		Leave Hamilton	Leave St. George's
7:15				
7:45 sd	9:12	For Saturday service on Route 3, see Hamilton - Grotto Bay timetable (connections are available at Grotto Bay to/from St. George's)		
8:45	10:12			
9:45	11:12			
10:45	12:12		11:30	11:30
11:45	1:12		12:30	12:30
12:45	2:12		1:30	1:30
1:45	3:12		2:30	2:30
2:45	3:42 sd		3:30	3:30
3:45	4:12		4:30	4:30
4:45	5:12		5:30	5:30

Running time from Hamilton to St. George's is approx. 58 mins.
sd - Trip originates/terminates in St. George's on school days only

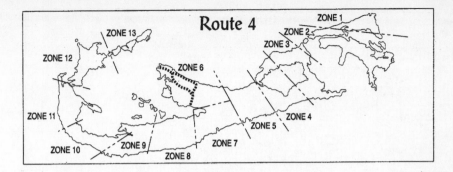

Route 4

ROUTE #4 (HAMILTON - SPANISH POINT) *via St. John's Road*					
MON TO FRI		**SATURDAY**		**SUNDAY**	
Leave Hamilton	Leave Spanish Point	Leave Hamilton	Leave Spanish Point	Leave Hamilton	Leave Spanish Point
	6:42 sj				
	7:12 sj				
	7:27 sj				
7:30 sj	7:42 sj				
7:50 sj	8:02 ns		7:27 sj		
8:10 sj	8:22 sj	8:00 sj	8:12 sj		
8:30 sj	8:42 ns	8:30 ns	8:42 ns		
9:00 sj	9:12 ns	9:00 sj	9:12 ns	8:45 sj	8:57 ns
10:00 sj	10:12 ns	10:00 sj	10:12 ns	10:15 sj	10:27 ns
11:00 sj	11:12 ns	11:00 sj	11:12 ns	12:45 sj	12:57 ns
12:00 sj	12:12 ns	12:00 sj	12:12 ns	2:45 sj	2:57 ns
1:00 sj	1:12 ns	1:00 sj	1:12 ns	4:45 sj	4:57 ns
2:00 sj	2:12 ns	2:00 sj	2:12 ns	6:15 sj	6:27 ns
3:00 sj	3:12 ns	3:00 sj	3:12 ns		
4:00 sj	4:12 ns	4:00 sj	4:12 ns		
4:30 sj	4:42 ns	4:30 ns	4:49 ns		
4:45 sj	5:02 sj	5:05 sj	5:17 sj		
5:05 sj	5:17 ns	6:00 sj	6:12 ns		
5:15 sj	5:27 ns				
5:30 sj	5:42 ns				
6:00 sj	6:12 ns				

Running time from Hamilton to Spanish Point is approx. 12 mins.
ns - Trip operates via North Shore Road
sj - Trip operates via St. John's Road
Outbound buses travelling via North Shore Road will return via Black Watch Pass.
Inbound buses travelling via North Shore Road will return via Langton Hill.

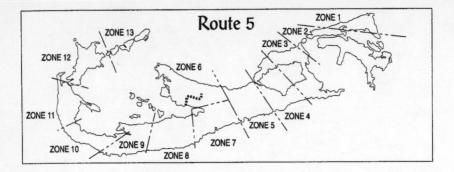

Route 5

ROUTE #5 (HAMILTON - POND HILL) via Parson's Road and Glebe Road			
MON TO FRI		**SATURDAY**	
Leave Hamilton	Leave Pond Hill	Leave Hamilton	Leave Pond Hill
	6:30		
	7:00		
7:20	7:30		
7:50	8:00	7:50	8:00
8:20	8:30	8:50	9:00
8:35	8:45	9:50	10:00
8:50	9:00	10:50	11:00
Every hour until		11:50	12:00
12:50	1:00	12:50	1:00
1:50	2:00	1:50	2:00
2:50	3:00	2:50	3:00
3:50	4:00	3:50	4:00
4:20	4:30	4:50	5:00
4:50	5:00	5:50	6:00
5:05	5:15	6:20	6:30
5:20	5:30		
5:50	6:00		
6:20			
Running time from Hamilton to Pond Hill is approx. 10 mins.			

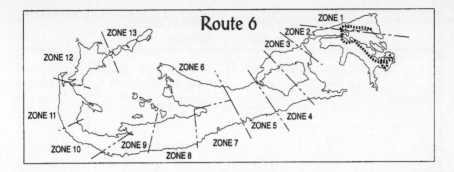

Route 6

ROUTE #6 (ST. GEORGE'S - ST. DAVID'S) *via USNAS Main Gate*					
MON TO FRI		**SATURDAY**		**SUNDAY**	
Leave St. George's	Leave St. David's	Leave St. George's	Leave St. David's	Leave St. George's	Leave St. David's
	7:20 sd				
6:55 sd	7:39 *	7:15	7:40		
7:15	7:40	8:15	8:40	8:15	8:40
8:15	8:40	9:15	9:40	9:15	9:40
9:15	9:40	10:15	10:40	10:15	10:40
10:15	10:40	11:15	11:40		
11:15	11:40	12:15	12:40	12:15	12:40
12:15	12:40	1:15	1:40	1:15	1:40
1:15	1:40	2:15	2:40	2:15	2:40
2:15	2:40	3:15	3:40	3:15	3:40
3:15	3:40	4:15	4:40	4:15	4:40
4:15	4:40	5:15	5:40	5:15	5:40
5:15	5:40	6:15	6:40	6:15	6:40
6:15	6:40				

Running time from St. George's to St. David's is approx. 25 mins.
* - Trip operates to Hamilton via Route 3
sd - Trip operates on school days only

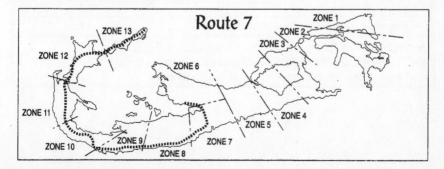

Route 7

ROUTE #7 (HAMILTON - BARNES CORNER)
via South Shore Beaches

MON TO FRI		SATURDAY		SUNDAY	
Leave Hamilton	Lv. Barnes Corner	Leave Hamilton	Lv. Barnes Corner	Leave Hamilton	Lv. Barnes Corner
	7:10				
	7:20				
	7:30				
7:00	7:40				
7:15 sd	7:50				
7:30	8:05		7:19		
	8:20		7:49		
8:00 pr	8:35	8:00	8:19		
	8:50	8:15	8:49		
8:30	9:05	8:30	9:04		
8:45	9:20	8:45	9:19		
Every 15 mins. until		Every 15 mins. until		9:30	
4:00	4:35	4:00	4:34	10:00	
4:10	4:50	4:15	4:49		10:19
4:20	5:05	4:30	5:04	10:30	
4:30	5:20	4:45	5:19		11:19
4:40	5:35	5:00	5:34		
4:50	5:50	5:15	5:49	Every 30 mins. until	
5:00	6:05	5:30	6:04	5:00	
5:10	6:20	5:45	6:34		
5:20	6:35	6:00	7:08 sb		5:49
5:30	6:50	6:30 sb	7:38 sb	6:00	
5:45	7:09 sb	7:00 sb	7:49		6:19
6:00	7:50	7:15	8:49		
6:30 sb	8:50	8:15	9:49		
7:15	9:50	9:15	10:49		
8:15	10:47				
9:15					

pr - Trip operates via Port Royal School; this trip does not serve Barnes Corner
sb - Trip operates to or from Sonesta Beach; does not serve Barnes Corner
sd - On school days, trip operates only as far as Sonesta Beach

ROUTE #7 (HAMILTON - DOCKYARD)
via South Shore Beaches, Somerset and Maritime Museum

MON TO FRI		SATURDAY		SUNDAY	
Leave Hamilton	Leave Dockyard	Leave Hamilton	Leave Dockyard	Leave Hamilton	Leave Dockyard
	6:50 mb				
	7:00 mb				
	7:10 mb				
	7:20 mb				
	sv 7:30 mb		7:00 mb		
	7:45 mb		7:30 mb		
	8:00 mb		8:00 mb		
7:00	8:20 we		8:20		
	8:50		8:50		
8:00 pr	9:20	8:00	9:20		
8:30	9:50	8:30	9:50		
9:00	10:20	9:00	10:20		10:00 mb
9:30	10:50	9:30	10:50	9:30	10:50
10:00	11:20	10:00	11:20	10:00	11:20
Every 30 mins. until		Every 30 mins. until		Every 30 mins. until	
3:00	4:20	3:00	4:20	3:00	4:20
3:30	4:50	3:30	4:50	3:30	4:50
4:00	5:20	4:00	5:20	4:00	5:20
4:20 mb	5:50	4:30	8:20	4:30	5:50
4:30	6:20	5:00	9:20	5:00 mb	
4:50 mb	8:20	5:30 mb	10:20	6:00 mb	
5:00	9:20	6:00 mb			
5:20 mb	10:20	7:15			
5:30		8:15			
6:00 mb		9:15			
7:15					
8:15					
9:15					

Running time from Hamilton to Dockyard is approx. 62 mins.

mb - Trip operates to or from Somerset Terminal; does not serve Dockyard

pr - Trip operates via Port Royal School route; does not serve Turtle Cove area

sv - Trip operates via Sound View Road

we - Trip operates via West End School route; does not serve Somerset Main Road between Crocket Lane and Sound View Road

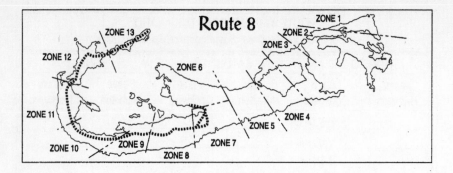

Route 8

BUS ROUTE #8C (HAMILTON - CEDAR HILL)					
via Middle Road					
MON TO FRI		SATURDAY		SUNDAY	
Leave Hamilton	Leave Cedar Hill	Leave Hamilton	Leave Cedar Hill	Leave Hamilton	Leave Cedar Hill
	7:45				
7:45	8:15	7:45	7:45		
8:45	8:45	8:45	8:45		
9:45	9:45	9:45	9:45	9:45	
10:45	10:45	10:45	10:45	10:45	10:45
11:45	11:45	11:45	11:45	11:45	11:45
12:45	12:45	12:45	12:45	12:45	12:45
1:45	1:45	1:45	1:45	1:45	1:45
2:45	2:45	2:45	2:45	2:45	2:45
3:45	3:45	3:45	3:45	3:45	3:45
4:45	4:45	4:45	4:45	4:45	4:45
5:15	5:45	5:20	5:45	5:45	5:45
5:45	6:45	5:45	6:45	6:45	
6:45		6:45			

Buses leaving Hamilton marked "8-Dockyard" or "8-Somerset" will run via Cedar Hill.
Buses from Cedar Hill are the regular Route 8 trips departing Dockyard at five mins. past the hour.

BUS ROUTE #8 (HAMILTON - SOMERSET)
via Middle Road and Southampton Princess

MON TO FRI		SATURDAY		SUNDAY	
Leave Hamilton	Leave Somerset	Leave Hamilton	Leave Somerset	Leave Hamilton	Leave Somerset
	6:15				
	6:30				
6:45	6:45				
	6:55				
	7:05				
7:15	7:15				
	7:25	6:45	6:45		
	7:35	7:15	7:15		
7:45	7:45	7:45	7:45	7:45	7:45
8:15	8:00 xp	8:15	8:15	8:45	8:45
8:45	8:15 sv	8:45	8:45	9:45	9:45
9:15	8:45	9:15	9:15	10:15	10:15
Every 30 mins. until		Every 30 mins. until		Every 30 mins. until	
4:15	3:45	4:15	4:15	4:15	4:15
4:35	4:15	4:45	4:45	4:45	4:45
4:45	4:45	5:10 sv	5:15	5:15	5:15
4:55	5:15	5:15	5:45	5:45	5:45
5:05 sv	5:45	5:45	6:15	6:45	6:15
5:10 xp	6:15	6:15	6:45	7:45	6:45
5:15	6:45	6:45	7:45	8:45	7:45
5:20	7:15	7:45	8:45	9:45	8:45
5:45	7:45	8:45	9:45	10:45	9:45
6:15	8:45	9:45	10:45		10:45
6:45	9:45	10:45	11:59		
Every hour until	10:45	11:45			
11:45	11:59				

sv - Trip operates via Sound View Road
xp - Trip operates between Barnes Corner and Crow Lane

BUS ROUTE #8 (HAMILTON - DOCKYARD)
via Middle Road, Southampton Princess and Maritime Museum

MON TO FRI		SATURDAY		SUNDAY	
Leave Hamilton	Leave Dockyard	Leave Hamilton	Leave Dockyard	Leave Hamilton	Leave Dockyard
	6:35				
	7:05				
	7:35		7:35		
6:45	7:50 xp		8:05		
7:15	8:05 sv	7:15	8:35		
7:45	8:35	7:45	9:05		
8:15	9:05	8:15	9:35		9:35
8:45	9:35	8:45	10:05		10:35
9:15	10:05	9:15	10:35		11:05
9:45	10:35	9:45	11:05	9:45	11:35
10:15	11:05	10:15	11:35	10:15	12:05
10:45	11:35	10:45	12:05	10:45	12:35
11:15	12:05	11:15	12:35	11:15	1:05
11:45	12:35	11:45	1:05	11:45	1:35
12:15	1:05	12:15	1:35	12:15	2:05
12:45	1:35	12:45	2:05	12:45	2:35
1:15	2:05	1:15	2:35	1:15	3:05
1:45	2:35	1:45	3:05	1:45	3:35
2:15	3:05	2:15	3:35	2:15	4:05
2:45	3:35	2:45	4:05	2:45	4:35
3:15	4:05	3:15	4:35	3:15	5:05
3:45	4:35	3:45	5:05	3:45	5:35
4:15	5:05	4:15	5:35	4:15	6:35
4:45	5:35	4:45	6:35	5:15	
5:10 xp	6:05	5:15			
5:45	6:35	5:45			
6:15	7:05	6:15			
10:45	11:50	10:45	11:50	10:45	

Running time from Hamilton to Dockyard is approx. 62 mins.
sv - Trip operates via Sound View Road
xp - Trip operates express between Barnes Corner and Crow Lane

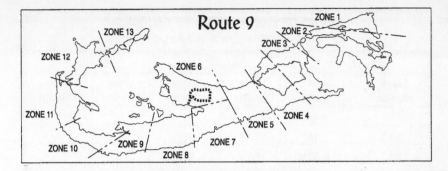

Route 9

BUS ROUTE #9 (HAMILTON - PROSPECT) via National Stadium and Palmetto Road					
MON TO FRI		SATURDAY		SUNDAY	
Leave Hamilton	Leave Prospect	Leave Hamilton	Leave Prospect	Leave Hamilton	Leave Prospect
7:15	7:25				
8:15	8:25				
8:45	8:55	8:15	8:25		
9:15	9:25	9:15	9:25		
10:15	10:25	10:15	10:25	10:30	10:40
11:15	11:25	11:15	11:25		
12:15	12:25	12:15	12:25		
1:15	1:25	1:15	1:25		
2:15	2:25	2:15	2:25		
3:15	3:25	3:15	3:25		
4:15	4:25	4:15	4:25		
4:45	4:55	5:15	5:25		
5:15	5:25	5:45	5:55		
5:45	5:55				
6:15					
Running time from Hamilton to Prospect is approx. 10 mins.					

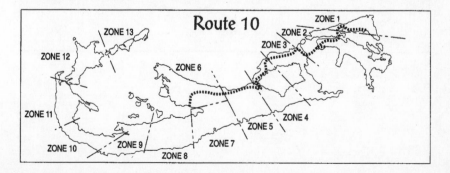

Route 10

BUS ROUTE #10 (HAMILTON - ST. GEORGE'S)
via Palmetto Road, Aquarium and Perfume Factory

MON TO FRI		SATURDAY		SUNDAY	
Leave Hamilton	Leave St. George's	Leave Hamilton	Leave St. George's	Leave Hamilton	Leave St. George's
	6:15				
7:15	7:15	7:15	7:15		
8:15	8:00 xp	8:15	8:15		
9:15	8:15	9:15	9:15		
10:15	9:15	10:15	10:15	10:15	10:15
11:15	10:15	11:15	11:15	11:15	11:15
12:15	11:15	12:15	12:15	12:15	12:15
1:15	12:15	1:15	1:15	1:15	1:15
2:15	1:15	2:15	2:15	2:15	2:15
3:15	2:15	3:15	3:15	3:15	3:15
4:15	3:15	4:15	4:15	4:15	4:15
5:00	4:15	5:15	5:15	5:15	5:15
5:10 xp	5:15	6:15	6:15		
5:15	6:15				
6:15	7:15				
7:15	8:15				
8:15	9:15				
9:15	10:15				
xp - Express service					

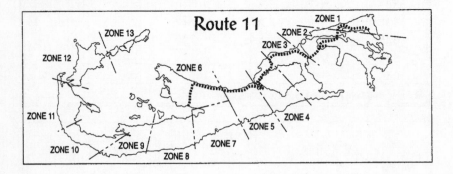

Route 11

BUS ROUTE #11 (HAMILTON - ST. GEORGE'S)
via Blackwatch Pass, Aquarium and Perfume Factory

MON TO FRI		SATURDAY		SUNDAY	
Leave Hamilton	Leave St. George's	Leave Hamilton	Leave St. George's	Leave Hamilton	Leave St. George's
	6:45				
	7:00				
	7:30				
6:45	7:45	6:45	6:45		
7:45	8:00 xp	7:45	7:45	7:45	7:45
8:00	8:30	8:30	8:30	8:45	8:45
8:45	8:45	8:45	8:45	9:45	9:45
9:00	9:00	9:00	9:00	10:45	10:45
9:30	9:30	9:30	9:30	11:45	11:45
9:45	9:45	9:45	9:45	12:45	12:45
Every 15 mins. in conjunction with Route #10				1:45	1:45
11:45	11:45	11:45	11:45	2:45	2:45
12:00	12:00	12:00	12:00	Every hour until	
12:30	12:30	12:30	12:30	9:45	9:45
12:45	12:45	12:45	12:45	10:45	
Every hour on the hour, 15 minutes and 30 mins. after each hour until					
4:35	4:45	4:45	4:45		
4:45	5:00	5:00	5:00		
4:55	5:30	5:10	5:30		
5:05	5:45	5:30	5:45		
5:10 xp	6:45	5:45	6:45		
5:25 sd	7:45	6:45	7:45		
5:35	8:45	7:45	8:45		
5:45	9:45	8:45	9:45		
6:45	10:45	9:45	10:45		
7:45	11:45	10:45	11:45		
Every hour until		11:45			
11:45					

Running time from Hamilton to St. George's is approx. 50 mins.
sd - Trip operates direct from Hamilton to St. David's then continues to St. George's
xp - Trip operates express between Sheely Bay Plaza and Hamilton

Index